New perspectives on industrial disputes

Industrial disputes in the UK underwent radical change in their extent and nature during the 1980s. This means that previous orthodoxies in the area need to be reconsidered.

This volume provides new insights on industrial disputes, using the most current research. It assesses the respective roles of union organisation and management in generating, deterring and winning or losing disputes. Diverse methods of analysis are brought to bear on the merits of the new labour laws of the 1980s and arbitration in the UK and North America, particularly in deterring disputes. Consequences of disputes are also evaluated, using UK evidence on pay and labour costs from both a large-scale survey and from case studies. The focus of the material is on the UK, but the book also draws on comparative evidence from North America.

David Metcalf is one of the UK's leading experts on collective bargaining, strikes and trade unions. **Simon Milner** is an emerging authority on industrial disputes with particular expertise in the impact and use of arbitration.

This volume will appeal to industrial relations academics and students, labour lawyers, labour economists, personnel managers, human resource professionals, arbitrators, union officials and researchers.

New perspectives on industrial disputes

Edited by
David Metcalf and Simon Milner

ROUTLEDGE

London and New York

First published 1993
by Routledge
11 New Fetter Lane

Simultaneously published in the USA and Canada
by Routledge Inc.
29 West 35th Street, New York, NY 10001

Typeset in 10/12 Times by Megaron, Cardiff, South Wales
Printed and bound in Great Britain by
T J Press Ltd, Padstow, Cornwall

British Library Cataloguing in Publication Data
A catalogue reference for this book is available from the British Library.

Library of Congress Cataloging in Publication Data
has been applied for.

ISBN 0-415-09151-9

Contents

List of figures

List of tables

Acknowledgements

The basis for this volume is the work of the Industrial Relations Group of the Centre for Economic Performance at the London School of Economics. It consists of papers presented and discussed at a Conference on Industrial Disputes held on 23 and 24 March 1992 in the Centre's headquarters at the School. Participants at the conference included representatives from the Economic and Social Research Council, the Department of Employment, the Confederation of British Industry, the Trades Union Congress, the Engineering Employers Federation and the media in addition to academic colleagues.

We would like to thank all the participants who contributed to a constructive and stimulating conference. Particular thanks go to the discussants: Geoffrey Owen, David Grant, Carlo Dell'Aringa, Tony de Launay, John Benson, Andrew Oswald, Sid Kessler, Paul Edwards and Paul Gregg.

Research funding is gratefully acknowledged and was supplied by the Economic and Social Research Council, which finances the Centre for Economic Performance, the Department of Employment, the Leverhulme Trust, the LSE Staff Research Fund, the Villas Foundation, and the Industrial Relations Section of Princeton University.

Thanks also go to the administrative and technical support staff at the CEP including Phyllis Gamble, Sue Gerrard, Adam Lubanski, Suzanne Martin, Marion O'Brien, Kate Perry, Nigel Rogers and Jill Walters. We are particularly indebted to Philomena McNicholas for helping to organise the conference and to Clare Mumford for her efficient assistance in the editing of the papers.

1 New perspectives on industrial disputes

David Metcalf and Simon Milner

In 1991, there were fewer working days lost through strike action than in any year since records began in 1893. Moreover, the actual number of stoppages recorded by the Employment Department – 369 – was the lowest since 1933 (see *Employment Gazette* May 1992 and Chapter 11 of this volume). The massively reduced intensity of strike activity since the 1970s is perhaps the most celebrated element in the changing industrial relations scene in the last decade. There are a number of convergent explanations for this decline including, *inter alia*, the rise and persistence of high unemployment, restrictive legislation introduced since 1979, the fall in trade union membership and the newly assertive role of management. Whilst providing new insights into these well-known changes in British industrial relations in the 1980s and 1990s, this volume also probes more deeply, and with a wider ambit, into the sphere of industrial disputes.

Industrial disputes must be distinguished from the wider expanse of industrial conflict. Edwards (1992), in his extensive and illuminating review of the whole area of industrial conflict, emphasises the distinctions between organised and unorganised, individual and collective forms of conflict. This book is concerned almost exclusively with collective, organised disputes such as strikes, action short of strikes and the use of dispute procedures, therefore excluding absenteeism, sabotage and the like.

Rival theories concerning the causes of disputes, strikes in particular, are perhaps the longest running source of debate in this area. The respective merits of economic, institutional, sociological and political models of strikes have been well worked over in the past, albeit with no agreement (Kennan 1986, Edwards 1992). The causes of disputes are analysed from some different angles in this book – including the role of management and the effectiveness of legal and quasi-legal dispute deterrents. However, the main feature of the book is to provide perspectives on issues concerning disputes which have not been as comprehensively tackled as causes to date.

The book is structured into three general sections. Three chapters examine aspects of management and unions concerned with industrial disputes. Four chapters focus on dispute deterrents. And two deal with the consequences of disputes. Although each chapter of the book examines the issue of disputes from a quite different angle, there are certain themes and rationales which underpin all parts of the book.

THEMES AND RATIONALES

Disputes as the critical edge of industrial relations

Even though the incidence of the most immediate form of conflict, strikes, is now at a very low ebb (such that soon students might not be asked 'Why are there strikes?' in exams but instead 'Are there strikes?' or 'Why aren't there strikes?'), there are still very good reasons for studying disputes. The most straightforward is that strikes are not the only manifestation of bargaining disputes, so the study of action short of strikes or the use of dispute procedures can broaden an analysis of bargaining breakdowns.

More important, however, is the notion that disputes can be seen as representing the critical edge of collective industrial relations. One fundamental tenet of research is to connect outcomes with mechanisms. Disputes, whether numerous or rare, are without doubt one of the generic 'outcomes' of collective bargaining. Therefore the study of disputes can act as a thematic conduit for different analyses of the mechanisms and constituent parts of industrial relations. Whether discussing the merits of a particular legal environment, a certain type of arbitration or the pay-off to strikes in terms of higher or lower wage settlements, a connecting thread running through the chapters is the notion that a knowledge of the mechanisms of disputes heightens the understanding of industrial relations. Whilst some of the chapters are firmly rooted in the industrial dispute debate – whether causes, processes and/or consequences – a majority of the chapters provide a wider perspective on key issues within industrial relations.

Management of industrial relations

Distinguished observers of the industrial relations scene, like Kessler and Bayliss (1992), characterise the last decade as one where managerial prerogatives were reasserted. The consequences for industrial disputes are addressed from very diverse perspectives in different chapters. Two main types of managerial story are illuminated here. First, how have managers operating in established companies reacted to new found roles and opportunities in the 1980s afforded to them by high unemployment and the new labour legislation? Second, we examine the actions of managers at newly established sites, commonly known as greenfield sites, in the context of 1980s and 1990s industrial relations. Managerial attitudes, styles and policy reactions to the changing industrial relations scene are addressed directly by two sets of authors.

Dunn and Wright (Chapter 3) concentrate on managements' response to, and role in, the demise of the closed shop in 'old era' workplaces. Old era plants are those which in the 1970s were prime examples of traditional, confrontational industrial relations often conducted via the closed shop. The authors investigate the role of management in the decay of one of the most potent symbols of 1970s-style dispute-ridden industrial relations.

In contrast, Guest and Rosenthal (Chapter 2) assess literature on the 'new era' workplaces establishing their ideal industrial relations systems on greenfield sites. Inherent in this ideal is that conflict will be managed away through, for example, employee involvement and new payment systems. Guest and Rosenthal highlight in particular the maturation of industrial relations on new sites, or what happens when 'green turns brown', and the potential impact this might have on previously dispute-free relations.

Although not overtly concerned with the changing role of management in industrial relations, four of the other chapters also shed light on this area. Closely related to the Guest and Rosenthal chapter are Milner's survey of 'new style deals' (Chapter 7), which provides the data for his analysis of final-offer arbitration, and Machin, Stewart and Van Reenen's study of multi-unionism (Chapter 4). Milner's chapter provides evidence on the success of attempts by management (and in some cases unions) often on greenfield sites to design and adopt dispute procedures which in theory promote agreement.

By concentrating on the link between single or multiple bargaining units and multi-unionism, Machin *et al.* emphasise the influence of the structure of the bargaining relationship between unions and management on industrial relations outcomes. This chapter links with the Dunn and Wright chapter. Both are concerned with the mechanisms, attitude towards and impact of change towards new arrangements from old era industrial relations involving closed shops and/or multiple bargaining arrangements.

The interaction of management prerogatives and the new legal framework is emphasised by Simpson and Elgar (Chapter 5), in particular the extent to which managers have made (or not made) use of new statutory powers to restrict industrial action during disputes. Richardson and Rubin (Chapter 10) have a different focus. They examine a recent dispute in the engineering industry to see how management, faced with a successful union campaign, was able to use its revitalised prerogatives to control the cost of consequences of a reduction in the working week. Their chapter spotlights the catalytic effect the campaign had on the determination with which managers sought to introduce new working practices and make other changes in order to 'pay' for the cut in hours.

Transformation of the legal framework

Legislative changes concerning industrial relations must rank as one of the most well-known policy manifestations of recent Conservative governments. The general conclusions from the academic debate on the impact of the legislative changes on the incidence and conduct of disputes is that the law has had some definite impact, although not always in the anticipated direction (Brown and Wadwhani 1990, Edwards 1992, Martin *et al.* 1991, Metcalf and Dunn 1991). However, the extent of influence remains unclear. Further it is difficult to disentangle the direct and indirect effects of the law. The two chapters concerned overtly with the impact of the law on industrial relations provide new perspectives on the controversy.

Although using distinctive methods of investigation, the chapters by Manning (Chapter 6) and Simpson and Elgar (Chapter 5), provide complementary insights into the impact of the changing legal framework. Manning provides an innovative non-technical discussion about the predictions of different economic models concerning the impact of compulsory pre-strike balloting provisions (introduced by the Trade Union Act 1984) on strike activity, union democracy and union bargaining power. The prominent feature of Manning's analysis is that the potential impact of the balloting law can vary widely, dependent on which economic model is applied and what assumptions are adopted.

In contrast to Manning's theoretical economics approach, Simpson and Elgar are interested in the actual, observed attitudes and behaviour of employers and unions towards the new legal environment. Their analysis comes explicitly from a legal perspective, examining the nuances as well as the main thrust of the law. This labour lawyers' chapter concludes that the impact of the law on strikes varies considerably across industries and industrial relations contexts. Their finding is quite consistent with Manning's chapter in that it highlights that alternative theories of disputes (for instance) may apply to different industrial relations settings. Both these very diverse perspectives on the law highlight that the industrial relations context is a crucial influence on the impact of the law on outcomes. For example, Manning emphasises the way in which alternative union structures may have a bearing on the effect of compulsory balloting and Simpson and Elgar show how ballots impact differently across industries.

Simpson and Elgar also demonstrate that it is important not just to consider the direct influence of the law on parties which have made use of the new provisions but also to consider the demonstration and deterrent effects of the law. Certain well-known cases have no doubt demonstrated the potential power of new legal provisions to curtail effective industrial action, such as the Stockport *Messenger*, P & O Shipping, and Dock Labour Scheme disputes (also discussed by Dunn and Wright). Just as interesting as the public court battles are the 'dogs that don't bark' – those groups of workers who under a less restrictive legal framework may have resorted more readily to industrial action. Some assessment of the muzzling effect of the law is clearly a key element to determining its impact.

Dunn and Wright's findings add support to the Simpson and Elgar conclusions about the diversity of legal impact. They argue that there have been two main managerial strategies – active or passive – over the decline of the closed shop. Managers in the majority of firms surveyed, which had entrenched closed shops in 1979, have been content to see the demise of their closed shops without actually contributing much to their downfall. They argue that new laws banning the closed shop clearly had a role to play in its decline, but that this influence was mainly indirect rather than explicit such as through legal challenges to extant closed shops.

Although principally concerned with the consequences of the engineering hours dispute, Richardson and Rubin also demonstrate how the law can influence the conduct of a dispute. The overall form of the campaign, to target individual companies or workplaces rather than aim for a national strike, was guided by the strictures of the pre-strike balloting rules introduced in 1984, and amended in the Employment Act 1988. The amended rules stipulate that in multi-plant disputes, there have to be separate ballots in each workplace and separate majorities for individual action to retain legal immunity. This makes a national strike impossible unless membership is such that there are strike majorities in virtually all workplaces. In the engineering industry multi-unionism is an added complication. The requirement to have a separate majority applies to each union in each workplace. So, the unions had little alternative but to take selective rather than national action. Selective action was not necessarily to their disadvantage. The law may have made it easier for the unions to adopt what, irrespective of legal requirements, were the best tactics.

A further feature of the campaign was that, after the initial strikes, a majority in a ballot supporting strike action over a shorter working week was generally sufficient for management to concede a reduction in hours, without the need for industrial action. This evidence links in well with Manning's theoretical discussion of the importance of ballots in providing information about worker militancy to both union leaders and employers, such that the action itself may be prevented. Nevertheless questions remain concerning whether or not the ballots actually do provide an accurate estimate of militancy. This is because there is a considerable moral hazard problem – non-militants have an incentive to vote 'yes' to strike action if they believe this will exact a more beneficial settlement without the need to take industrial action. Manning discusses the possible ramifications of such behaviour.

The influence of legal framework is also one feature of Olson's chapter (8) on interest arbitration in North America, although not connected to changes in the legal framework in the UK in the last twelve years. The spread of arbitration arrangements, both conventional and final-offer arbitration, in the US is very much determined by public policy in different states, in the context of the right to strike and legally binding collective agreements. This contrasts markedly with the development of final-offer arbitration (FOA) arrangements in the UK, as analysed by Milner, which have spread in the context of voluntarily signed, not legally binding collective agreements. The different experiences with FOA in these two countries must in part be explained by the alternative legal environments. This suggests that the influence of the law on disputes can also be assessed using comparative evidence from a number of countries as well as by studying changes in the law in one country.

Different approaches

A principal feature of this book is the constructive use of different approaches to illuminate this broad area of industrial disputes. Edwards (1992) stresses the range of approaches that have been used in other studies of industrial conflict, however these studies are rarely seen as complementary. By contrast part of the 'new perspective' that this book attempts to provide is the diversity of methods and approaches within and across its chapters.

Analytical methods employed include detailed case studies, large-scale interview-based studies, statistical analysis of both very large and much smaller data sets, a literature survey and theoretical expositions. Two chapters (7 and 10) also include both statistical analysis and information from interviews on the chosen subject.

There is interest in both attitudes and behaviour, as illustrated respectively by Simpson and Elgar who are principally concerned with managerial and union attitudes towards the changing legal framework and Machin *et al.* who investigate the statistical relationship between multi-union bargaining structures and outcomes.

Different approaches are used to investigate an issue in associated chapters. The distinctive approaches of Manning and Simpson and Elgar have already been noted. Likewise different perspectives on the consequences of strikes are provided by Metcalf, Wadsworth and Ingram (Chapter 9) and Richardson and Rubin. The former undertake a statistical analysis of data from the CBI Databank. By contrast the latter employ a case study approach to the catalytic impact of the engineering hours campaign on management.

SUMMARY AND CONCLUSIONS

Having highlighted the broad themes and feature of the book, it should be stressed that the work provides analyses of considerably more issues than the ones drawn out above. Summaries of the main elements and their conclusions are outlined below.

Management and unions

In Chapter 2, Guest and Rosenthal examine the industrial relations experience of greenfield sites established in the 1980s based on a careful review of existing literature. They set the experience of these workplaces within the wider context of the approach to management at such sites. Two particular features of the chapter relate specifically to industrial disputes.

First there is the issue of unionised and union-free greenfield sites. The authors analyse why there are variations by examining the strategic considerations that influenced the initial management decision about union recognition. Following from this, they also examine the human resource policies designed to avoid any felt need for unions among the workforce. The second issue concerns industrial action. There has been very little industrial action at greenfield sites established in the 1980s. Explanations for this are sought in the general pattern of industrial conflict in the 1980s, the human resource policies pursued at greenfield sites and the policy and practice of unions.

The free hand given to management to control industrial relations at a greenfield site is the antithesis of managing in the 1970s in firms with high unionisation and a closed shop. Yet, Dunn and Wright's chapter on the demise of the closed shop illustrates that it was managers operating in the latter who underwent the most extensive 'liberating experience' in the 1980s. Indeed they argue that the fading of the closed shop is the most potent symbol of this unbridling. So whilst Guest and Rosenthal examine what unrestrained management does, Dunn and Wright analyse how the 'shackles' of closed shop practices were broken, what role management played in this and how they have reacted to their new found freedom to manage.

Using a sample of employers' associations and unionised companies, interviewed both in 1978–9 and 1990–1, this chapter (3) explores a range of other issues connected to the decay of the closed shop. There are brief discussions of the policy arguments surrounding the closed shop in terms of its functions for unions and management, and the legal developments since 1980 which saw the final outlawing of the practice in 1990. The pre-entry closed shop is treated as a separate issue, given the additional costs associated with its restriction on labour supply and skill demarcation. A particularly interesting section concerns a controversy over the recent Department of Employment claim that 1.3 million people are covered by pre-entry shops, a figure higher than both the 1979 (850,000) and 1964 (750,000) estimates.

Multi-unionism, alongside the closed shop, is widely perceived as one of the structural characteristics of industrial relations which has a detrimental impact on bargaining outcomes, including disputes. This issue has become increasingly important in light of recent moves towards single table bargaining (in multi-union settings) associated with progression from old era to new era industrial relations. The particular impact of multi-unionism in single or multiple bargaining arrangements is investigated in Chapter 4 by Machin, Stewart and Van Reenen using data from the 1984 Workplace Industrial Relations Survey.

Outcomes analysed include wages and financial performance as well as the incidence of industrial action. Where multiple unions are present it is found to be important to distinguish between whether they bargain separately or jointly, and the most important effects are isolated where separate bargains occur. The results suggest that plants with multi-unionism and separate bargaining arrangements pay higher wages, have worse financial performance and are more prone to strike action lasting at least one day than their counterparts with one union or multiple unions with single table bargaining.

Dispute deterrents

Some analysis of dispute deterrence is crucial to a rounded understanding of the whole disputes area, and yet it is often overlooked in favour of discussions of why disputes occur. We recognise that the three chapters in the first section of the book also have some bearing on dispute deterrence. Conclusions which follow from these chapters are that management could aim to deter disputes through removing the closed shop, promoting dispute-free relations in greenfield sites or instituting single table bargaining. However, the four chapters in this section concern themselves much more explicitly with the value and efficacy of more direct deterrents.

Two chapters examine the impact of the law on industrial disputes. Simpson and Elgar's study analyses the actual use of newly enacted legal powers in negotiations and disputes. Their concern is to examine afresh claims made by various commentators about the effects of employment legislation passed between 1980 and 1990. The initial focus of the research concerned unions at head-office level and employers' associations. This provides a valuable insight into how unions and employers have developed labour relations policies and strategies in the light of a changing legal environment.

The second stage of their research involves surveys of union and management negotiators carried out by questionnaire and structured interviews. It is at this level that the influence of the legal framework on the process of negotiations and disputes can be assessed. Differences between national and local perspectives on the law also become apparent. Chapter 5 presents results in the form of a general overview and reports on particular sectors – engineering, printing and publishing, education and other public sectors. It identifies those areas of the law which have had a significant influence and evaluates the nature of those influences. Simpson and Elgar state that the law has been an important factor in industrial relations in some sectors, but its impact is complex and not always in the direction of deterring industrial action.

Manning, in Chapter 6, provides an assessment of what economic theories concerning asymmetric information predict concerning the impact of compulsory pre-strike ballots on strike activity. This analysis spotlights the strategic decisions made by employers when setting offers and workers when voting over those offers (and) in strike ballots. A key development of Manning's model is to challenge the commonly accepted notion that ballots provide better information to employers such that strike incidence should be reduced. Essentially previous commentators have ignored the endogenous nature of the information extraction process – workers use different rules in deciding whether or not to reject an offer with and without balloting. Although Manning concludes that strike incidence is probably reduced by the introduction of balloting, he further states that there is a suspicion that this is not a general result. Chapter 6 also looks at the wider implications of pre-strike ballots for union democracy, wages and employment.

An alternative to legal restrictions on industrial action as a deterrent to disputes is some form of arbitration. Chapters 7 and 8 provide complementary insights into the effect of different types of arbitration on collective bargaining. Milner provides the first empirical investigation of the very recent experience in the UK private sector with final-offer arbitration, as one feature in so-called new style deal agreements. This type of arbitration is specifically designed to deter disputes (i.e. its own use) more effectively than conventional arbitration, which has been accused of 'chilling' negotiations.

Evidence from a postal survey of seventy-two new style deal plants, covering nearly 300 bargaining rounds, and interviews at eight plants which have experienced impasses under the procedure, is used to test the theory. The data suggest that overall final-offer arbitration is not more effective than conventional arbitration at preventing bargaining disputes. However, where multi-stage dispute procedures involving conciliation, mediation and arbitration exist, final-offer arbitration is superior to conventional arbitration in deterring disputes. Milner also examines possible explanations for the apparent underperformance of final-offer arbitration in deterring disputes thus far in the UK.

Olson provides a comparative perspective on the North American experience of interest arbitration, examining both final-offer and conventional arbitration. He provides a thorough review of empirical and theoretical research into the impact of interest arbitration on public sector bargaining. The main points of debate concerning the behaviour of negotiators and arbitrators under different arbitration arrangements, and the effect of arbitration on wages and benefits are drawn out. Olson concludes his wide ranging chapter with a discussion of future research directions which are applicable to the UK as well as the US and Canada.

The consequences of disputes

Interest in disputes has focused mainly on the causes and processes of strikes and there has been only sporadic interest in the consequences of breakdowns in bargaining (Knowles 1954, Gennard 1982). The penultimate and final chapters of this book look directly at the consequences of strikes, from a union perspective (Metcalf, Wadsworth and Ingram) and a management perspective (Richardson and Rubin).

Using data on nearly 9,000 separate wage settlements in British manufacturing in the 1980s drawn from the CBI Pay Databank, Metcalf *et al.* provide new information on wage settlements with and without strikes. They report that in seven out of ten years (1979–80 to 1988–9) real wage settlements involving a strike were higher than those without a strike. On average for the decade as a whole real pay increases where there was a strike were 0.7 per cent a year higher than settlements without a strike. In certain industries the strike/no strike differential is significantly greater. For instance, in Metal Manufacturing real settlements with a strike were 4.2 per cent a year higher on average than those without a strike. The authors emphasise, however, the need to control for other determinants of wage settlements before determining the actual pay off due to striking. Once such controls are made it is possible to calculate how long a strike is worthwhile from the union's viewpoint. The authors calculate that if the pay-off to striking lasts for thirty years or more and the discount rate is 0.02 even a strike of three weeks is worthwhile. But if the pay-off only lasts one year and the discount rate is 0.10, no strike of a day or longer would pay for itself.

In August 1989 the UK engineering unions launched an unusual and imaginative campaign of strike action at selected factories in pursuit of their claim for a reduction in the standard working week below thirty-nine hours. By the end of 1990, the unions claimed that 1,300 agreements had been signed, securing a thirty-seven hour week for 600,000 workers. Richardson and Rubin analyse the impact of this campaign on firms' competitiveness. In particular the study sought to determine the reactions of management to the campaign and the subsequent hours cut.

Research was three-pronged involving investigation of around 400 agreements signed to incorporate the hours cut, a small number of factory visits to glean more on the perspective of managers on the process surrounding the shorter working week and a survey of over 150 firms to provide more extensive and representative coverage. The authors strongly challenge the popular belief that the campaign represented a defeat for the employers. They argue that the hours cut acted as a catalyst for management to make further assaults on remaining restrictive practices, other organisational slack and inefficiency. The workers achieved a shorter week, but management had considerable success in offsetting the implied rise in labour costs by modifying working practices. Indeed, in some cases both parties gained, because shorter hours with new working practices were more productive than old hours and old practices.

Strike data

A final original perspective on industrial disputes is the new series of strike activity over the last century reported in Chapter 11. Most strikers are union members. Therefore time series running from 1893 to 1991 for strike frequency, workers involved and days lost have been calculated on a 'per union member' basis as well as on the traditional 'per employee' basis. Fresh information on average strike duration is also shown. The primary aim of Chapter 11 is to present the data as background material for the rest of the book, but some highlights in the series are also noted.

REFERENCES

Brown, W. and Wadwhani, S. (1990) 'The economic effects of industrial relations legislation since 1979', *National Institute Economic Review*, 131, (1): 57–70.

Edwards, P. (1992) 'Industrial conflict: themes and issues in recent research' *British Journal of Industrial Relations*, 30, (3): 361–404.

Gennard, J. (1982) 'The financial costs and returns of strikes', *British Journal of Industrial Relations*, 20, (2): 247–56.

Kennan, J. (1986) 'The economics of strikes', in O. Ashenfelter and R. Layard (eds), *Handbook of Labor Economics*, Vol. II, Amsterdam and New York: Elsevier.

Kessler, S. and Bayliss, F. (1992) *Contemporary British Industrial Relations*, London: Macmillan.

Knowles, K.G.J.C. (1954) *Strikes: a Study in Industrial Conflict*, Oxford: Basil Blackwell.

Martin, R., Fosh, P., Morris, H., Smith, P. and Undy, R. (1991) 'The decollectivisation of trade unions? Ballots and collective bargaining in the 1980s', *Industrial Relations Journal*, 22, (3): 197–208.

Metcalf, D. and Dunn, S. (1991) 'Labour legislation 1980–1990: philosophy and impact', Centre for Economic Performance, LSE, Working Paper No. 12 (revised).

2 Industrial relations in greenfield sites

David Guest and Patrice Rosenthal

Greenfield sites are of interest to students of industrial relations and management policy because they provide an opportunity to examine the kind of industrial relations management would ideally like. In setting up a new plant, managers have what is essentially a *tabula rasa*, an opportunity to start afresh, freed from the constraints of tradition and custom and practice. What sort of industrial relations will they pursue? Will they recognise trade unions and engage in traditional collective bargaining? If not, what does industrial relations, or what may perhaps be more appropriately termed employee relations, look like in the absence of a trade union? And can policies and practices associated with greenfield sites be sustained over time? In other words, what happens when greenfield sites turn brown?

There is a popular stereotype that at greenfield sites managers practise, and sustain over time the practice of new forms of human resource management, either in the absence of unions or with a single carefully selected and controlled union; that they do so on the basis of a model based either on American high-technology companies or Japanese manufacturers; and that in doing so they obtain highly positive performance outcomes, judged both on human resource and industrial relations criteria and on a wider range of performance criteria. One outcome that is not expected is any form of industrial dispute between company and workforce.

The aim of this chapter is to test this popular stereotype by reviewing, within a broad conceptual framework, what is already known about the subject. The review additionally highlights the key issues, identifies gaps in our knowledge and provides the point of departure for research being undertaken at the LSE's Centre for Economic Performance.

WHAT IS A GREENFIELD SITE?

The term 'greenfield site' has been used loosely in the past and has clear connotations of a new plant established in a rural or semi-rural environment. Beaumont and Townley (1985) have argued that it will be a manufacturing plant and it will typically have innovative employment policies. However, this seems to prejudge the issue and is therefore too limiting. For our present purposes it will be more useful to focus on the following features:

1 it will be a new site, located some distance away from existing sites belonging to the same organisation.
2 it will be part of a larger organisation rather than a completely new venture.

This second criterion imposes a major but deliberate limitation. Many, indeed most new organisations are single establishments. However, most are also small and, if they survive, stay small. Storey (1983) has studied new firms in the north-east of England and found that over 30 per cent of new manufacturing firms fail to survive for four years, the median number of employees is ten and there is at best a 0.75 per cent chance of a wholly new business employing 100 employees after a decade. From data on trade union recognition we know that industrial relations, defined in terms of collective arrangements with trade unions, has a better chance of thriving in larger establishments. By the time they exceed the official, albeit perhaps unrealistically large figure for a small firm of 200 employees, almost none of the new single-site establishments will also be able to call themselves greenfield sites any longer. They are therefore excluded from our operational definition for the purposes of our research.

Most research has focused on new manufacturing plants. Yet much growth has occurred in the service sector. Our definition must therefore embrace new supermarkets, new insurance offices and new banks which may be located in new buildings but which will often be sited in town centres rather than green fields. Finally, we would exclude the nature of the human resource management/industrial relations (HRM/IR) policies from our definition since they would appear to be a dependent variable.

THE ANALYTIC FRAMEWORK

The analysis of industrial and employment relations in greenfield sites must include consideration of inputs or influences on policy choices, some way of classifying the resultant policies and practices and a concern for the range of outcomes. Each is briefly considered.

Influences on policy

Previous research points to a long list of possible influences on human resource management and industrial relations policy.

Industrial Sector We know that there are variations on a range of industrial relations indices between and within sectors. For example, trade unions are more likely to be found in manufacturing than in the private service sector (we will not be discussing the public sector). Furthermore, within manufacturing, unions are more prevalent in motor manufacturing than in electronics.

Size Unions are more likely to be found in larger organisations (Millward and Stevens 1986). At some new plants management may deliberately plan to keep the number of employees below about 500 in the belief that smaller plants are associated with greater job satisfaction, and lower labour turnover, absence and conflict.

Location One of the attractions of the original concept of the greenfield site was the argument that rural areas had less militant trade union traditions. There are variations between regions in levels of trade union membership. These are heavily influenced by, but operate independently of sector and size. Companies may wish to locate in less unionised and less militant areas. One survey which explored this (ACAS Wales 1986) concluded that the key influences on choice of location, for a sample of new foreign-owned plants in Wales, were proximity to markets, availability of premises and availability of labour. These overrode industrial relations considerations, despite some initial concern about industrial relations reputation.

National/government policy Companies may be encouraged to establish new plants because of a range of government policies. These include regional incentives, industrial relations policy, educational and training policy, the tax regime and labour costs. Recently the government in the UK has made much of the need to avoid the damaging impact of the Social Chapter on inward investment. It has also emphasised over the past decade its eagerness to free managers of legal and trade union constraints. Indeed the EETPU, in its evidence to a House of Commons Employment Select Committee inquiry in 1986, accused the government of covertly encouraging foreign investors to ignore union calls for representation rights (Industrial Relations Review and Report, IRRR 1986).

This variable is important in any debate about whether greenfield sites established in the 1980s are different from those set up in earlier years. It is worth remembering that even the most militant plants were once greenfield sites. So will those plants opened in the 1980s in a political context more hostile to trade unions than in the past drift as they age towards a typical pattern of medium-size plant industrial relations or will they retain the often distinctive employment policies and practices established at the outset?

Labour market considerations and type of workforce Unionisation and therefore collective industrial relations is more likely among male full-time workers in craft-type jobs than among clerical female part-time workers (Stevens and Wareing 1990). In greenfield sites it may be possible to shape the structure of the workforce through job design and at the point of selection. This in turn will be governed by the nature of the labour market. It has, for example, been argued (Garrahan and Stewart 1992) that firms like Nissan have been able to take advantage of high levels of local unemployment to select and retain a workforce that operates effectively with their distinctive set of policies.

Country of origin Non-union policies in the UK and indeed in Ireland (Toner 1987) have been particularly associated with American multinationals. Considerable attention has also been paid to industrial relations policies in Japanese plants. Focus on country of origin assumes that some distinctive features of 'home' patterns are likely to be exported, at least in part, to the UK greenfield site. In the present context, the key factor is likely to be the kind of industrial relations the firm is accustomed to both in its home territory and in any previous experience of new plants, particularly in the UK. Thus the normal American experience will be of no union. The Japanese will be accustomed to a form of 'in-house' union. The North Europeans will be most familiar with a heavily institutionalised set of arrangements with a single union.

Corporate culture Many of the best-known US non-union firms reflect the strong culture developed by their founder, or sometimes by a particularly strong subsequent leader. This culture stamps its mark on all parts of the organisation. A major and as yet unresolved research issue has been the relative influence of corporate against national culture on local practice (Hofstede 1980). Clearly, however, there are likely to be variations in the extent to which organisations have a strong culture and the extent to which they wish to transplant that culture to plants in other countries.

Plant leadership Industrial relations policies may be influenced by the particular leader of the plant and the management team at the time when the plant is established. The first HRM director may also play a key part in establishing policy and practice. One issue is whether the key managers are exported from the host organisation or recruited locally.

The production system and the product market These two factors will be closely interrelated and may have an important bearing on the type of industrial relations that is sought. For example a firm providing components on a 'just-in-time' basis will place a high premium on smooth, uninterrupted and high quality production. In such circumstances it must avoid industrial unrest or problems of quality and availability of labour.

All these factors, together no doubt with others, combine to influence the HRM/IR strategy. Much, probably too much, has been written on this subject. One consequence of this is that many more people are now aware of the importance of developing a strategy; at a greenfield site, unlike at some established plants, there is genuine scope for strategic choice and the opportunity to think through the preferred set of HRM/IR policies in advance. Of course the factors listed above do not indicate total freedom of choice. There may be national legislative requirements. Managers may also feel constrained by other factors; for example, new car plants are highly visible and become natural targets for the trade unions. Managers may therefore feel that they want to recognise a union on their terms rather than when, through unforeseen circumstances the union may be in a stronger position to dictate. Previous experience may also lead to the view that collective arrangements, if carefully organised, provide more orderly arrangements than any alternatives. The strategic choice is therefore not straightforward. Even those who opt to avoid a union may then have to consider what alternative arrangements to provide and what steps must be taken through positive HRM policies to obviate any felt need for unions among the workforce. Finally we must bear in mind that the existence of strategic choice does not imply that managers are invariably either aware of the choices or weigh them in any deliberate manner.

THE FORM OF INDUSTRIAL RELATIONS

There have been various attempts to classify contemporary industrial relations strategies (see, for example, Purcell and Sisson 1983, Purcell 1987, Keenoy 1990) and the relevant debate will not be repeated here. These attempts normally identify policy choices along one or two dimensions. Purcell and Sisson (1983), for example, classify personnel and industrial relations strategies along two dimensions of individualism and collectivism, giving them four main policy types. Guest (1989) has identified a range of policy choices about the management approach to trade unions at greenfield sites which can be summarised on a continuum from unitarist anti-unionism to support for a traditional, possibly multi-union presence. Another dimension which Guest and others identify reflects the approach to human resource management, ranging from sophisticated and strategically integrated at one extreme to a set of often ad hoc and certainly less clearly thought out policies at the other.

Dimensions of this sort are inevitably arbitrary and over-simplistic, but do help to identify and classify some of the main choices and to locate and compare organisations. For our present purposes, since we are particularly interested in industrial relations and human resource management in greenfield sites, probably the most useful approach is to take the two related dimensions of policies on unionisation and HRM policies. Along one dimension we therefore have policy preferences ranging from 'anti-union' through 'controlled unionism', which in practice means that unions are tolerated and even welcomed but on management's terms, to 'independent unionism', which implies that unions exist on their own terms and within an essentially pluralist framework. Along this continuum we might expect to find a managerial preference for policies which focus primarily on individuals, on groups and on collective arrangements.

Along the second dimension we again have three categories. The first is 'no coherent HRM strategy and ad hoc personnel policies'. However, it seems sensible to follow the increasingly popular pattern of separating two approaches to HRM. One, which is sometimes termed 'hard' HRM, is primarily concerned with efficient use of human resources and cost minimisation. The other is more concerned with full use of human resources and is sometimes termed 'soft' HRM. The preferred approach can often be traced back to whether the organisation's main concern was initially for managerial and professional staff, in which case they are more likely to emphasise the 'soft' version; or for shop-floor production work, in which case they are more likely to emphasise 'hard' HRM. The distinction between these approaches is likely to be reflected most clearly

Table 2.1 National stereotypes, HRM strategy and unionisation

	Ad hoc weak HRM	*'Hard' HRM efficiency focus*	*'Soft' HRM utilisation focus*
Anti-union (individualistic)	UK?	UK/USA?	USA
Controlled unionisation (group)	UK?	Japan	Japan
Independent unionisation (collective)	UK/North Europe?	North Europe?	North Europe

in the form of control system in use and in the ideology about the role of work in facilitating personal growth.

If we use these two dimensions and link them to national stereotypes we might find the information in Table 2.1. Within this sort of classification system it becomes possible to locate the expected policies of the typical firm from specific countries if they conform to the popular stereotype. For example, American firms would be expected to fit in the top right-hand triangle in the table. Japanese firms would be somewhere in a block in the middle. The location of European firms is less clear but we might predict that North European countries, with their tradition of social democracy, present a clear alternative which would actively welcome trade unionism, albeit in the form of a single union. They would therefore fit somewhere near the bottom end of the table. What is less clear is how to locate the typical British firm. The reason for this is the absence of a distinctive national approach. This absence produces the range of possibilities indicated in the table and raises the important empirical question of whether there is a preferred UK-firm pattern of HRM/IR in greenfield sites. These assumptions of national patterns are over-simplistic stereotypes but their value lies in providing hypotheses for empirical work and a context within which to explore the existing research evidence.

The next sections look first at the evidence on the number and extent of greenfield sites in the UK and then use the existing evidence to address the stereotypes outlined above.

WHERE ARE THE GREENFIELDS?

There is no central source of information about greenfield sites in the UK. We know that new firms and new plants have played a major part in employment growth in the past decade. But most of the growth has occurred in very small firms, often in the service sector. We do know more about investment by foreign firms through information collected by the Invest in Britain Bureau (IBB) of the Department of Trade and sometimes from data collected by foreign embassies. According to 1991 figures (*Financial Times* 20 September 1991) foreign-owned manufacturing companies accounted for 13 per cent of manufacturing employment, 19 per cent of net manufacturing output and 21 per cent of capital expenditure. The figure of 13 per cent represents a fall from 15 per cent of manufacturing employment in 1989, according to Income Data Services (IDS 1992) figures. The total number of employees working for foreign-owned firms fell from 974,000 in 1979 to 724,000 in 1989. This occurred because the growth caused by the influx of new plants was more than offset by a decline in employment in established US multinationals.

The IBB reported that in 1990, there were in the UK 120 new US investment projects, 63 German, 37 Japanese and 27 French. The IBB figures help to put the scale of Japanese investment in perspective. It is nevertheless highly significant in terms of the total Japanese pattern of investment in Europe. In recent years, the UK has accounted for 41 per cent of the financial value of the direct EC investment of both Japan and the USA. This is both because the scale of Japanese investments in the UK are numerically greater than in other EC countries and of higher average value. Looking specifically at Japanese manufacturing companies, which have attracted much of the research attention, there were some seventeen new investments in the UK in the 1970s but this rose to 145 in the 1980s. By 1990, there were seventy-eight Japanese plants employing more than 200 employees.

Some of the most thorough work on new manufacturing plants has been reported by Beaumont (1987). Based on Scottish Development Agency data, he reports that in 1981 there were 288 foreign-owned firms in Scotland, 170 of which were US-owned. A majority had started prior to 1950. Each plant employed on average 326 workers compared with 103 for UK-owned plants. More recent data from Welsh Development International reveals that in 1960 there were about thirty foreign-owned companies based in Wales. By 1992 there were about 350 such companies, employing more than 67,000 people (Welsh Development International, personal communication).

We must be careful not to overestimate the importance of these foreign-owned firms. Stone and Peck (1991) claim to have approached all inward investing manufacturing companies that had established plants in the north-east of England during the 1980s and which employed more than twenty people. A third were UK-owned firms. Nevertheless, 19 per cent of the plants but 40 per cent of the employment was accounted for by Far East firms, which in practice means predominantly Japanese. The 105 plants had created 15,000 jobs or 5 per cent of total manufacturing jobs in the region. Since the north-east has been one of the favoured regions for investment, this implies that the impact of new plants on employment has not been as great as sometimes believed.

Finally, Beaumont (1987) cites data from two new towns in Scotland, Irvine and Glenrothes. He found that approximately half the manufacturing plants in each town had been started between 1979 and 1985. Most were single independent establishments and most were British-owned. During the same period, Glenrothes had obtained only one new foreign-owned plant and Irvine nine.

Two further points may help to set the assumptions about greenfield sites in perspective. First, manufacturing sites account for only about 20 per cent of Japanese investment in the UK. About half has gone into the financial sector. Second, the pattern of investment in manufacturing may be changing. Recently there has been a shift towards joint ventures or takeovers (*Financial Times* 20 September 1991). Third, as the pattern of investment changes resulting in the possible need for a more skilled workforce, Japan may lose interest in opening new plants. Many Japanese firms have reported concern about UK skill shortages and general skill levels. Perhaps as a result, recent JETRO (Japanese External Trade Organisation) figures indicate that at present 137 Japanese companies are considering investment in Germany, compared with only 107 in the UK (*Financial Times* 4 June 1992). At the same time, firms in the north-east complain that Japanese firms are poaching the skilled workers. In all this it becomes ever more important that company HRM/IR systems operate successfully if the UK is to remain an attractive location for inward investment.

In analysing the industrial relations and human resource policies in greenfield sites, the existing literature focuses almost entirely on manufacturing. It falls into three main and partly overlapping categories: first, a general interest in industrial relations in greenfield sites, reflected in particular in the question of trade union recognition and the existence of innovative HRM policies; second, a focus on specific sectors and most notably electronics and the motor industry; and third, an analysis of the impact of foreign-owned firms and in particular Japanese and American firms, but to a lesser extent German ones too. Our review will follow this pattern.

RESEARCH ON INDUSTRIAL RELATIONS AND HUMAN RESOURCE MANAGEMENT IN GREENFIELD SITES

Research on greenfield sites has its origin in the USA. There, it was initially associated with the move from the rust belt to the sun belt but also with the quality of working life movement. Foulkes (1980) has outlined how existing non-union firms carefully selected the location and size of new plants in the USA to ensure that they would be non-union and would obtain a suitable workforce. Lawler (1978, 1986), who has done the most extensive work on the American experience, has drawn up a list of characteristics found in several of the apparently successful greenfield plants. These overlap to a considerable extent with the set of policies and practices Foulkes (1980) reported in his study of personnel policies in large non-union companies.

These characteristics include a flat structure based on high trust; job enrichment or autonomous work groups as the basis of job design; team and group activity; an open consultative system with extensive two-way communication and likely use of regular attitude surveys; very careful selection based on best practice psychological tests and realistic job previews; an internal labour market and career structures; extensive training and development; skill-based and normally generous reward systems; security and stability of employment; egalitarianism and single status conditions; and a pleasant physical working environment. These policies and practices have come to be associated with greenfield sites in the United States, with successful electronics and other high-technology firms and subsequently with the 'full utilisation' approach to human resource management. They are based on individual commitment to the organisation and leave little scope for trade unionism. Where grievances occur there will be elaborate systems for individual expression of concern, but no collective arrangements. Industrial disputes are likely to be non-existent. This approach presents one paradigm for the study of greenfield sites. It is, stereotypically, what greenfield sites are thought to emulate.

These stereotypes have been partly confirmed in some of the case study reports of greenfield sites in the UK. In the early 1980s the Work Research Unit (1982) of the Department of Employment described the innovative practices at sites such as Carreras Rothman in Spennymore and the Berkshire Brewery in Reading. More recent accounts of sites such as Toshiba (Trevor 1988) and Nissan (Wickens 1987) confirm the pattern of greenfield practices. While illustrating what can be achieved, these case studies provide no indication of whether these practices are typical of greenfield sites.

In an attempt to find out whether new plants in general conform to this pattern, Beaumont and Townley (1985) conducted surveys of practices in two samples of greenfield sites, one in Scotland, the other in the north-west of England. They obtained a count of the number of new practices of the sort outlined above and correlated the total score against a number of independent variables. In Scotland, there was a greater number of these practices in firms which were US-owned, non-union and had larger personnel departments. However, there was no significant correlation with age of plant, suggesting that these practices were no more likely in newly established plants (Beaumont 1985). This may reflect the date of the data collection, in 1984. Otherwise, the stereotypes are supported. Further support comes from the study of the Scottish electronics industry by Sproull and MacInnes (1989). Multivariate analysis revealed three significant influences on the presence of a recognised union, namely size, age of plant and single status. A single status system is one of the core elements of a human resource policy, suggesting that where a human resource policy existed trade unions were more likely to be absent.

In the north-west England survey, the results were very different. The practices associated with HRM were more prevalent in larger, unionised plants with a specialist personnel department and which were part of a larger multi-plant organisation. The small number of American firms did not have a significant influence on the overall results although their practices were closer to the pattern found among the American plants in Scotland. We must treat these results carefully since we do not know which variables were ticked in each sample, the list of variables included a variety of joint committees which might be more common in unionised than non-unionised plants and the statistical analysis is limited. However, the results imply that UK-owned greenfield sites, particularly small single establishment firms, do not conform to the American stereotype. The American-owned greenfield sites may do, but they were no more likely to do so than the older American firms.

One of the key issues for greenfield sites is how well they cope with the ageing process. Lawler has revisited a number of the earlier greenfield sites in the USA and although he presents no systematic data, he reports that 'virtually every plant has thrived and continues to be managed in a very participative way' (Lawler 1990: 10). However, like other writers, he notes that these plants face a number of what might be termed second generation problems. These include the problem of managing change, associated with a risk of complacency; an underestimate of the investment required to sustain effective teams; the problem of skill-based pay 'topping out' after about four years; and the problems of developing both staff and managers in stand-alone manufacturing sites offering little scope to move on to other activities in the wider organisation. Taking his assessment a step further, Lawler (1991) argues that these greenfield sites have been largely successful in providing workers with the information and autonomy to maintain involvement in their jobs and to do them effectively but the new challenge lies in creating self-managed organisations where workers contribute well beyond the narrow confines of their own jobs.

At a more mundane level new plants face the challenge of moving to a more stable bureaucracy. The risk is that something will be lost as the excitement and novelty and sense of opportunity in a greenfield site disappears. It is perhaps then that they become more vulnerable to industrial relations problems. These problems can be exacerbated by external economic factors and also by the maturing of the workforce. Promotion expectations may be hard to meet. Those selected as young impressionable workers grow older and wiser but cannot be replaced; in short, a new set of issues arises. The analysis of industrial relations arguably becomes more important once a plant has aged a little and the real challenges begin.

We have very little systematic evidence on the impact of ageing on HRM/IR in the UK. However, there does appear to be some substance to the fears for greenfield sites. A report (IRRR 1984) on Cadbury's plant at Chirk fifteen years after its establishment as a greenfield operation in 1969 found that a single union agreement had given way to separate recognition for some white-collar staff. There had been some minor industrial relations difficulties. But on the positive side, industrial relations generally were rated as being very good and some further innovations in policy and practice had been introduced. A study by Newell (1991) of workforce attitudes in four UK- and European-owned greenfield sites a few years after their opening revealed that the workforce attitudes were no more positive than those of typical UK workers. The main problem appears to have been that workers were encouraged to have unrealistically high expectations at the outset which the company was unable to realise. Essentially, this appears to be a problem with the processes of recruitment, selection and socialisation.

Sproull and MacInnes (1989), in their study of the UK electronics industry, reported considerable stability of union recognition over the three years between 1984 and 1987. Among the forty-seven plants in their sample recognising a trade union, twenty-four had accepted recognition at the time when the plant opened, ten recognised them during the first five years of operation, six between six and ten years and seven only after eleven years. Most of this recognition subsequent to opening had occurred in the 1970s and there was very little evidence of it occurring in the harsher climate of the 1980s. The evidence therefore appears to be mixed but points to some variety of outcome as new plants age.

RESEARCH ON SPECIFIC INDUSTRIES

The electronics industry is reputed to have been most enthusiastic in adopting human resource management. This is a function of its relative youth and its association with a number of American organisations such as IBM, Hewlett Packard and Digital which have been in the forefront of human resource management and non-union systems both in the USA and the UK.

Much of the research has been conducted in Scotland. In 1991 the Scottish electronics industry employed 47,000 workers (The *Guardian* 8 October 1991). Over half the plants were foreign-owned, 80 per cent by American firms. About fifty of the firms in the industry originated locally. In 1988, thirty-nine of these each employed fewer than 100 workers. Sproull and MacInnes (1989) have reviewed the impact of the shift 'from ships to chips' on trade unionism. Their postal survey obtained responses from 144 plants employing 87 per cent of the industry's workforce. They found that although 64 per cent of the plants they studied were non-union, most of these were small, so that 62 per cent of workers in the industry were employed in establishments that had some form of union recognition. They also found that American plants were just as likely to be unionised as UK-owned plants, mainly because size was a key factor and American plants tended to employ much larger numbers on average. Significantly in the present context, however, they, like Beaumont and Harris (1990), found that those established in the 1980s were much less likely to be unionised. Therefore, although this research is useful in challenging popular assumptions about the electronics industry in Scotland in general, it does seem possible that the 1980s greenfield sites are different. Given the other results, these findings also raise again the question of whether the difference is a function of the young age of the plants or a significant new pattern associated with the changed climate and/or the changes in management strategy in the 1980s.

A second industry which is of interest is the car industry. Taking account of the influences cited earlier and its strong industrial relations traditions, it would be plausible to assume that any new plants would be unionised. There have been a few new plants opened in the 1980s, largely by foreign-owned firms and in particular by the Japanese. The employment patterns in some cases, such as the Nissan plant in Sunderland, are well known. However, there are also a number of new plants in the engine and components industries which have also been traditionally highly unionised. One of the new plants opened by Lucas in the 1980s is non-union and based entirely on individual contracts. Recent plants opened by some Japanese firms have voted to be non-union. So the picture is not clear-cut.

The third sector is finance and insurance. Large numbers of foreign and UK firms established a significant presence in the City and elsewhere in the UK during the 'big bang'. Not all have subsequently thrived. It is generally assumed that almost all of these are non-union. Yet some employ quite large numbers, raising the question of what sort of employment practices they have adopted. Again, there is a stereotype – large amounts of performance-related pay and the threat of arbitrary dismissal. Some evidence to reinforce the existence of a distinctive pattern of human resource management in financial institutions was provided by White and Trevor (1983), who looked at three Japanese City firms and found that they did not conform to the Japanese stereotype, preferring to operate a dual labour market and a system in which scope for advancement and participation in key decision-making was denied to UK employees. More recently, a case study based on two Japanese firms finds that they have adapted their policies, limiting the number of Japanese staff and providing more access to positions of power for UK employees (Evans 1991). We need more research before we can write with any confidence about patterns of HRM in new finance sector sites. They deserve as much attention as manufacturing plants since they are probably more representative of the future pattern of employment.

INDUSTRIAL RELATIONS AND HUMAN RESOURCE MANAGEMENT IN FOREIGN OWNED ESTABLISHMENTS

The hypothesis outlined earlier, based on popular stereotype, is that American firms are typically non-union, that new Japanese plants are single union but with special arrangements and that North European firms will typically adopt traditional collective bargaining but with a single union. These industrial relations considerations will be associated with distinctive patterns of human resource management practice.

Research in the USA by Fiorito, Lowman and Nelson (1987) has suggested that the presence of a range of company HRM policies is associated with union failure to organise at specific plants. Beaumont and Harris (1990) attempted to explore this in the UK by examining the characteristics of failed union attempts to organise. Using data from WIRS2 for the period 1979 to 1984, they found that among plants which were still non-union in 1984, organising attempts were slightly *more* likely in plants which showed any evidence of HRM practices as measured by the presence of joint consultation, share ownership schemes and increases in employee involvement. Arguably these are poor indicators of HRM, more especially joint consultation, which was much the most important predictor of the three but which is not typically associated with American firms. They also found that organising attempts were much more likely in UK- as opposed to foreign-owned plants. However since this study only covers unsuccessful attempts at organising it must be treated with caution.

The evidence of Sproull and MacInnes (1989), cited earlier, appears at first sight to dent the assumptions about US firms. Their study found that in the Scottish electronics industry, the plants recognising a trade union ranged from 44 per cent among establishments which were part of a larger British-owned firm, 40 per cent in American firms, and 30 per cent in European firms to 0 per cent in Japanese firms. The same study also shows that new plants, including new American plants, are less likely to be unionised and that none of the Scottish semi-conductor plants, all of which are foreign-owned, are unionised. There may not have been a long-established tradition of non-unionism in American plants in Scotland, but one appears to have developed in the 1980s.

Much research has been conducted on Japanese firms (see, for example, Oliver and Wilkinson 1988, White and Trevor 1983). Since the first zip-making plant was established in 1972, Japanese firms have set up or taken over about 150 manufacturing plants, employing about 40,000 people. They have also set up well over fifty banks and brokerages in the City (*Financial Times* 20 September 1991). Yet there is disagreement about how best to label their industrial relations and human resource management. The earlier studies described them as 'piecemeal pragmatism' (White and Trevor 1983). Others, such as Oliver and Wilkinson and Wickens (1987) have outlined a distinctively Japanese set of practices. In industrial relations terms, these include the single union with a special agreement, often including no strikes and possible pendulum arbitration. There will be careful selection and training and considerable flexibility of roles. There will also be use of teamwork and a system of open and extensive communication. The existence of all these characteristics has been empirically confirmed by Morris (1988) in a study of plants set up in the mid-1980s, and by Oliver and Wilkinson (1988).

Oliver and Wilkinson (1989) attempted to survey all Japanese firms in the UK. They found that the expected Japanese practices were widely used. For example, 95 per cent had flexible work arrangements, 93 per cent had group working, 83 per cent used an extensive system of communications, 75 per cent had single status and 73 per cent used quality circles. Although they obtained a limited response, meaning that the results must be treated with some caution, a slightly later survey broadly supported their findings (IRRR 1990).

More recently the assumption that these practices are typical of Japanese firms has been challenged. Stone and Peck (1991) have queried whether the Japanese do in fact use many of the innovative practices which are claimed, suggesting that often the responses may reflect misunderstanding of questions or a desire to please. They also argue that 'nationality of ownership is a relatively poor predictor of (HR) patterns'. Nevertheless, 'Japanese firms are perhaps more common in the more sophisticated group'. Garrahan and Stewart (1992) have argued that Japanese firms in the north-east, and more especially Nissan, have only succeeded because of the external labour market situation – location in high unemployment areas – and careful selection which this situation permits. It seems equally probable that these counter-claims are in turn over-simplifications. In this context it is interesting to note that Oliver and Wilkinson (1989) found that comparable British firms were almost as likely to be using the 'Japanese' practices as the Japanese. What this strongly implies is that the use of a particular technique is less important than the way it is used and how successfully it is integrated into a coherent HRM strategy. In many of the Japanese plants this has been achieved, using total quality management as the key integrating mechanism.

Beaumont, Cressey and Jakobsen (1990) have examined the practices in a sample of half the German firms operating in the UK, 25 per cent of which had been started in the 1980s. They do not appear to conform readily to the North European stereotype. Seventy-six per cent were non-union – almost exactly the proportion of 'parent' companies that were unionised – and only a quarter had anything resembling a works council. The probability of a trade union presence predictably increased with size, the median size for the whole sample being only eighty-five. It appears that German firms maintain very loose controls over the personnel and industrial relations policies of their UK subsidiaries.

Purcell *et al.* (1987) used WIRS2 to compare UK- and foreign-owned firms on a number of personnel practices. They found that the foreign-owned ones were far more likely to use innovative techniques, to take communication and consultation more seriously and generally to behave in a manner more likely to conform to good personnel practice. This reinforces the findings of the Beaumont and Townley study with respect to Scotland.

What all this research indicates is that although there may be a tendency towards the national or industrial stereotype, the picture is far from clear. 'Newness' may possibly be more important than 'foreignness' in explaining IR/HRM policies in greenfield sites. This is of course no surprise. It is unreasonable to assume homogeneity among firms from a particular country. What it also reveals is the scope for choice, again emphasising the importance of management strategy and in particular strategy at the time when a new plant is established. Greenfield sites of the 1980s do on balance appear to be distinctive in their industrial relations. What we do not know is whether they are distinctive because they are new or because they reflect an enduring break with the past. Will they sustain their new practices or will they go the same way as so many green fields of the past and turn muddy and brown and develop familiar industrial relations?

INDUSTRIAL RELATIONS AND HUMAN RESOURCE MANAGEMENT OUTCOMES AT GREENFIELD SITES

In this section we will concentrate on IR/HRM outcomes. They can be considered at a number of levels. The first concerns the system and its stability. Do those plants which start out with a particular system sustain it over time? The most obvious aspect of this is the question of whether non-union plants stay non-union and whether single union plants stay single union. A second issue is how far the arrangements, such as they may be, for negotiation, consultation, communication and grievance handling are altered over time.

The second level of issue concerns the product of this system in what might be termed conventional industrial relations terms. In other words, are there disputes, what evidence is there of grievances and how far are employees participating in the consultative and communication processes? Are employees comfortable with the system and satisfied with their jobs and with their employment?

At the third level, a range of outcomes typically assumed to flow from effective HRM should be considered. These will include levels of labour turnover and absence, the number of ideas emerging from quality circles and related techniques, amount of unplanned overtime working and stability of employment. Taking this one step further, we might want to consider business performance criteria. Has the plant expanded according to its expected schedule, is the quality of the product acceptable in the marketplace and how does the productivity and competitiveness of the plant compare with other plants, perhaps in other countries?

At present it is much easier to ask these questions than to answer them. We can only take a superficial look on the basis of the available sketchy evidence.

Stability of the industrial relations arrangements

There is little indication that IR procedures change significantly in more than a handful of cases. If we confine our analysis to greenfield sites opened in the 1980s, the picture from the Sproull and MacInnes (1989) study in Scotland, which found one case of recognition and one case of de-recognition, is probably fairly typical. However, a few cases have been reported, including the Cadbury plant at Chirk cited earlier, which reveal the kind of pressures that can lead to change. Three of these cases can illustrate the points.

The first case is a Japanese plant in Wales where the management took a decision as the plant grew that it would prefer a union to simplify and organise its communication and consultation processes and consequently took the initiative in seeking a collective agreement. The second concerns Isola Werke, a German electronics firm employing 170 staff in Scotland. It opened in 1985 but by 1991 the AEU had organised 60 per cent of the workforce. Management insisted that the works council retain sole representative and negotiating rights but allowed 60 per cent of the employee seats on the council to go to AEU members. It also conceded that failure to agree at the council could lead to calling in the full-time official. The union in turn had to agree to support the company objectives by displaying adaptability and co-operation.

The third case concerns United Dairies. It opened its new Westgate plant in West London, employing about 100 workers, as a non-union plant in 1987. As the first non-union plant in the company, this was meant to serve as a model with single staff status for everyone, flexible team working, a flat hierarchy and no union. The non-union status was confirmed after an eighteen-month review. However, friction arose over working conditions and working arrangements. In particular there was concern among the workforce that they were required to undertake overtime work without pay because they were on staff status. An initial reaction was high labour turnover and a subsequent one was that the TGWU was able to organise over half the workforce. By early in 1991, management was forced to concede 'limited recognition', which consisted of the right to be consulted about changes in working conditions and the right to make representations on annual pay. Although the evidence on the German plant is too limited, the United Dairies example illustrates the potential for unionisation if management fails to ensure good industrial relations. Taken together these cases illustrate the variety of pressures at greenfield sites that can lead to union recognition.

Disputes, industrial conflict and worker satisfaction

Evidence of industrial disputes in greenfield sites is hard to find. Metcalf and Milner (1992) studied seventy-two cases of 'new style deals'. Two-thirds were in plants established in the 1980s, half were Japanese- or American-owned and 43 per cent were in the electronics sector, so they fit in well with the popular image of the new 1980s IR/HRM. Although the variations in the procedures make the results hard to compare, twenty-seven of the 212 wage rounds where a disputes procedure was available went to impasse. This figure of 12.7 per cent is not particularly low compared with private sector firms as a whole. However, industrial action took place in just five cases in the form of two strikes and three overtime bans, which is well below the national average. Since the sample is likely to contain many if not most of the sizeable 1980s greenfield sites where trade unions are recognised, it confirms the absence of significant industrial conflict.

A somewhat older study by ACAS Wales (1986) examined twenty-six foreign-owned firms operating in Wales. Fourteen had started during the 1980s and all the remainder in the 1970s. In the ten years prior to the study, seven of the twenty-six companies had experienced industrial action in the form of strikes or overtime bans.

Research, usually on a plant by plant basis, often reveals high levels of satisfaction among staff, more particularly at foreign-owned establishments. Toner (1987) in Eire, compared foreign-owned greenfield sites and comparable locally owned older plants and found higher satisfaction among those at the new and non-union plants. Surveys at the Cadbury plant revealed fairly high levels of satisfaction. The work of Newell (1991), cited earlier, provides an interesting contrast, suggesting that high satisfaction will only be achieved with an integrated human resource policy giving careful attention, among other things, to the management of expectations.

In summary, greenfield sites of the 1980s do appear to be largely free of industrial disputes. In so far as many are non-union, the whole concept of an industrial dispute begins to look outdated. Good industrial relations needs to be redefined either in terms of quality of working life criteria of the sort found in the Social Chapter or in terms of human resource outcomes.

Human resource management outcomes

There is very little systematic evidence on criteria such as labour turnover and absence. The ACAS Wales study cited absenteeism levels of about 4 per cent and claimed that this was close to the average for Wales. Reports on Toshiba and Nissan reveal absence levels, including sickness absence of about 2.5 per cent. Anecdotal evidence points to care taken to sustain employment stability at foreign-owned greenfield sites. However, in the face of recession, some changes are beginning to appear. For example, Unisys have shut their Scottish plant, opened in 1980, resulting in the loss of nearly 700 jobs and Seagate have closed their Scottish disk drive repair plant with a loss of 220 jobs. Another American closure was the Wang plant in Scotland but it was taken over by Compaq with a net increase in the numbers employed. Stone and Peck (1991) refer to two north-east foreign-owned plants which were sold to UK-owned companies but they do not cite the country of origin.

Japanese firms have been reluctant to close plants or make compulsory redundancies. However, Hitachi required major cutbacks in their Welsh plant and asked for volunteers aged above thirty-five. The current recession has affected a number of plants. NSK and Komatsu in the north-east of England used extended Christmas and New Year breaks at the end of 1991 as a way of cutting back production and Fujitsu have slowed the expansion plans for their new plant.

On the basis of these limited cases, it appears that the Americans are more ready to abandon sites, even when, as in the case of Unisys, there is a research and development capacity as well as production. The Japanese seek ways to maintain employment levels without compulsory redundancies.

Plant performance data for greenfield sites are very hard to identify. Profit levels are inappropriate criteria to assess plant-level performance because of the flexibility of accounting procedures. Productivity indices would be more useful. If we are only comparing across greenfield sites then the age factor can be discounted. But once again we lack any systematic data. There is, however, a certain amount of anecdotal evidence about the performance of Japanese plants compared with similar plants in Japan. These accounts range from some which suggest productivity levels are the same to others which indicate that they are up to some 20 per cent lower. At a more general level, recent CBI data suggest that foreign-owned firms have contributed disproportionately to the rise in UK manufacturing productivity. This reflects the figures cited earlier about differences in employment and output.

CONCLUSIONS: THE RESEARCH AGENDA

This review has revealed how little we know about policies and practices at greenfield sites and about their impact on HRM/IR outcomes and organisational performance. Most of the reported research focuses on policy and practice and ignores industrial relations and performance outcomes. At present it is impossible to conclude with confidence that the HRM/IR polices adopted by these firms are any more effective than more traditional systems. Almost all the evidence is drawn from cross-sectional surveys of manufacturing industry, with a strong bias towards Scottish and Japanese plants. There is some suggestion that survey data seriously oversimplify the picture (see for example, Stone and Peck 1991). There is also little or no evidence about how HRM/IR policy and practice adapts over time. This points to the need for a different research agenda linking inputs, in terms of policy and practice, with outputs in terms of indicators of co-operation and conflict and levels of performance and doing so in the service sector as well as in manufacturing. And it points to the need for a form of reconstruction of cases to identify how the system has changed if at all and why. Only then will we be in a stronger position to reach conclusions about the sustainability and impact of the industrial relations and human resource management at establishments opened in the 1980s. And only then will we be able to judge whether industrial relations at these plants have moved beyond industrial disputes.

REFERENCES

ACAS Wales (1986) *Successful Employment Relations: The Experience of Overseas Companies in Wales*, Cardiff: ACAS Wales.

Beaumont, P. (1985) 'New plant working practices', *Personnel Review*, 14, (1): 15–19.

—— (1987) *The Decline of Trade Union Organization*, London: Croom Helm.

Beaumont, P., Cressey, P. and Jakobsen, P. (1990) 'Some key industrial relations features of West German subsidiaries in Britain', *Employee Relations*, 12, (6): 3–8.

Beaumont, P. and Harris, R. (1990) 'Union recruitment and organizing attempts in Britain in the 1980s', *Industrial Relations Journal*, 21, (4): 274–86.

Beaumont, P. and Townley, B. (1985), 'Greenfield sites, new plants and work practices', in V. Hammond (ed.) *Current Research in Management*, London: Frances Pinter.

Evans, C. (1991) *Internationalization, Corporate Strategy, and Human Resource Management in the Japanese Financial Services Organization*, MSc dissertation, Department of Industrial Relations, London School of Economics.
Fiorito, J., Lowman, C. and Nelson, F. (1987) 'The impact of human resource policies on union organizing', *Industrial Relations*, 26, (2): 113–26.
Foulkes, F. (1980) *Personnel Policies in Large Non Union Companies*, Englewood Cliffs, NJ: Prentice-Hall.
Garrahan, P. and Stewart, P. (1992) 'Work organization in transition: the human resource management implications of the Nissan way', *Human Resource Management Journal*, 2, (2): 46–62.
Guest, D. (1989) 'Human resource management: its implications for industrial relations and trade unions', in J. Storey (ed.) *New Perspectives on Human Resource Management*, London: Routledge.
Hofstede, G. (1980) *Culture's Consequences: International Differences in Work-Related Values*, Beverley Hills, CA: Sage.
Industrial Relations Review and Report (IRRR) (1984) 'A greenfield agreement 15 years on', *IRRR*, 314: 6–10.
—— (1986) 'Industrial relations in foreign-owned companies', *IRRR*, 378: 14–15.
—— (1990) 'The Japanese in Britain: Employment policies and practice', *IRS Employment Trends*, 470: 6–11.
Keenoy, T. (1990) 'HRM: a case of the wolf in sheep's clothing?' *Personnel Review*, 19, (2): 3–9.
Lawler, E. (1976) *High Involvement Management*, San Francisco: Jossey Bass.
—— (1978) 'The new plant revolution', *Organizational Dynamics*, 6, (3): 3–12.
—— (1990) 'The new plant revolution revisited', *Organizational Dynamics*, 19, (2): 5–14.
—— (1991) 'The new plant revolution: a second generation approach', *Organizational Dynamics*, 20, (1): 5–14.
Metcalf, D. and Milner, S. (1992) 'Final offer arbitration in Great Britain: style and impact', *National Institute Economic Review*, 142, November.
Millward, N. and Stevens, M. (1986) *British Workplace Industrial Relations, 1980–1984*, Aldershot: Gower.
Morris, J. (1988) 'The who, why and where of Japanese manufacturing investment in the UK', *Industrial Relations Journal*, 19, (1): 31–40.
Newell, H. (1991) 'Field of Dreams: Changing Employee Relations through Greenfield Sites', PhD thesis, Oxford University.
Oliver, N. and Wilkinson, B. (1988) *The Japanization of British Industry*, Oxford: Blackwell.
—— (1989) 'Japanese manufacturing techniques and personnel and industrial relations practice in Britain: evidence and implications', *British Journal of Industrial Relations*, 27, (1): 73–92.
Purcell, J. (1987) 'Mapping management styles in employee relations', *Journal of Management Studies*, 24, (5): 533–48.
Purcell, J., Marginson, P., Edwards, P. and Sisson, K. (1987) 'The industrial relations practices of multi-plant foreign owned firms', *Industrial Relations Journal*, 18, (2): 130–7.
Purcell, J. and Sisson, K. (1983) 'Strategies and practice in the management of industrial relations', in G. Bain (ed.) *Industrial Relations in Britain*, Oxford: Blackwell.

Sproull, A. and MacInnes, J. (1989) 'Union recognition, single union agreements and employment change in Scottish electronics', *Industrial Relations Journal*, 20, (1): 33–46.

Stevens, M. and Wareing, A. (1990) 'Union density and workplace composition', *Employment Gazette*, August: 403–13.

Stone, I. and Peck, F. (1991) *The Labour Market Impact of New Inward Investment on the Northern Region*, Newcastle: Department of Employment/Newcastle Polytechnic.

Storey, D. (1983) 'Regional policy in a recession', *National Westminster Bank Quarterly*, November: 44–5.

Toner, W. (1987) *Union or Non Union – Employee Relations Strategies in the Republic of Ireland*, Unpublished PhD thesis, London School of Economics.

Trevor, M. (1988) *Toshiba's New British Company*, London: PSI.

White, M. and Trevor, M. (1983) *Under Japanese Management*, London: Heinemann.

Wickens, P. (1987) *The Road to Nissan*, London: Macmillan.

Work Research Unit (1982) *Meeting the Challenge of Change; Case Studies*, London: Department of Employment.

3 Managing without the closed shop

Stephen Dunn and Martyn Wright

An epitaph has already been written (Metcalf 1989a). Snuffed out finally by Conservative law in 1990 and disowned by the Labour Party and TUC, the closed shop may seem a ghost of trade unionism past, glimpsed in quaint corners like Smithfield Meat Market. Even the Institute of Personnel Management (IPM) has regretfully let it go. In response to the 1989 Green Paper, the IPM offered 'no objection to the demise of the remaining remnants of the closed shop' (1989: 2), but listed its virtues nevertheless.

We pick out the IPM because its stubborness in finding practical good in such arrangements echoes the 1970s, when bosses were said to have loved the closed shop (Hart 1978). The echo is faint, admittedly. Throughout the 1980s it was muffled by the free marketeers' condemnation of trade union monopolism (e.g. Hayek 1984, Hanson and Mather 1988). Round up the usual suspects and the closed shop was invariably among them: icon and proxy of union power. Yet the IPM's persistence in finding virtue where the market liberals find none raises interesting questions. If, for example, the closed shop has largely gone, do managers miss it? Does its absence create industrial relations problems? Or, to stop its disappearing, have managers tacitly supported closed shop arrangements, despite their unlawfulness? Or have managers now been converted to the free market doctrine? Have they come to see the closed shop only in terms of damage, leaving the IPM as a lonely and erroneous voice? Or was the 'bosses love the closed shop' thesis always a myth, cultivated to reduce managerial cognitive dissonance at a time when there seemed no escape from the practice? Is it now buried unmourned as employers bask in a new freedom to manage provided by Conservative law and union decline?

In tackling these questions, we draw on research conducted at LSE in 1978–81 and in 1990–2. The earlier project attempted to establish the extent and impact of the closed shop just as the Thatcher government took power (see Dunn and Gennard 1984). The present research replicates the previous sample of large unionised companies and employers' associations (about ninety organisations in all). Thus we have two linked batches of 'vignettes' through which we aim to explore how the management of industrial relations has changed in the intervening decade. We are particularly, but not exclusively, interested in whether managing without the closed shop is an issue. Our method is the same as that used before. Semi-structured interviews have been conducted with senior industrial relations personnel or, more likely these days, human resource specialists. We appreciate that such people have a particular view which may not coincide with that of line managers or other specialists. But at least we can claim consistency across the two surveys. Before reporting our findings, however, and linking them with other research, we need to ask whether the closed shop is really dead.

IS THE CLOSED SHOP DEAD?

Legislation

The closed shop is legally dead. Like Rasputin's assassins, the government put a lot of effort into the task. The fact that it took ten years to complete suggests that the Conservatives, again like Rasputin's assassins, were wary of their victim's strength. The attack was two-pronged (Dunn 1985).

One thrust crippled collective action. Under early legislation, a union forfeited its immunities if members in one plant or company took steps (boycotts, writing unfriendly letters, tampering with contract negotiations) to force the closed shop on *another*. Later, action in support of *any* closed shop became unlawful (Employment Act 1988). This encompassed, for instance, a strike by union members to win a closed shop agreement at their own workplace, or to prevent its withdrawal, or to fix a demarcation line.

A second thrust bled the strength from the closed shop by bolstering individual rights. Unfair dismissal protection for those fired or harrassed as 'nonners' was initially extended from religious to conscientious objectors, and to existing non-members. Later a ballot test was imposed on closed shops; otherwise everybody enjoyed the above right. Finally (again the 1988 Act) no employee could be fairly dismissed or penalised for non-membership in any circumstances.

The 1988 Act closed the pincer. Yet a comprehensive right not to belong to a union did not quite exist. Job applicants remained unprotected. Especially those working in or seeking access to pre-entry trades and industries, where a union card was the passport to employment, could still be denied a job because they could not get, did not want, or lost the correct card. The Employment Act 1980 had attempted to curb union arbitrariness in this matter by offering redress to people unreasonably excluded or expelled from membership. Even so, the survival of such entry control ten years later prompted the Conservatives to target it as the last flicker of legal life in the closed shop (Department of Employment 1989). Their *coup de grâce* was aimed at ending hiring discrimination against non-unionists and members of 'wrong' unions whereupon the closed shop in all its forms was officially pronounced dead.

The fall

But is it really dead? At the last count 2.6 million people thought they were still in closed shops (Stevens, Millward and Smart 1989). The finding, extrapolated from a NOP poll commissioned by the Department of Employment, suggests slippage between law and practice. True, it represents a halving of the closed shop population since its high point at the end of the 1970s (Dunn and Gennard 1984). However, the proportional drop is somewhat less. About 25 per cent of union members were covered in 1989, compared to around 40 per cent a decade earlier. Yet, either way, this seems an awful lot of people contained within legally indefensible arrangements. No employer involved can fairly sack anybody for trying to escape membership. No union involved can lawfully strike to coerce an employer into getting rid of the escapee. No unionists can lawfully strike to prevent their employers tearing up a closed shop agreement. Even 'Coventry bans' and other social sanctions to compel membership risk legal penalties. How does the closed shop survive?

One possible answer is that the legal penalties are not draconian enough to stop law-breaking. For instance, non-members get sacked and employers and/or trade unions, if 'joined' in the action, pay up the compensation. The unfair dismissal evidence does not support this. Or else the strike threat makes employers fearful of abandoning closed shop agreements. However, we know enough about the hazards of injunctions, fines and sequestration and the increasing wariness of unions about unlawful behaviour to reject such a proposition. A second possibility is that sackings for non-membership occur regularly but victims do not complain. Given the vigil that organisations like the

Freedom Association have long kept for such victims and the punitive levels of compensation available, this too seems unlikely.

A more plausible answer is that the surviving practices are sleeping dogs which are allowed to lie, unmolested by the courts. By this we mean that, within many of them, union membership may be a deeply ingrained habit and that rare nonconformity is corrected by a quiet word. In others, perhaps, where unionism is less well entrenched, it may be that managers and stewards collude to minimise the disturbance when dissenters appear, maybe allowing them to leave the union while keeping up the pretence that non-membership is unacceptable. Such closed shops may often be at the very margins of the definition. As Dorothy Parker said about President Coolidge's death: 'how could they tell?'. The difference between a live and a defunct closed shop can be equally elusive. If so, the NOP poll reported by Stevens *et al.* (1989) is a problem. It may conceivably overestimate the true extent of live closed shops. For instance, repondents who acknowledged being in a closed shop tended to have long service in their current job. Years before, when they were recruited, union membership may have been an explicit and invariable condition of employment. But how good was their information about enforcement in 1989? How many thought they were still in a closed shop because they once had been and nobody had told them otherwise?

In fact the poll offers some information on enforcement. But this merely adds to the puzzle. When asked what would happen if they were to lose or resign their union membership, a quarter of respondents in closed shops did not reply, perhaps indicating the lack of knowledge suggested above. More surprisingly, 28 per cent thought nothing would happen. Indeed only 20 per cent considered that they would be dismissed, forced to resign or transferred. Stevens *et al.* refer to these findings as showing a 'formidable array of sanctions' (1989: 620). Yet, in effect, they reveal that, put to the acid test of closed shopness, only a smallish minority of arrangements pass. Thus, if we strictly define the practice as a situation in which retaining your job depends on union membership, then in 1989 the NOP poll revealed, not 2.6 million, but just over half a million in closed shops. Perhaps, therefore, the legislation has had a greater effect than is often thought. The safest conclusion seems to be that the 'sleeping dog' hypothesis has some merit.

The NOP poll was unusual in asking workers about the closed shop. Other surveys have tended to rely on management. The latest of these comes from the National Institute of Economic and Social Research (NIESR) (Gregg and Yates 1991). It uncovers an accelerating closed shop decline in the second half of the 1980s, especially after the 1988 Act. Specifically, '22 per cent of companies with a closed shop agreement in

1984 had abolished it by 1990 while another 16 per cent had partially removed such arrangements' (1991: 366). Of course, this leaves a majority which have not done these things. Gregg and Yates speculate that the inertia represents a lag in the law's impact, or indicates that management has only acted where the closed shop was calculated to be detrimental to the business. The latter speculation accords with the 'sleeping dog' view, notably when Gregg and Yates surmise that, because legislation makes enforcement difficult, closed shops tend to be ineffectual and their formal removal is not necessary (1991: 367).

Our research helps clarify the picture. It generally supports Gregg and Yates's suppositions. The pattern is that many formal post-entry closed shops, particularly those regulated by the kind of Union Membership Agreement (UMA) which emerged in the late 1960s and late 1970s, have faded, are defunct or have been withdrawn without much fuss. This lack of resistance suggests, as was suspected, that UMAs were often paper closed shops (Dunn 1981 and 1985, Terry 1982, Hyman 1989). They came into existence because management and shop stewards sought procedural tidiness and they lacked any depth of rank and file support. As a result, when management withdrew support, the will to enforce the practice unilaterally was absent and the UMAs collapsed.

Yet there remain bedrock closed shops which have survived both the law and managerial policy adjustments. Managers are not coy about these. Even where UMAs have been withdrawn, informal practices are acknowledged to continue in certain workplaces or among certain types of employee. They are sustained by traditional solidarity ('Would you like to take your knees home in a carrier bag?'), often in older plants where the practice emerged long ago and they are left alone by management provided nobody has to be sacked. As one manager said: 'The closed shop exists because it doesn't exist'.

An exception to this pattern concerns the pre-entry shop. Generally management has been keener to get rid of this type of arrangement mainly because entry control, demarcation and union job territories hamper the search for flexibility. Such practices tend to be deeply entrenched and subject to arcane custom and practice. Removing them is not merely a matter of shredding an agreement. Rather it involves dislodging a craft ethos. Managers freely admit that the task is slow and sometimes hazardous as the bitter disputes in printing, merchant shipping, independent television and the docks testify. Even so, most managers interviewed thought they had made progress. Responses ranged from 'We've scratched the pig in a couple of places' to 'We've broken control of entry'. In the latter case, the manager claimed to have bulldozed the training school on one site in a symbolic move against the old apprenticeship system.

The mysterious resurrection

The pre-entry issue has a strange coda. According to the 1989 NOP poll, the closed shop population was equally divided between pre- and post-entry arrangements (Stevens *et al.* 1989). Superficially this might seem to confirm the argument above that the post-entry shop, previously regarded as the much commoner type, had declined far more quickly than the obdurate pre-entry variety. The trouble is that these findings ostensibly mean a dramatic rise in pre-entry shops in the late 1980s. In fact the numbers in pre-entry shops appeared higher than at any time since figures have been available. At the start of the 1960s, for example, the estimate was below 750,000 (McCarthy 1964: 37). At the end of the 1970s it was about 840,000 and already subject to erosion (Dunn and Gennard 1984: 18). In the mid-1980s the Workplace Industrial Relations Survey (WIRS2) information put the total at 500,000 (quoted in Stevens *et al.* 1989: 617), reflecting, among other things, the employment fall in pre-entry areas. A rough estimate based on WIRS data but modified to take account of the further decline of these industries since 1984, but not of abolished arrangements, puts the pre-entry population at 480,000 in 1989. Yet in the same year the NOP poll showed it to be 1.3 million.

Stevens *et al.* explain this anomaly by saying that previous estimates were based on managements under-reporting the practice and by pointing to the discrepancies between management and shop steward claims in the WIRS2 survey (1989: 618). Accordingly the apparent rise was not real but the product of differing research methods, the assumption being that individual workers provided better information. However the true problem, partially acknowledged by Stevens *et al.*, lay in their questionnaire. Employees were asked: 'If someone were to be recruited now to do your job, would they have to be a union member (a) before being considered for the job, or (b) before taking up the job, or (c) after starting the job?' Those who responded positively to (a) or (b) were classified as being in pre-entry shops. Yet in neither case is the defining feature of the pre-entry shop, entry control, mentioned. In a true pre-entry arrangement, if the category is to have any meaning, the union concerned has to put a qualification on membership that stops most people getting into both the union and the job. This may be apprentice training or it may be family or community connections or it may be a quota system. Neither option (a) nor option (b) attempt to uncover such restrictions. Option (a), for instance, would most simply be interpreted to mean that the personnel manager tells job applicants during the interview that they must be willing to join the union or they stand no chance of being selected. Why should it be interpreted to mean that the union might refuse to accept the applicant into membership because he/she had no apprenticeship or the wrong father? Option (b) is an even feebler instrument for identifying the pre-entry shop. 'Before taking up the job' could merely mean that during induction the shop steward or supervisor gives new recruits a union form to fill in. In other words the difference between option (b) and option (c), which Stevens *et al.* take as identifying the post-entry shop, could merely be a matter of union efficiency. How soon does the shop steward get round to doling out a union application to recruits? It has nothing to do with exclusiveness, the desire to bar people from the union and thus restrict the supply of labour. Stevens *et al.* try to fudge this by saying that option (a) uncovers 'hard' pre-entry shops while option (b) locates 'soft' ones. But in effect all they have done is redefine the pre- and post-entry shops to suit their question.

This is more than nit-picking. The NOP survey provided ammunition for the 1989 Green Paper's attack on pre-entry arrangements (Department of Employment 1989: 4–6) and the subsequent legal change. The 1.3 million figure was accepted uncritically to show that entry control was a bigger obstacle to economic success than had previously been realised. Yet the Green Paper's summary of the pre-entry shop's economic impact was derived from a completely different set of statistics. If we were to accept the NOP findings, the WIRS2 data used by many researchers (e.g. Metcalf and Stewart 1992) are very wrong, showing a mere 400,000 covered by pre-entry arrangements. Therefore their calculations of the pre-entry impact are rendered useless. The government cannot use the two data sets in tandem without opening itself to accusations of wanting to have its cake and eat it too.

To sum up our discussion of the extent of the closed shop, the practice is not dead. But the post-entry shop is shrivelling to its hard core, while pre-entry arrangements have wilted under management heat in recent years. Now we turn to the changing relationship between management and the closed shop. Throughout we wish to emphasise the difference between the pre-entry and post-entry types. Too often they are conflated. The Americans, more precisely and more wisely, give them unambiguous tags. The weaker post-entry type is referred to as a 'union shop'. The 'closed shop' label is confined to circumstances where entry control exists.

MANAGING WITH AND WITHOUT THE CLOSED SHOP

How bosses came to love it

In the late 1970s a Warwick Industrial Relations Research Unit survey of manufacturing revealed that far more managers found advantages in the closed shop than found disadvantages (Hart 1978, Brown 1981: 118). Indeed three-quarters supported the practice, while half could think of no disadvantages. These results seemed to indicate a sea change in employer attitudes since McCarthy's pioneering study published in 1964. He depicted the closed shop as a trade union weapon, wielded where industrial relations were tough, to secure strike solidarity and craft exclusiveness or to prevent casualisation. If management conceded the practice, it tended to come only after a period of unilateral enforcement by union members or as a result of a bitter strike campaign when the costs of further resistance were calculated to outweigh the price of capitulation. Afterwards came management toleration or perhaps habituation.

The change uncovered by the Warwick survey was partly associated with the reforms recommended by the Donovan Commission (1968). In the main, employer advantages related to the post-entry shop. The arrangement was seen to add stability and comprehensiveness to procedures at a time when management wanted to support union representatives in a joint search for orderly conduct and authoritative agreements. Writ large, this meant that union officials or shop stewards would be more likely to sign and police unpopular agreements on, say, productivity if they knew that their members could not quit the union in protest. Rather they had to remain under union discipline. Good examples of this hope were to be found in British Rail and the Post Office where, in a period of profound reorganisation, management and unions came to closed shop agreements against a backdrop of unofficial action and troublesome splinter unions (Dunn and Gennard 1984: 60–7).

But not all advantages were about controlling the rank and file. In a number of shrinking and peaceful sectors, employers, and particularly their associations, were keen to preserve the viability of their industrial unions and to protect them from more militant predators by granting a closed shop. Examples were clothing, footwear and parts of textiles (Dunn and Gennard 1984: 80–1). More generally, the LSE survey found that 44 per cent of managers interviewed in manufacturing companies thought the closed shop useful in preventing outside unions encroaching on existing union territories (1984: 83). It was, for instance, fairly common for companies to conclude a closed shop agreement with a single union on a greenfield site before the first worker was hired. The aim was to prevent subsequent inter-union strife (1984: 80).

How bosses grew blasé about it

The advantages uncovered in the late 1970s can easily be exaggerated. Deeper probing revealed a more complex picture. Against a background of spreading trade unionism and industrial discontent, managers appeared to be locked into a world of narrow industrial relations choices where 'making the best of things' and 'live and let live' represented the limits of ambition. Many of the benefits attributed to the closed shop were expressions of the 1960s hope that procedural solutions existed to tackle the problems of low productivity, unofficial strikes and multi-unionism. As the 1970s wore on, however, managers seemed to become more jaundiced about anticipated gains. They still claimed them, as might be expected when they had recently signed UMAs. But, when asked to provide concrete evidence, they were often stumped. Also their behaviour suggested a degree of scepticism about the closed shop. For a start, a significant minority of unionised companies remained hostile to the practice and resisted demands. Others opposed white-collar closed shops. Even those that accepted UMAs were reluctant to concede them unless union density was high, which indicated perhaps that combating multi-unionism was not the priority. Once the overwhelming majority of employees have joined a union, a company either has multi-unionism or does not. The closed shop scarcely helps (Dunn and Gennard 1984: 83–4). Above all, instances of management initiating the practice were rare. Even on the crest of the closed shop wave, its appearance waited on trade union demand.

The most plausible explanation of management behaviour in the late 1970s is that post-entry shops were conceded because the disadvantages seemed nugatory when union density was high, while possible benefits were a bonus if they materialised. In other words, the closed shop was a sideshow in what one manager interviewed in 1990 called 'the old industrial relations circus'. In that sense management grew increasingly blasé about it, almost to the point of indifference. Whether companies regarded their industrial relations as bad or good, they calculated that, where unions were well entrenched, the practice would hardly affect matters one way or the other. Familiarity bred contempt for its theoretical dangers (Dunn and Gennard 1984: 67–70, 85–8 and chapter 6).

Why bosses ought to hate it

While managers were becoming increasingly blasé about the closed shop, certain observers were warning of these theoretical dangers with increasing vigour. The message was amplified as market liberal ideas coalesced into Thatcherism. Indeed the closed shop became central to the moral panic which the Conservatives generated around trade unionism (Dunn 1985: 82–4).

Put briefly, the market liberal view is that, as trade unions exploit monopoly power, the closed shop allows them to do it more ruthlessly. The strike and the strike threat become more lethal and restrictive practices tighten into 'Old Spanish Customs'. Among the consequences for the economy are fewer jobs, lower productivity and lower profits than would otherwise prevail. The stylised facts of this process come in two varieties. First, the higher labour costs in closed shop firms galvanise management into capital investment and/or hiring better quality workers. Productivity may thus rise in those firms. But the effects are felt in non-closed shop sectors which face an oversupply of lower quality labour and an undersupply of capital. Thus the initial victims of the closed shop are those firms and workers in open areas. If true, this might explain why managers with closed shops appeared blasé about them. Second, and more simply, closed shops mean featherbedding. Labour is more expensive, less efficient and more resistant to technical change even than in unionised firms where no closed shops exist. For such firms, product market competition waits in ambush round the corner. Either way the result is harmful. Burton (1978), for example, calculated that trade unions in general and the closed shop in particular reduced potential GDP by 12 per cent and advocated that the government should borrow in order to buy out the practice once and for all before it strangled the economy (see also Hanson, Jackson and Miller 1982, Hayek 1984).

Comparing this message to those received from companies in the 1970s, it seems that market liberals and managers lived in separate universes. Yet there were some points of contact. In their analysis, market liberals did not necessarily distinguish between pre- and post-entry shops. The darkness of monopoly power covered them both. Nevertheless it is clear that, if these adverse effects did indeed flow from the practice, the pre-entry shop was the likely main culprit. Certainly some companies were able to recognise the problem. Managers were reluctant, for example, to allow new pre-entry arrangements to take root. Indeed, while post-entry agreements mushroomed between the early 1960s and late 1970s, the pre-entry population grew only slightly. Moreover, even though firms in pre-entry trades and industries often seemed anaesthetised against the restrictions imposed upon them, the stirrings of a reaction were detectable. In merchant shipping, 'flagging out' to avoid the National Union of Seamen (NUS)'s labour pool shop was already commonplace. In the docks, non-registered ports were taking an increasing amount of business from those that were harnessed into the Dock Labour Scheme. In printing, computer technology was starting to eat into the National Graphical Association (NGA)'s craft qualification and labour supply shops (Dunn and Gennard 1984: chapter 3). All these moves continued with growing management success, and some bloody battles, in the 1980s.

In the 1980s too, more precise economic evidence, based on data sets like WIRS1 and 2, became available. Broadly it appeared to show that, if firms did indeed love or even felt blasé about the closed shop, the dalliance hurt them. Looking back at the first half of the 1980s, establishments with closed shops seemed to be faring worse in terms of financial performance, pay levels, productivity, strikes and job loss than unionised places without closed shops and non-union establishments. The evidence varied in robustness but it tended to point the same way (see, for example, Blanchflower and Oswald 1988 and Metcalf 1989b). Some of it (notably Blanchflower and Millward 1988 on job loss) indicated that the closed shop effects worsened between 1980 and 1984. For market liberals, this would be nice evidence of market retribution, the competitive ambush round the corner to shake management from its connivance in trade union monopolism.

The end of the affair

Such research suggests that far from helping to incorporate unions into the managerial process, as left-wing commentators (e.g. Hyman 1979) suggested, the closed shop in fact helped incorporate management into a trade union ethos of featherbedding and restrictionism, just as the simpler set of market liberal stylised facts predict. Its decline would suggest managers have seen the error of their ways. However, before we offer our own evidence on the matter, we enter an important caveat.

The stock in trade of the above research is to control for other variables in order to isolate closed shop effects. Closed shops are compared with other unionised workplaces and with non-union firms. Some analysts also attempt to separate pre- and post-entry effects, which seems to be a vital addition. But much rarer is any attempt to differentiate post-entry shops from open shops with high union density. For those of us who are keen to pin down the closed shop's precise role, the differentiation is important. It is also important in judging the performance of management over the past twenty years.

A careful attempt to make such a differentiation is provided by Metcalf and Stewart (1991). Earlier work by Stewart had separated the wage mark-ups of pre- and post-entry shops over open union and non-union establishments (1987 and 1991). In this exercise, the authors again isolated a pre-entry premium, but detected no post-entry premium over and above that found where union density was high but no closed shop existed (pp. 9–10). If the finding were to be repeated in relation to other claimed closed shop effects, then a number of inferences follow.

First, those firms that became blasé in the 1970s about conceding post-entry shops, on the grounds that union power would not be increased where union density was high and rising, were making a rational calculation. Second, we would expect significant managerial advantages to accrue from the removal of pre-entry shops, but not from the end of post-entry arrangements, unless this was accompanied by a collapse of union membership. (The only survey evidence we have on this latter point is from Gregg and Yates (1990) who found that on average union density fell by 9 per cent (1985–90) in companies which reported a partial closed shop removal (pre- and post-entry not separated): not trivial, but not a collapse.) Third, if managers recognised this pattern of advantage, they might have been expected to risk more to get rid of pre-entry arrangements than post-entry. Fourth, and putting the previous two another way, those improvements in company performance associated with the decline in union power (see, for example, Metcalf 1989c) might have something to do with dismantling pre-entry shops but are less likely to result from the ending of post-entry types.

Recent evidence has shed some, but not enough, light on the fourth proposition. Using the NIESR data set, Gregg and Machin found that the union pay premium fell slightly on average in companies where a closed shop had disappeared (1991). Unfortunately the data could not tell us whether the defunct practice was pre- or post-entry. The same source allowed Gregg, Machin and Metcalf (1991) to relate closed shop removal to productivity growth, although in this case they did not uncouple such removal from reported instances of union de-recognition so that the explanatory variable remained a composite 'changes in union status'. They found that companies where union status had changed enjoyed an average 9 per cent higher productivity growth in 1988 and 1989 than non-union companies, which was almost double the corresponding figure for firms where union status had remained the same.

Again it was not possible to tell what kind of closed shops had been terminated.

So, although the above research tells us that the closed shop's waning is associated with improved company performance, a more detailed story needs to be told. Gregg and his colleagues are sensitive to this. They are reluctant to attribute monolithic powers to the closed shop and therefore to make easy causal links based on the assumption that these powers are swept away wherever a closed shop disappears. For example, the disappearance may follow, rather than contribute to, union enfeeblement. Or tearing up one UMA in a company covered by many closed shops may be a signal to the whole workforce that management intends to reassert its prerogative, even if the act itself is only of symbolic importance and even if the other closed shops are not the target (Gregg *et al.* 1991: 12–14).

Our own research is intended to help confirm or deny this kind of speculation. The pattern that emerges from our 1990–1 'vignettes' is not as easy to identify and interpret as that of a decade ago. Then managers appeared much more constrained than now in their industrial relations attitudes, behaviour and aspirations. Liberation from trade union power has subsequently set them running in all directions or sometimes more energetically on the same spot.

Preliminary analysis suggests a clearer pattern surrounding the pre-entry shop than the post-entry, although it has some interesting shapes. We have already mentioned the big industrial and legal conflicts that accompanied the demise of pre-entry shops in newspapers, shipping and the docks (described in McIlroy 1991: 69–72, 108–16, 143–51). These were probably the bitterest private-sector disputes of the 1980s. Employers bore the cost of confrontation because they could clearly see and desperately needed the gains of victory (Gregg, Machin and Metcalf 1991: 13): competitive advantage in the crowded provincial newspaper market, escape from the Fleet Street jungle, survival of cross-channel ferries in the coming age of the Tunnel, and consolidation of potential labour cost savings on the abolition of the Dock Labour Scheme.

These key events support the four propositions we listed above. More intriguing, however, are situations that do not fit. Take printing. Firms in the general trade appear far less hawkish towards the comprehensive labour supply/craft qualification shop than those in national and provincial newspapers. Employers still go to the craft union for labour and, even though non-unionism has grown among manuals in the British Printing Industries Federation (BPIF) sector from about nil to 10–15 per cent, there seems a widespread acceptance of entry control. Why? The answer is partly that firms are content to remain all in the same boat. New technology has had less impact on skills than in newspapers. So firms still seem keen to keep skilled labour out of competition as long as it still remains relatively scarce. The other part of the answer relates to Gregg, Machin and Metcalf's notion of 'signals'. Both union and managers picked up the signals from the newspaper sector. The union in particular has 'bent over backwards' to avoid further legal entanglements, to co-operate in work practice changes and to allow dilution, in order to hang on to its labour supply function. Entry control operates with the back door ajar. In short the pre-entry shop has survived because management has been able to make sufficient progress towards its goals without confrontation. Indeed it may be that employers' reluctance to attack labour supply arrangements makes the union more co-operative than it otherwise would be.

Yet erosion is clearly detectable. By their nature, employers' associations tend to reflect the conservative tendency of established small to medium-sized companies whose entire business lies within the industry. They see more merit in supra-company institutions, even the pre-entry shop, than do the new small firms trying to break into the market and large conglomerates with diverse interests. In the latter case, corporate pressure on subsidiaries to achieve financial targets lower managers' toleration of familiarly comfortable industrial relations processes. We noted, for example, considerable hostility to the print unions from managers in this type of company, a satisfaction at having marginalised them and sometimes a rejection of the employers' association as a link with a past best forgotten.

The general printing trade is unusual in still displaying a robust, multi-employer pre-entry system. As has already been mentioned, employer 'runaway' and technological change have been slowly eating into such systems for many years. The Conservative laws merely quickened the process. Yet some others, on a smaller scale, still endure. In construction, for example, while union membership has been collapsing, contract electricians have maintained traditional jointly regulated practices with considerable employer support. Even though the Electrical Contractors' Association usually denies that the arrangement is a pre-entry shop, it does ensure virtually 100 per cent union membership and it clearly aspires to do an entry control task by excluding 'cowboys' without the approved craft qualification. For employers the rationale is, of course, regulation of competition. For employees it means that they miss out on the spectacular rises and are protected from the spectacular falls in hourly rates that, say, self-employed bricklayers experienced in the 1980s. Also in construction there remain cohesive, itinerant gangs of tunnellers and scaffolders whose work is dangerous and whose entry controls are a law unto themselves. But these probably fall into the same category of eccentricity as the London wholesale markets in a land which time forgot (Metcalf 1991).

The disintegration of the major industry-wide pre-entry arrangements almost everywhere but in printing and acting, where the Equity pool shop survives on a wing and a prayer, means that numerically the most important entry control arrangements nowadays are the fragmented craft qualification shops found in tool rooms and maintenance sheds across many industries, together with the queueing systems that some unions operate to regulate access to certain high-paying firms in specific localities. Both are somewhat down-market compared to the old Fleet Street or docks. In the case of maintenance crafts, overall control of labour supply has long been beyond union grasp. In effect controlling entry from outside is no more than a card check. The real impact is on the internal labour market where restrictions on upgrading semi-skilled workers and on multi-skilling have been the intent. Here, as we have already indicated, a quiet war of attrition is being waged. Yet because the workers involved are often few in comparison with a company's entire workforce, elimination of entry control is not necessarily a priority or a matter for major conflict. Managers have admitted to us that, in pursuing a wider reform of industrial relations and working practices, they have advanced along lines of least resistance and left these small redoubts to be mopped up later.

Turning to the post-entry shop, generalisation is much more hazardous. From the four propositions we discussed earlier, we might expect that management has tended to see its removal as insufficiently rewarding to risk confrontation with the unions involved, and not to claim major gains where it has disappeared, provided union membership has not collapsed as well. There may also be, of course, managers who want to preserve their post-entry shops and who would regard their disappearance as a loss rather than a gain.

Picking up and disposing of this last point first, we encountered a few twinges of regret that the law has ended UMAs. Where industrial unions struggle for independence in declining sectors, like clothing, footwear, textiles, knitting and so on, employers' association officials often feel a sympathy for union recruitment problems where labour turnover is high. But this sympathy is muted compared to the 1970s when the real worry was that a big militant union would intrude and turn their placid lagoon to bloody froth. Now predator unions do not seem to be a concern, partly because industry unions and would-be predators have sometimes merged without great disturbance, and partly because the words 'predator' and 'trade union' tend not to be a credible combination nowadays. The fear just no longer exists. It is worth noting, for example that the much publicised single union deals of the 1980s, unlike those of the 1970s, contain no closed shop clause. Sole recognition is calculated to offer enough in the way of union security.

Of other reasons why bosses loved the closed shop, we could find hardly a trace of the argument about strengthening union officials against rank and file militants, dissidents and unofficial strikers. 'Order' and 'discipline' are not words in vogue with management in the era of 'commitment', 'flexibility', 'total quality management' and 'team working'. And the idea that management would need to rely on union officials or stewards to control their employees might be taken as a slur. They may still do so, of course, but none admitted it. Rather they emphasised the marginalisation of shop stewards, the abolition of full-time convenors, and the opening of new channels of communication with the workforce, undistorted by union 'voice'.

Overall our conclusion is that the withdrawal of the post-entry shop does not cause management problems. Rather than tacitly supporting it to stop it disappearing, managers tacitly support it where it refuses to disappear: where it represents the will of the membership and is part of the furniture.

Moving on to consider whether managers identified gains from the elimination of the post-entry shop, the British Rail case is illuminating. Recall that in the late 1960s the Rail UMA was signed partly in the hope that union leaders would be better placed to discipline unofficial strikers. Ironically, it was torn up in 1982 because union leaders wanted to use it to coerce strike-breakers during an official strike. It might be thus inferred that managerial gains were expected. However, despite a slight leakage of membership, union resistance to organisational change has continued, and, again ironically, it is the most closed group, the engine drivers, that is regarded as the most co-operative.

The general point which this illustrates is that getting rid of the post-entry shop does not appear to bring automatic benefits to management. Most managers recognise the fact. Indeed the post-entry shop seems to survive (usually informally and often as a 'sleeping dog') or else die, irrespective of changes in industrial relations goals and practices. We have found, for example, firms that preach Total Quality Management with religious fervour and have downgraded the role of the union drastically, yet 100 per cent membership remains universal among manuals, despite the withdrawal of UMAs. We have encountered firms that have, literally one decisive day, summoned up the courage to tell their unions that 'the nonsense must stop' and revolutionised industrial relations overnight. Yet they have left post-entry shops as they are. We have interviewed managers who continue to do things in the old way, despite commercial difficulties, and who see the unions as a major obstacle, but scarcely consider the post-entry shop to be a factor. In short, managers might perceive their unions to be strong or weak, co-operative or combative, and they might regard the presence or absence of informal practices as symbolic of that stance. Only exceptionally, however, do they calculate that withdrawing an agreement would make any difference, even if it too was a symbolic act to mark a new determination to change industrial relations. If managers are increasingly managing without the post-entry closed shop, it is more a matter of getting round to complying with the law and the gradual slackening of social enforcement than a need to destroy its theoretical power. The speed with which this happens appears to depend more on how law-abiding the firm feels it ought to be or on the personal values of senior managers or union members than on industrial relations goals or strategic shifts in management style.

CONCLUDING REMARKS

Epitaphs for the closed shop are premature but only slightly so. They are certainly less premature than the latest Department of Employment figures would suggest. Our 1990 evidence shows that previous arguments about managers liking the closed shop sometimes still hold true, even in pre-entry areas. But generally the love has faded and by and large management does not regret its passing. In pre-entry circumstances, some firms have fought significant battles to rid themselves of entry controls. Others have conducted a quieter war of attrition against them. Elsewhere, however, post-entry shops have tended to fade peacefully. In these cases managers are prone to see neither great gains nor losses from the practice's disappearance. The managerial indifference which marked the rise of the post-entry closed shop in the late 1970s, seems also to have attended its fall in the 1980s.

REFERENCES

Blanchflower, D. and Millward, N. (1988) 'Trade unions and employment change: an analysis of British establishment data', *European Economic Review*, 32.

Blanchflower, D. and Oswald, A. (1988) *The Economic Effects of Trade Unions*, London: Employment Institute.

Brown, W. (ed.) (1981) *The Changing Contours of British Industrial Relations*, Oxford: Blackwell.

Burton, J. (1978) 'Are trade unions a public good/bad? The economics of the closed shop', in L. Robbins (ed.) *Trade Unions: Public Goods or Public 'Bads'*, London, IEA, Reading 17.

Department of Employment (1989) *Removing Barriers to Employment*, Green Paper, London: HMSO, Cm 655.

Donovan Commission (1968) *Royal Commission on Trade Unions and Employers' Associations 1965–1968, Report*, London: HMSO, Cm 3632.

Dunn, S. (1981) 'The growth of the post-entry closed shop since the 1960s: some theoretical considerations', *British Journal of Industrial Relations*, 19, (3): 275–96.

—— (1985) 'The law and the decline of the closed shop', in P. Fosh and C. Littler *Industrial Relations and the Law in the 1980s*, Aldershot: Gower.

Dunn, S. and Gennard, J. (1984) *The Closed Shop in British Industry*, London and Basingstoke: Macmillan.

Gregg, P. and Machin, S. (1991) 'Changes in union status, increased competition and wage growth in the 1980s', *British Journal of Industrial Relations*, 29, (4): 603–11.

Gregg, P., Machin, S. and Metcalf, D. (1991) 'Signals and cycles: productivity growth and changes in union status in British companies, 1984–1989', Centre for Economic Performance, LSE, Discussion Paper 49, August.

Gregg, P. and Yates, A. (1991) 'Changes in trade union and wage setting arrangements in the 1980s', *British Journal of Industrial Relations*, 29, (3): 361–76.

Hanson, C., Jackson, S. and Miller, D. (1982) *The Closed Shop*, Aldershot: Gower.

Hanson, C. and Mather, G. (1988) *Striking Out Strikes*, Hobart Paper 110, London: IEA.

Hart, M. (1978) 'Why bosses love the closed shop', *New Society*, 15 February.

Hayek, F. (1984) *1980s Unemployment and the Unions*, Hobart Paper 87, London: IEA, 2nd edition.

Hyman, R. (1979) 'The politics of workplace trade unionism', *Capital and Class*, 8.

—— (1989) *The Political Economy of Industrial Relations*, London and Basingstoke: Macmillan.

Institute of Personnel Management (1989) *Green Paper on Removing Barriers to Employment*, Comments, London: IPM.

McIlroy, J. (1991) *The Permanent Revolution: Conservative Law and the Trade Unions*, London: Spokesman.

McCarthy, W. (1964) *The Closed Shop in Britain*, Oxford: Blackwell.

Metcalf, D. (1989a) 'Epitaph for the closed shop', Centre for Labour Economics, LSE, Working Paper No. 1154, later published in *Personnel Management*, September 1989, under the title: 'Can the closed shop ban open new doors for unions?'.

—— (1989b) 'Trade unions and economic performance: the British evidence' *LSE Quarterly*, 3, (1): 21–42.

—— (1989c) 'Water notes dry up: the impact of the Donovan reform proposals and Thatcherism at work on labour productivity in British manufacturing industry', *British Journal of Industrial Relations*, 28, (1): 1–32.

—— (1991) 'Smithfield meat market: the ultimate pre-entry closed shop', *Work, Employment and Society*, 5, (2): 159–79.

Metcalf, D. and Stewart, M. (1992) 'Closed shops and relative pay: institutional arrangements or high density?', *Bulletin of Oxford Institute of Economics and Statistics*, 54, (4): 503–16.

Stevens, M., Millward, N. and Smart, D. (1989) 'Trade union membership and the closed shop in 1989', *Employment Gazette*, November.

Stewart, M. (1987) 'Collective bargaining arrangements, closed shops and relative pay', *Economic Journal*, 97: 140–56.

—— (1991) 'Union wage differentials in the face of changes in the economic and legal environment', *Economica*, 58: 155–72.

Terry, M. (1982) 'Organising a fragmented workforce: shop stewards in local government', *British Journal of Industrial Relations*, 20, (2): 1–19.

4 Multiple unionism, fragmented bargaining and economic outcomes in unionised UK establishments

Stephen Machin, Mark Stewart and John Van Reenen

Bargaining structure is an important determinant of economic outcomes, whether in the labour economics context of union–firm bargaining models (Oswald 1985, Ulph and Ulph 1990), in the macroeconomic literature on cross-country economic performance (Calmfors and Driffil 1988, Rowthorn 1992) or in other areas of economics and industrial relations.[1] One of the most important, but understudied, aspects of bargaining concerns the number of bargaining units and the bargaining structures that accompany them.

The issue of multiple unionism is sometimes cited, often with little supportive evidence, as a source of detrimental effects on economic outturns. It is, however, rarely acknowledged that where multi-unionism exists, the unions involved may bargain either separately or jointly. As Marginson and Sisson (1989) state 'What claims about multi-unionism frequently ignore is the existence of effective joint arrangements in many multi-union situations. It may well be that it is fragmented bargaining arrangements, and not multi-unionism per se, which are the major source of the industrial relations problems attributed to multi-unionism' (Marginson and Sisson 1989: 1).

In this chapter we present some establishment-level evidence on this subject using data from the 1984 Workplace Industrial Relations Survey.[2] We address a number of issues, but place particular emphasis on the potentially different impacts of separate and joint bargaining structures amongst establishments with multiple unions. We attempt to compare economic outcomes that prevail under these two forms of multiple unionism with those under single unionism and, where appropriate, non-union outcomes. Specifically, we look at whether otherwise comparable UK establishments had different wages, financial performance and propensities to experience various forms of industrial action under different forms of bargaining structure.

The results that emerge are quite striking. It appears that, in line with the Marginson-Sisson (1989) quote above, what matters is fragmented bargaining and not multiple unionism per se. In 1984 multi-union workplaces with fragmented bargaining structures paid higher wages, had inferior financial performance and were more likely to experience strikes of at least a day by manual workers. In multi-union situations where joint bargaining took place these outcomes were no different from the single union situation.[3]

The rest of this chapter is structured in the following way. The first section discusses some economic and industrial relations explanations of why the presence of multiple unions and multiple bargaining may have an impact on economic performance. A second section then presents and discusses the basic unadjusted statistics. Then we draw on and describe some econometric results reported in our earlier work (Machin, Stewart and Van Reenen 1991) that estimate differences controlling for other relevant factors. A final section offers some concluding remarks.

ECONOMIC AND INDUSTRIAL RELATIONS THEORIES

A number of theories have emerged from the fields of economics and industrial relations concerning the possible effects of multiple unionism and fragmented bargaining. Some years ago, the concerns of industrial relations specialists were highlighted in the Donovan Commission Report (1968), which spoke of the problems created for economic stability by the 'hiatus between workplace realities and union officials' knowledge of them' (Batstone 1988: 5). The underlying problem appears to be that the prospect of industrial strife is exacerbated by the proliferation of potential points of conflict associated with large numbers of bargaining groups. Unions themselves have often regarded fractured bargaining as a tool of managerial divide and rule. For example, in the 1980 Workplace Industrial Relations Survey, when asked about reasons for preferring a single bargaining unit the most popular answer from the workers' representatives was that it 'Avoids divide and rule/strengthens union group' (Daniel and Millward 1983, Table II.25).

On the other hand, there are some advantages associated with fragmented bargaining. By giving expression to the diversity of workers' normative aspirations, it may enhance workplace democracy and so have desirable economic effects (Fox and Flanders 1970). Trying to collapse the disparate grievances and preferences of very different work groups into one bargain may cause more problems than it solves. Indeed, over 60 per cent of both union and management respondents to the question over their preference for separate bargaining structures in the 1980 Workplace Industrial Relations Survey cited this very reason ('Issues/Problems vary').

Two of the important recent advances in economic theory have been the renewed interest in union bargaining and the modelling of strike incidence on the basis of asymmetric information. Despite the relevance of these, they have rarely been applied to the analytically tricky problems of multi-unionism. Asymmetric information models (e.g. Hayes 1984, Kennan 1988) assert that disputes occur when the two parties have different beliefs over, for example, the expected profitability of the firm. To the extent that multiple unionism, and in particular multiple bargaining, increase the danger of conflicting perceptions of the true situation, these theories would predict a higher incidence of industrial disputes under multiple-union bargaining structures.

The most impressive attempt to integrate modern bargaining theory with multiple unionism is by Horn and Wolinsky (1988), who look at the situation where two unions bargain with a single firm. The advantage of separate bargaining from the unions' view is that they bargain for a share in the profits twice and can effectively leapfrog each other's pay claims. The disadvantage to the unions is that management can try to substitute labour from one union during a dispute with the other. Horn and Wolinsky conclude that separate bargaining will result in higher wages when workers are very difficult to substitute in the production process. This is because the firm will get very little revenue from hiring only one group of workers and both unions can demand a share in the relatively large revenues that are generated when they are the last group to settle. The implication of this is that skilled workers, who are harder to substitute, should gain more in terms of higher pay than less skilled workers under separate bargaining. We examine this conjecture in the empirical work that follows.

DESCRIPTIVE STATISTICS ON THE THREE ECONOMIC OUTCOMES

The data source we use is the 1984 Workplace Industrial Relations Survey. This is a nationally representative survey of just over 2,000 establishments, the sampling frame being the 1981 Census of Employment. It provides very detailed industrial relations information, enabling us to derive measures of multiple unionism and fragmented bargaining at workplace-level, and also gives information on a number of economic outcomes. We concentrate on the relationship between multiple unions and the pay of three manual groups of workers (skilled, semi-skilled and unskilled), managerial perceptions of financial performance and measures of industrial action for both the manual and non-manual workforce.

Table 4.1 Descriptive statistics on pay conditional on bargaining structure

	Type of union bargaining structure			
	Non-union	*Single*	*Joint*	*Separate*
Average log (pay)				
Skilled	4.834	4.914	4.999	5.079
Semi-skilled	4.591	4.704	4.811	4.854
Unskilled	4.344	4.519	4.648	4.642
Pay distributions (proportion of plants)				
Skilled pay				
<£97	0.151	0.127	0.020	0.020
£97–154	0.624	0.580	0.635	0.480
>£154	0.224	0.294	0.346	0.501
Number of plants	286	282	153	201
Semi-skilled pay				
<£97	0.449	0.310	0.119	0.182
£97–154	0.487	0.579	0.765	0.616
>£154	0.065	0.112	0.116	0.202
Number of plants	279	243	142	183
Unskilled pay				
<£97	0.670	0.527	0.384	0.362
£97–154	0.285	0.419	0.547	0.536
>£154	0.045	0.063	0.069	0.103
Number of plants	326	272	142	194

Notes

1 Private-sector establishments: unweighted means and proportions and numbers of establishments.

2 In the survey, the pay variable is weekly pay of a typical worker and is grouped into eleven bands. In the table, these eleven bands are aggregated into three, corresponding to the lowest four, the middle three and highest four pay bands.

3 The proportions allow for multiple responses across pay bands. So, if managers state two responses 0.5 of a plant is allocated to each band, if three responses are given 0.333 is allocated to each of the three bands and so on.

Multiple unionism was quite common in 1984. Thirty-five per cent of union sector establishments had more than one recognised manual union and, of these, about half had more than one bargaining unit (Millward and Stevens 1986, Table 3.7). The relative constancy of multiple unionism since the first Workplace Industrial Relations Survey of 1980 was one of the striking features of the 1984 survey (the percentage of union plants with multiple unionism for manuals was 35 per cent in both years).[4] It is also the case that multiple unionism and multiple bargaining structures are more prevalent in larger plants, manufacturing and where closed shop arrangements co-exist (see Machin *et al.* 1991, Table 2).

Table 4.1 reports some descriptive statistics on the pay levels of the three groups of manual workers conditional on bargaining structure.

Comparisons are drawn between non-union, single union and multi-union situations where joint or separate bargains occur. The first panel of the Table reports mean (log) pay levels for skilled, semi-skilled and unskilled workers in private-sector establishments in the survey.[5] As is well known, the mean level of pay is higher in the union sector for all pay groups. Similarly, pay is highest for skilled workers, next highest for the semi-skilled, and lowest for unskilled workers.

Perhaps more interesting is the variation with respect to bargaining structure. A clear hierarchy of mean pay levels emerges. Establishments with multiple unions pay more on average than those with single unions for all three skill groups. Furthermore, for skilled and semi-skilled workers, mean pay is higher for multiple unions who bargain separately *vis-à-vis* multi-unionism with joint bargaining. Interestingly, average unskilled pay levels between these two groups are almost identical. If we assume that the more skilled workers are less substitutable, this is exactly what would be predicted by the Horn and Wolinsky (1988) model discussed in the previous section.

For reasons of maximising response, pay levels in the Workplace Industrial Relations Survey are grouped into eleven bands. Figure 4.1 plots the pay distributions for skilled workers.[6] The pattern is very striking. Moving from non-union through to separate bargaining both raises the mean and compresses the distribution of pay. Hence, multiple unionism (especially where fragmented bargaining takes place) appears to raise pay but equalises skilled pay levels across establishments with more than one recognised trade union. To draw this out more fully, the pay responses, amalgamated into three bands, are reported for each of the three skill groups in panel 2 of the table.[7] Fifteen per cent of non-union plants stated that their skilled workers earned less than £97 per week; the corresponding percentages for single unions, joint bargaining and separate bargaining were 13 per cent, 2 per cent and 2 per cent respectively. At the other end of the distribution, less than a quarter of plants (22.4 per cent) in the non-union group stated that skilled workers earned in excess of £154 per week, whilst over half (50.1 per cent) of the separate bargains group earned over this amount.

The second economic outcome we consider is establishment-level financial performance. The management respondents in the survey were asked the following question:

> How would you assess the financial performance of this establishment compared with other establishments in the same industry? Would you say it was (i) a lot better than average; (ii) a little better than average; (iii) about average; (iv) a little below average; (v) a lot below average?

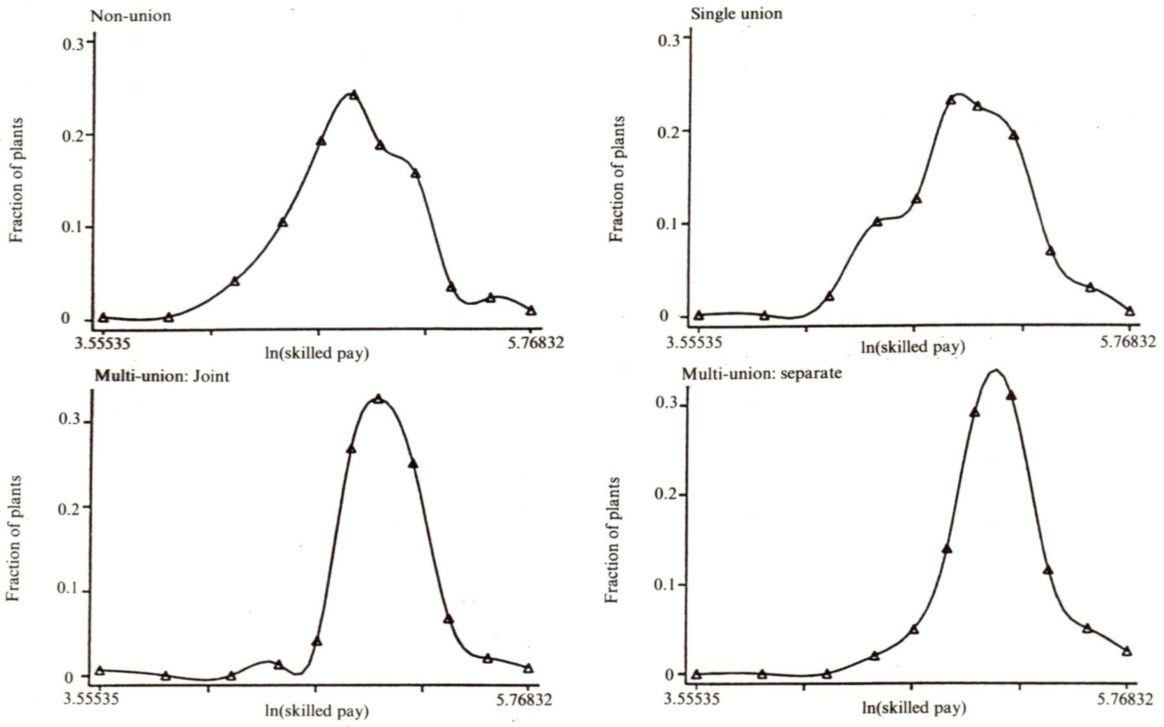

Figure 4.1 Skilled pay distributions

Figure 4.2 plots the distribution of responses conditional on bargaining structure. A fairly clear pattern is revealed. Managers in non-union establishments are far more likely to state that their plant has above-average financial performance; this is much less the case for all union-sector plants. Concentrating on the below-average responses we see a monotonic pattern with lower proportions in the non-union sector and the highest amongst multiple unions who bargain separately.

The third and final outcome variable that we consider concerns the incidence of industrial action in the twelve months preceding the survey.[8] Several forms of industrial action are possible, ranging from non-strike action such as overtime bans, go-slows and works-to-rule up to strike action of one day or more. Figures 4.3a and 4.3b plot incidence frequencies for manual and non-manual worker responses. Plants with multiple unions appear to be more likely to have experienced all forms of industrial action as compared to single union establishments. This holds for multi-union plants who bargain jointly or separately and for both manuals and non-manuals. Unlike skilled and semi-skilled wages and financial performance, it is not clear that there is any divergence associated with fragmented bargaining, at least in the raw data.

So it appears that the nature of bargaining has discernible effects on these three economic variables. Multiple union plants appear to have different economic performance (higher pay, inferior financial performance, more industrial action) than single union plants. Over and above this, there is also some evidence that multiple union plants with fragmented bargaining structures also pay higher wages (for relatively skilled workers) and have inferior financial performance.

Informative as these descriptive statistics are, there may be other factors at play. We know from elsewhere that a whole host of other factors which could be correlated with bargaining structure – e.g. size, workforce composition, ownership status – are important factors that determine pay at the establishment-level (see, *inter alia*, Stewart 1987, 1991, Blanchflower *et al.* 1990). Similar arguments are true for determinants of financial performance (Machin and Stewart 1990) and industrial action (Blanchflower and Cubbin 1986, Booth and Cressy 1990). It is important to see whether the pattern of results in Table 4.1 stands up to controlling for these factors, and we turn to this in the next section of the paper.

ECONOMETRIC RESULTS

Table 4.2 reports union-sector estimates of the impact of multiple unionism and bargaining when one controls for a number of factors.

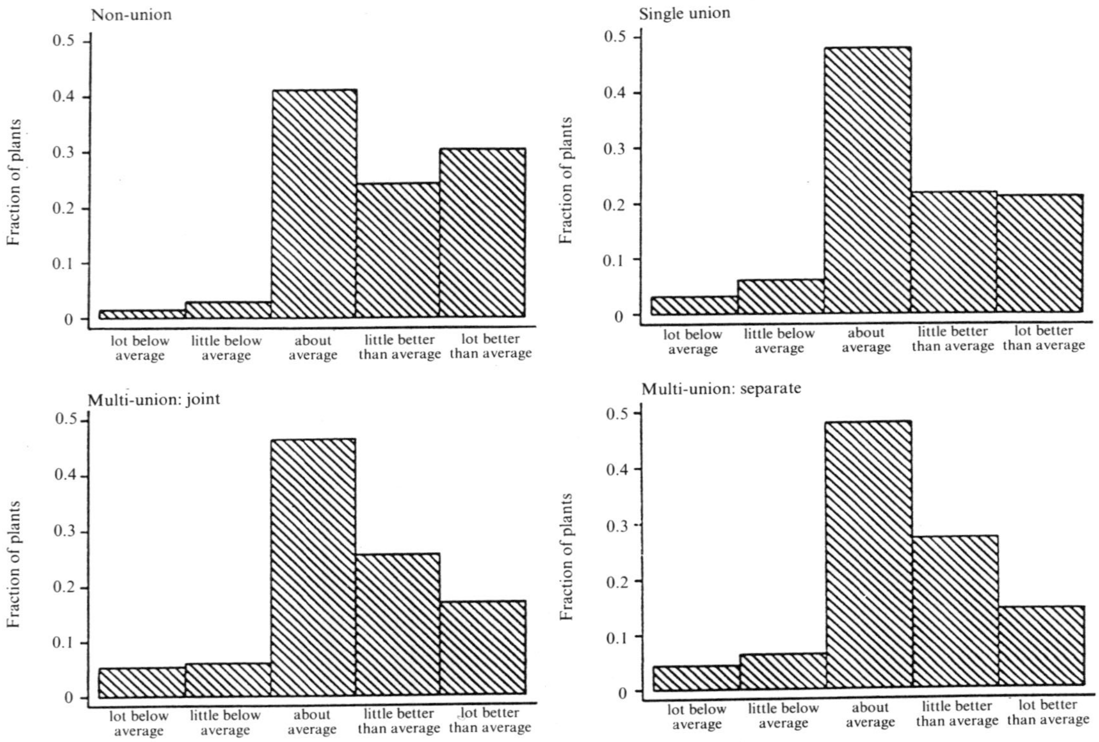

Figure 4.2 Financial performance responses

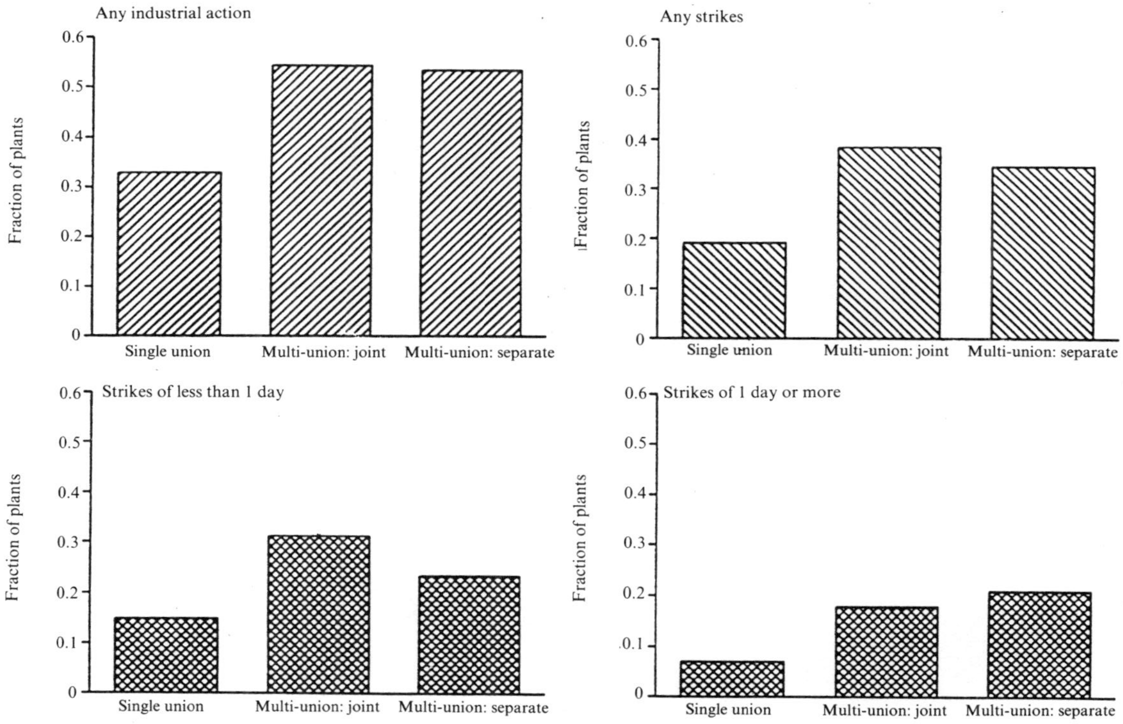

Figure 4.3a Incidence of industrial action, manuals

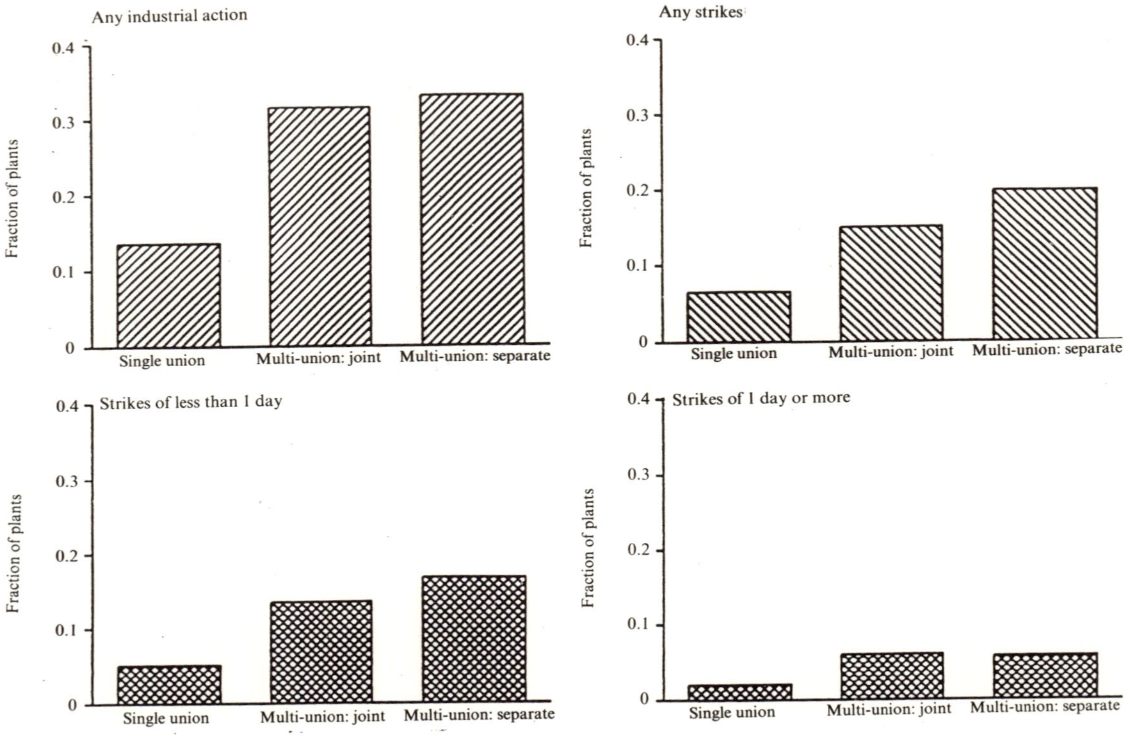

Figure 4.3b Incidence of industrial action, non-manuals

The precise control variables are detailed in the notes to the table. Two kinds of results are reported for each of our outcome variables. The first draws a comparison between multiple unions who bargain separately and jointly and otherwise comparable single union situations. The second compares separate bargaining with single bargains, where the single union and multiple joint bargaining categories are amalgamated.

The coefficient estimates reported in Panels 1 and 2 of the table can be rephrased as the percentage wage mark-ups[9] associated with the two comparisons described in the table. Panel 2 is preferred statistically because in all cases reported in Panel 1 the coefficient on the joint bargaining variable is never significantly different from zero in conventional statistical terms. To illustrate the magnitude of these effects, the estimates in Panel 2 suggest, *ceteris paribus*, that skilled workers who bargain separately receive 8.3 per cent higher wages than those who have a single bargaining unit. Corresponding figures for semi-skilled and unskilled are 5.0 per cent and 5.3 per cent.[10] Hence the essential pattern embodied in the raw statistics of higher fragmented bargaining mark-ups for skilled workers is maintained.[11]

It is also true that the broad contours of the raw statistics hold in more rigorous econometric models of financial performance.[12] In Panel 4 there is some (relatively weak) evidence that separate bargaining is negatively related to establishment-level financial performance. The magnitude of the effect is such that an establishment with separate bargaining is 8.4 per cent less likely to have above-average financial performance than a comparable single bargaining establishment.[13] A simple interpretation of this is that it merely reflects the fact that separate bargaining significantly raises wage costs.

Finally, in Panels 5 and 6 the results for industrial action are recorded. Looking at manuals, it is obvious that our control variables drive the effect of multiple unions and fragmented bargaining to zero for the any industrial action, strike action, and non-strike action categories. However, plants with fragmented bargains are still significantly more prone to serious strikes (those of one day or more) even after controlling for size, workforce composition and various structural characteristics of the establishment. The positive joint bargaining effect which was strong in the raw data is wiped out on the inclusion of these controls for other characteristics of the establishments (see Machin *et al.* 1991, Table 6 for more details). In probability terms, a serious strike is 10.2 per cent more likely to occur in separate bargaining establishments than in comparable single bargaining group establishments.

For non-manual workers, by contrast, it is the presence of multiple non-manual unions, irrespective of bargaining structure, that matters.

Table 4.2 The impact of bargaining structures on wages, financial performance and the incidence of industrial action

	Multiple unions	
	Joint bargaining	*Separate bargaining*
Panel 1 : ln (pay) comparisons with single unions		
Skilled pay	−0.040 (0.026)	0.062 (0.024)
Semi-skilled pay	−0.028 (0.028)	0.036 (0.026)
Unskilled pay	−0.023 (0.035)	0.042 (0.031)
Panel 2 : ln (pay) comparisons with single unions and multiple unions bargaining jointly		
Skilled pay	–	0.080 (0.021)
Semi-skilled pay	–	0.049 (0.022)
Unskilled pay	–	0.052 (0.027)
Panel 3: Financial performance comparisons with single unions		
Financial performance	−0.139 (0.140)	−0.256 (0.140)
Panel 4: Financial performance comparisons with single unions and multiple unions bargaining jointly		
Financial performance	–	−0.191 (0.119)
Panel 5: Incidence of industrial action comparisons with single unions		
Any industrial action for manuals	−0.142 (0.152)	0.043 (0.136)
Any strike action for manuals	0.048 (0.158)	0.046 (0.144)
Strike of < 1 day for manuals	0.054 (0.166)	−0.098 (0.153)
Strike of > 1 day for manuals	0.072 (0.192)	0.327 (0.175)
Any industrial action for non-manuals	0.419 (0.200)	0.448 (0.144)
Any strike action for non-manuals	0.304 (0.239)	0.424 (0.173)
Strike of < 1 day for non-manuals	0.378 (0.251)	0.420 (0.183)
Strike of > 1 day for non-manuals	0.378 (0.323)	0.335 (0.254)
Panel 6: Incidence of industrial action comparisons with single unions and multiple unions bargaining jointly		
Any industrial action for manuals	–	0.106 (0.119)
Any strike action for manuals	–	0.023 (0.122)
Strike of <1 day for manuals	–	−0.125 (0.129)
Strike of ≥1 day for manuals	–	0.288 (0.142)
Any industrial action for non-manuals	–	0.338 (0.133)
Any strike action for non-manuals	–	0.354 (0.156)
Strike of < 1 day for non-manuals	–	0.312 (0.165)
Strike of ≥ 1 day for non-manuals	–	0.347 (0.238)

Notes

1 Coefficient estimates with asymptotic standard errors in parentheses.
2 See Machin, Stewart and Van Reenen (1991) who report equations and describe estimation techniques in more detail.
3 Panels 1 and 2 are coefficient estimates from union sector semi-log wage equations estimated by Maximum Likelihood methods. Controls included are: 5 plant-size dummies, dummies for ownership, whether single site, majority-sex male, any payment by results, proportions of manual, skilled, semi-skilled, female and part-time workers, and dummies for pre-entry and post-entry closed shop arrangements for any manual workers.
4 Panels 3 and 4 are Ordered Probit coefficient estimates where the dependent variable is ranked from 0–4 indicating a range from well-below average financial performance, a little below average, about average, a little above average up to well above average financial performance. Controls included are: dummies for demand rising, whether at full capacity, whether the plant has a high share of its operating market and various industry controls.
5 Panels 5 and 6 are Probit coefficient estimates from incidence equations for different forms of industrial action. Controls included are: 5 plant-size dummies, proportion of female, manual and part-time workers and dummy variables indicating whether the plant was foreign owned, single-site or had a Joint Consultative Committee.

Both joint and separate bargaining have a significant positive effect on the incidence of industrial conflict (see Panel 5).

CONCLUDING REMARKS

In this chapter we have investigated the relationship between two aspects of bargaining structures (multiple unionism and fragmented bargaining) and various measures of economic performance. For the most part our results indicate that it is whether multiple unions bargain separately or not which matters rather than the existence of multiple unions per se. According to our analysis, pay is significantly higher for all manual skill groups, financial performance worse, and manual strikes of at least a day more likely to occur under fragmented bargaining. Since unions appear to have been weakened through the 1980s, but multi-unionism appears to have been relatively resilient (Gregg and Yates 1991), it would be interesting to see if the 1990 Workplace Industrial Relations Survey confirms the pattern discovered in the 1984 data. This survey will also permit investigation of other increasingly common forms of bargaining, in particular single-table bargains, that are not identified in the data considered in this paper.

Finally, these results suggest that one should be very cautious in claiming that multi-unionism per se has harmful economic effects. Of course, this conflicts with much of the received wisdom expounded in managerial and academic circles which rarely distinguishes between multiple unionism and fragmented bargaining and often lays the blame for poor performance firmly at the door of the existence of multiple unions with little or no concrete supporting evidence.

NOTES

1 An additional example that gives a prominent role to bargaining structure is the managerial literature on corporate control (Gould and Campbell 1987). The structure of the bargaining process also clearly underpins a great deal of work in industrial relations (see, for example, the papers in Bain 1983, or Batstone 1988).
2 This chapter draws on the more elaborate econometric investigation presented in Machin, Stewart and Van Reenan (1991) – interested readers are directed there for more details.
3 Although this is not the case for non-manual industrial action.
4 Though this does mask a shift between public and private sector establishments – see Millward and Stevens (1986) for more details.
5 These are computed by allocating midpoints to the grouped weekly pay data.
6 Consideration of the skilled pay distributions is sufficient for our purposes. Patterns were very similar for the other two groups, though distributions were shifted left due to lower average pay. (Figures showing this are available on request.)
7 Note that some respondents stated that they had workers whose pay fell into more than one pay band (this was quite common): the proportions are weighted in an appropriate way to allow for this.
8 As recommended by Millward and Stevens (1986) industrial action is defined as taking place if either managers or worker representatives indicated that it had occurred in the prior twelve months.
9 The coefficients reported in panels 1 and 2 are D = ln (1 + multi-single differential). To convert into percentage terms take [exp (D) – 1] × 100.
10 It is interesting to note that once one controls for the variables detailed in note 3 of the table, the unskilled pay premium for separate bargains becomes positive and significant.
11 We also experimented with the two other pay measures available in the data. Clerical workers' pay was no higher in plants with fragmented bargaining among non-manual unions; on the other hand, supervisory workers received a mark-up of over 9 per cent associated with fragmented manual union bargaining (this was based on classifying them into the union sector by manual union recognition – this is a problem in the dataset since we do not know whether they supervise manuals or non-manuals). This appears to corroborate the consistency of our results with the Horn-Wolinsky model as the clerical and supervisory groups are probably the most and least substitutable groups of workers that we are able to consider.
12 Because of the discrete nature of the dependent variable and the non-linear nature of the estimation technique these coefficients (and those in the industrial action equations) are not interpretable as percentage effects.
13 The estimated probability that an establishment with separate bargaining has above-average financial performance is 0.386 and the corresponding probability for a single bargaining establishment is 0.470: see Machin and Stewart (1990) for details on the computation of probabilities in this type of model.

REFERENCES

Bain, G. (ed.) (1983) *Industrial Relations in Britain*, Oxford: Blackwell.
Batstone, E. (1988) *The Reform of Workplace Industrial Relations: Theory, Myth and Evidence*, Oxford: Oxford University Press.

Blanchflower, D. and Cubbin, J. (1986) 'Strike propensities at the British Workplace', *Oxford Bulletin of Economics and Statistics*, 48: 19–39.

Blanchflower, D., Oswald, A. and Garrett, M. (1990) 'Insider power and wage determination', *Economica*, 57: 143–70.

Booth, A. and Cressy, R. (1990) 'Strikes with asymmetric information: theory and evidence', *Oxford Bulletin of Economics and Statistics*, 52: 269–90.

Calmfors, L. and Driffil, J. (1988) 'Bargaining structure, corporatism and macroeconomic performance', *Economic Policy*, 6: 13–62.

Daniel, W. and Millward, N. (1983) *Workplace Industrial Relations in Britain: the DE/ PSI/ESRC Survey*, London: Heinemann.

Donovan Commission (1968) *Royal Commission on Trade Unions and Employers Associations Report*, Cmnd 3623, London: HMSO.

Fox, A. and Flanders, A. (1970) 'The reform of collective bargaining from Donovan to Durkheim', in A. Flanders, *Management and Unions*, London: Faber and Faber.

Gould, M. and Campbell, A. (1987) *Strategies and Styles. The Role of the Centre in Managing Diversified Companies*, Oxford: Blackwell.

Gregg, P. and Yates, A. (1991) 'Changes in trade union and wage setting arrangements in the 1980s', *British Journal of Industrial Relations*, 29: 361–76.

Hayes, B. (1984) 'Unions and strikes with asymmetric information', *Journal of Labor Economics*, 2: 57–83.

Horn, H. and Wolinsky, A. (1988) 'Worker substitutability and patterns of unionisation', *Economic Journal*, 98: 484–97.

Kennan, J. (1988) 'The economics of strikes', in O. Ashenfelter and R. Layard (eds) *Handbook of Labour Economics*, Amsterdam: Elsevier, Volume 2: 1091–137.

Machin, S. and Stewart, M. (1990) 'Unions and the financial performance of British private sector establishments', *Journal of Applied Econometrics*, 5: 327–50.

Machin, S., Stewart, M. and Van Reenen, J. (1991) 'The economic effects of multiple unionism: evidence from the 1984 Workplace Industrial Relations Survey', Centre for Economic Performance, LSE, Discussion Paper No. 66, forthcoming, *Scandinavian Journal of Economics* (1993).

Marginson, P. and Sisson, K. (1989) 'Prospects for a single bargaining table: a review of bargaining arrangements on existing sites', Industrial Relations Research Unit Paper prepared for the TUC's Special Review Body.

Millward, N. and Stevens, M. (1986) *British Workplace Industrial Relations 1980–84*, Aldershot: Gower.

Oswald, A. (1985) 'The economic theory of trade unions: an introductory survey', *Scandinavian Journal of Economics*, 87: 160–93.

Rowthorn, R. (1992) 'Centralisation, employment and wage dispersion', *Economic Journal*, 102: 506–23.

Stewart, M. (1987) 'Collective bargaining arrangements, closed shops and relative pay', *Economic Journal*, 97: 140–56.

—— (1991) 'Union wage differentials in the face of changes in the economic and legal environment', *Economica*, 58: 155–72.

Ulph, D. and Ulph, A. (1990) 'Union bargaining: a survey of recent work', in D. Sapsford and Z. Tzannatos (eds) *Current Issues in Labour Economics*; London: Macmillan: 86–125.

5 The impact of the law on industrial disputes in the 1980s

Jane Elgar and Bob Simpson

THE CONTEXT

Concern over the extent of industrial action in Britain has been an item on the political agenda for most of the last three decades. During that time there has always been a body of opinion which held that changes in the law could influence the level of strike activity. In crude terms adherents to this view argued that a more restrictive legal framework would lead to less industrial action. The precedents available in the 1960s did not provide much support for this thesis as far as Britain was concerned. In the first place there was no clear, consistent correlation between the state of the law and the incidence of industrial action over the period since the legal reforms of the 1870s laid the foundations of modern collective labour law.[1] The imposition of compulsory arbitration from 1915 to 1919 and from 1940 to 1951 under wartime regulations which made industrial action a criminal offence, for example, signally failed to produce greater industrial peace.

More fundamentally, there was no established consensus on how to measure the relative importance of the law as an influence on the willingness of unions and others to organise, and workers to take, industrial action. Roy Lewis has recently drawn attention to the widely differing conclusions of distinguished academics on the reasons for the decline in strike activity in the period 1901–6 (1991: 61). That was the period after the *Taff Vale* case[2] in which the House of Lords held that a trade union had sufficient legal personality to be made liable in the civil law of tort for losses caused by organising industrial action, and before the Trade Disputes Act 1906 enacted 'immunities' against tort liabilities which included a complete immunity from tort liability for trade unions as such.[3] While Phelps Brown attributed this decline to the law (1959: 194–5), Clegg, Fox and Thompson explained it as the result of the depressed state of the economy and the development of alternative means of dispute resolution through collective bargaining (1964: ch. 9).[4]

One of the central objectives of the research on which this chapter is based was to attempt to establish a means of resolving such different conclusions in relation to the more recent past.

A further problem which confronts attempts to determine whether changes in the law on strikes are a key determinant of the level of strike activity is that it is difficult to isolate strikes from the rest of collective labour relations. Indeed it is arguably not sensible to try to do this. The real issue is the role of the law in industrial relations as a whole. What may be described as the orthodox academic critique of British industrial relations in the 1960s attributed a minor role to the law. The system was, it argued, a 'voluntarist' one characterised by the preference of both sides for social rather than legal sanctions so that the role of the law was 'abstentionist'.[5] What this meant, as far as industrial conflict was concerned, was that since 1906 – and subject to some important qualifications in respect of, for example, the wartime provisions referred to above – the law had mapped out a broad area within which the sanction of industrial action could be used in bargaining without being subject to legal restraint. If this analysis was correct, changes in the law to create a more restricted area for lawful use of the strike weapon would have little effect on actual behaviour because of employers' preference for not invoking legal sanctions.

From this perspective the proposals made for more restrictive strike laws in the mid-1960s, in evidence to the Donovan Commission[6] and by the Conservative party in its policy document 'Fair Deal at Work' (1968), were seriously flawed because they overlooked this crucial characteristic of industrial relations in Britain at that time. The law was nevertheless changed and radically changed in 1971 on the premise that: 'the government believes that legislation has an essential and positive role to play in the improvement of industrial relations' (Department of Employment 1970: para. 9). In particular, new opportunities were provided for both the state and employers to seek legal restraints on the organisers of industrial action, including trade unions as such.[7] But the evidence from the 1971–4 period provided strong support for the 1960s academic orthodoxy that in Britain there was a deep-rooted preference for not using the law to determine the boundaries for legitimate behaviour. The failure of the Industrial Relations Act 1971 (IRA) was a failure to change the attitudes of the parties – workers and unions on the one hand, employers and managers on the other – towards the function of the law (see Weekes *et al.* 1975).

The 'Social Contract' labour laws of 1974–6 on industrial action were stigmatised by the present government as a 'militants' charter'. But the intentions behind them were at the time a far more accurate reflection of the role that the parties wanted the law to play in industrial disputes than the policy underlying the IRA. In 1979 Lord Scarman described those intentions as follows:

> [t]he policy of the statutes is to exclude 'trade disputes' from judicial review by the courts . . . Briefly put, the law is now back to what Parliament had intended when it enacted the Act of 1906 – but stronger and clearer than it was then.[8]

It is therefore ironic to reflect that if the law was a more potent influence on the level of strike activity in the 1980s, that may well have been due in part – and maybe to a very significant extent – to a change in the wider role of the law and attitudes of the parties towards the use of legal sanctions which occurred as a result of developments in other areas of labour law, notably statutory employment protection rights, in the 1970s.

There is certainly some evidence of employers' being more prepared to resort to the law when involved in disputes in the second half of the 1970s. A significant example was the greater willingness of employers in the newspaper industry actively to pursue labour injunction applications in the late 1970s;[9] this may be seen as a forerunner of larger legal confrontations in the 1980s which many would regard as an important factor contributing to the decline in industrial action in national newspapers and indeed wider changes in industrial relations in that industry.

Our concern, therefore, was to investigate how the parties to industrial relations actually reacted to the availability of legal sanctions in situations of dispute or potential dispute throughout the 1980s. It might be argued that this approach to assessing the influence of the law on industrial disputes is over-elaborate and that all that is needed is to assemble data on strike activity in recent years and see if they bear any discernible relationship to the state of the law. That at least would give some idea of whether the law was an influence on the extent of industrial action, whilst not denying the possible contribution of other variables.[10] While an approach of this sort would need to look at trends over periods of years, it might nevertheless lead to some surprising conclusions which would suggest the need for a broader frame of reference. It must be remembered that the law on strikes is formed by a complex interplay of judge-made common law, legislation and the arcane intricacies of legal procedure. This body of law has fluctuated considerably over the last thirty years between the relatively liberal and the very restrictive. The Department of Employment statistics on the number of stoppages and days lost due to strike action do not clearly mirror those fluctuations.

Furthermore these official strike statistics fail to provide a complete picture of industrial action, not least because they exclude all forms of action other than strikes. This is a failing of increased importance in the light of the evidence of the extent of industrial action other than strikes in recent years (see Millward and Stevens 1986: ch. 10). Our research has confirmed that there are certain important groups of white-collar workers in particular who in the 1980s had been willing to take action short of a strike, but would be far less likely to come out on an indefinite, or in some cases even a limited strike. Some of this action has been very disruptive and therefore an effective dispute tactic which prompted some employers to resort to the law in an attempt to redress the balance.

Another defect in an analysis based on correlating dispute statistics with strike law is that restricting the relevant legal influences to the law on strikes provides a very incomplete measure of the full extent of the role of the law in this area. Wider legal developments can be an equally potent influence on whether disputes and industrial action take place. Some of these are found in other areas of labour law. For example, it is generally accepted that one of the objectives of some of the more important parts of the individual employment protection legislation enacted in the 1960s and 1970s was to reduce the incidence of industrial action. The official study on the early effects of the Redundancy Payments Act 1965 claimed that the reduction in days lost due to strikes over redundancies from over 5 per cent of the total number of days lost in 1960–5 to less than 2 per cent in the period 1966–9 was evidence of the success of the legislation (Parker *et al.* 1971). Later research by Daniel (1985) supports the conclusion that this Act had a seminal influence on the nature of the trade union response to redundancies; while redundancies have never become the subject of negotiated decisions, neither have they been the cause of extensive industrial action. The legal right to buy redundancies has materially contributed to effectively taking the subject off the list of major causes of industrial conflict. The same motive of reducing the incidence of disputes and days lost due to strikes was a major influence on the decision to create a statutory right not to be unfairly dismissed at the end of the 1960s.[11]

In the 1980s there were a number of other legal developments outside the boundaries of labour law which were of specific relevance to particular sectors, both as a cause of disputes and a constraint on the potential for lawful industrial action. Changes in the organisation of state education in both schools and colleges of further and higher education and the contracting out of the provision of services by local government and the National Health Service are among the more important examples. They are discussed more fully in the fourth section of this chapter. In short there is a very wide range of legal developments which are potential influences on the extent of industrial action. Any attempt to assess the impact of the law on strike activity must take them into account.

It is particularly important to bear these developments in mind in attempting to assess the impact of the Conservative government's labour legislation of the 1980s. This has been a subject of considerable interest, not least because of the persistent, simplistic claims made by the government for the legislation's beneficial effects (e.g. DE 1989: paras 1.1–1.7, 1991: ch. 1). From a legal perspective, some of the results alleged to follow from these changes in the law appear to rest on assumptions about how the parties concerned react to the law which at least require rather more in the way of hard evidence than is usually supplied. They also fail to take account of the possible influence of other relevant factors both legal and extra-legal.

THE RESEARCH

It seemed therefore that there was a need to obtain some rather more systematic evidence to test assumptions that have been made about the impact of the 1980s labour legislation on industrial disputes. In an attempt to provide this we have undertaken a wide-ranging survey of those involved in industrial relations, both on the employers' side and within trade unions. The objectives have been twofold: first to explore employers' and unions' experience of negotiations, disputes and industrial action, actual or threatened, and the role of the law in relation to this experience; second, to ascertain their more general perceptions of the impact of the law overall and the changes in collective labour law, in particular over the 1980s. For these purposes it is important to understand the different ways in which the law may take effect. There are essentially two distinct processes involved: first, how, if at all, employers make use of the law during negotiations and disputes, and second, how trade unions respond to bargaining within a more restrictive legal framework.

Our work on the use of the law by employers builds on previous research on the incidence of labour injunctions (Evans 1985, 1987). We have adopted a broader definition of 'use of the law' to include threatened use of the law as a bargaining tactic. That is the threat to seek a labour injunction or other legal remedies if industrial action occurs. This may well not give rise to any legal proceedings for various reasons. A remedy may be available without the need to go to court, e.g. withholding pay from workers who are not working normally.

Alternatively the threat to use the law – to restrain a strike called without a ballot, for example – may lead to the industrial action being called off. Either way this 'use of the law' may have an impact on the outcome of negotiations and disputes. To limit the research to an analysis of the incidence of labour injunctions would, therefore, give only a very partial and incomplete picture of the influence of the law.

A similarly broad approach has been taken to measure the influence of the law on trade union behaviour. The 1980s saw a number of high profile cases arising out of well-publicised disputes: the Stockport *Messenger* dispute in 1983–4 (see Gennard 1984); the miners' strike in 1984–5 (see *Industrial Law Journal* 1985); the Wapping dispute in 1986–7 (see Ewing and Napier 1986) and the seafarers' dispute with the P&O and Sealink ferry companies in 1988 (see Auerbach 1988). In these cases the courts imposed penalties of increasing severity on the unions for contempt of court in failing to comply with labour injunctions. Only a few unions have been penalised in this way. But all unions and not just these few have been forced to re-examine their rules and practices in a changed legal environment. Union negotiators and policy-making bodies have been faced with making strategic decisions which necessarily involved weighing up the potential legal consequences of adopting different courses of action.

The observations in this chapter on the influence of the law on employers and union behaviour in disputes are based on evidence from the first part of a two-stage research project. This was a survey of employers' associations and unions at national level designed to provide an overview of developments as seen from the top. (The second stage of the research focused on union and management negotiators.) The employers' associations were selected to provide a broad cross-section of the Standard Industrial Classification with members in a range of different product markets and service areas. Documentary information in the form of circulars to affiliates relating to the law and its application in disputes was provided and interviews were carried out with senior industrial relations personnel in some thirty associations. All major unions affiliated to the TUC, together with the main non-affiliates were contacted and most responded by providing documentary material on rule changes, guidance to negotiators on the implications of changes in the law and other relevant circulars. Interviews were carried out with national officers in about forty unions.

The overall objective of the research was first to draw some conclusions about whether changes in the law had contributed to a decline in industrial action and if so how this came about. More fundamentally it aimed to assess whether and if so to what extent the conduct of industrial relations changed in the 1980s as a result of legal influences, in particular the labour legislation of 1980–90.

THE LAW

It has already been noted that the research had a broad remit as far as the relevant 'law' is concerned. It sought to identify the full range of legal influences on industrial disputes and it is clear that these go some way beyond the changes made to the law on industrial conflict by the Employment Acts of 1980, 1982, 1988 and 1990 and the Trade Union Act 1984. These changes, however, inevitably provided the main focus for the research. The broad thrust of the central provisions is quite widely appreciated, but some of the changes are of considerable technical complexity and as a result often understood imperfectly, if at all. This part of the chapter provides a general summary of these changes and then locates them in the procedural context in which they operate.[12]

The 1980s changes

Strike ballots

In 1984 the Trade Union Act made the availability of the key immunities for organising official industrial action conditional on the prior holding of a ballot. The form of the ballot has to comply with detailed legal requirements and a majority of those voting have to support the proposed action to avoid loss of legal immunity. The prescriptive content of the law has been considerably expanded by the 1988 and 1990 Acts. One important change is the need for separate ballots and separate majorities at each place of work, although this is subject to a complex and near-incomprehensible exception. In 1990 the law was supplemented by a code of practice which is even more prescriptive, but lacks the force of law.

This has become by far the best known of the 1980s changes in the law. It is unusual in that while it restricts the application of the immunities – they do not apply unless ballot approval has been secured – it also prescribes a procedure to be followed to obtain legal protection. It could be seen, therefore, to legitimise industrial action. Investigating the effects of this provision is therefore of particular interest since it could possibly have the effect of increasing the incidence of strikes. Earlier changes in the law in 1980 and 1982 and later changes in 1988 and 1990 are qualitatively different. They all reduce the area within which strike organisers have the protection of statutory immunities from civil liability in the law of tort.

Trade unions' immunity

From one perspective the most important of these changes was the 1982 repeal of the total immunity which trade unions had from tort liability. Apart from the period 1971–4, court orders to restrain the organisers of industrial action could only be made against individuals – union officials or unofficial strike leaders. In the case of official action this made little difference in one respect. Court orders against the general secretary of a union had the effect of restraining the union from continuing the prohibited conduct just as if the order had in fact been made against the union – and the union would invariably pay the general secretary's legal costs. But the complete immunity did prevent successful actions for damages to compensate for commercial loss caused by industrial action which had been organised outside the area of the immunities. While unions would pay their officials' legal costs, they would not undertake to pay damages awarded against them. Damages claims were therefore rarely made. Exposing unions to liability has also exposed their funds to damages claims.[13] Since 1990 this may occur in a wider range of circumstances since the law now makes unions vicariously liable for a large area of unofficial action. The potential importance of this goes beyond the very small number of claims actually made against trade unions in the decade after the law was changed.

Trade disputes

Of similar general importance is the narrowing of the area within which any of the immunities which remain can apply. The area of legitimate industrial conflict is delineated in law by the definition of a 'trade dispute'. Only if action is taken 'in contemplation or furtherance of a trade dispute' can it fall within the boundaries of legal immunity. The definition of a trade dispute was narrowed in key respects in 1982. It is now limited to disputes between workers and their *own* employer which are at least *mainly* related to industrial relations issues as distinct from, for example, political opposition to government policy or any non-industrial relations subject matter. Subject to a very narrow exception the dispute must also occur within the United Kingdom. Apart from reducing the potential for international solidarity action virtually to disappearing point, these changes eliminate the possibility of workers' entering into disputes with other employers and call into question the status of any dispute with overtones of opposition to government policy.

Secondary action

A related policy objective is evident in the two-stage removal of immunity for organising secondary action in 1980 and 1990. In legal terms, secondary action is action taken by workers who are not in dispute with their employer. Public policy has changed and in Britain the legitimacy of different workgroups supporting each other is now completely denied. Even if taken in furtherance of a trade dispute between other workers and their employers, solidarity action has been deprived of legal immunity. The exceptions to this principle enacted in 1980 were in practice never applicable. Apart from the exception which is necessary to preserve a limited right to picket peacefully (see below), they were removed in 1990.

Union membership disputes

A rather different change in public policy has placed union security arrangements on the wrong side of the law by a series of different legal techniques. These include the removal of immunity from organising industrial action over the employment of non-union members by the same employer or other employers with whom the employer of the workers taking action has, or may have, commercial relations.

Picketing

Removal of immunity from acts done in the course of picketing, unless they fall within the narrow confines of the legal right to picket peacefully was in large part a knee-jerk reaction to the media image of picketing in the 1978–9 winter of discontent. In 1980 the right to picket peacefully was restricted to picketing at the pickets' own place of work. In legal terms, the importance of this change is much smaller than is popularly believed to be the case. But the loss of immunity for acts done in the course of picketing outside the scope of the right of peaceful picketing has the potential to undermine the lawfulness of organising any industrial action where picketing occurs.

Dismissal of unofficial strikers

The removal of immunity for organising industrial action over the dismissal of unofficial strikers in 1990 was in part a similar knee-jerk reaction to highly successful unofficial action in the 1989 summer of discontent.

The procedural context

The potential impact of these changes in what may be called for want of a better description 'strike law proper' can only be appreciated if the legal procedures within which the law takes effect are understood. Virtually all court hearings which arise out of actual or threatened industrial action are 'interlocutory' proceedings initiated by employers – occasionally others – who are adversely or potentially adversely affected by particular industrial action. These parties are invariably seeking 'labour injunctions', which are orders directing the defendant unions or individuals to withdraw calls for industrial action which have been made. Their claims are based on tort liabilities which the calls for industrial action allegedly involve and the absence of any immunity against liability for these torts. The considerable uncertainty as to the ambit of these torts and in particular the possible existence of liabilities against which no immunities are provided in any circumstances means that labour injunction proceedings may raise many difficult issues.[14] These are almost invariably resolved against the defendant unions and officials on the basis of preserving the status quo pending a full hearing of the case (which never takes place). Labour injunction applications do not normally fail unless the existence of immunity is fairly clear cut. After 1984 this means, *inter alia*, that if a union was legally responsible for organising the action, all the prescriptive details of the law on strike ballots have been satisfied. Although the courts have recognised the need for unions and workers to 'strike while the iron is hot', they have done little to give effect to this imperative in the exercise of the broad discretion which the labour injunction procedure gives (see Wedderburn 1991: ch. 7).

SECTORAL ANALYSIS

This section of the chapter analyses some of the information obtained during the fieldwork for the research together with other information about developments over the 1980s which has been obtained from secondary sources. For reasons which are further explained in the concluding section this information has been synthesised in a series of sectoral reports. What follows is a summary of four of these reports – on education, other public services, printing and publishing, and engineering and construction – which highlights the main points in relation to industrial disputes and the law.

Education[15]

In the 1980s the machinery for settling pay and other conditions for school teachers, lecturers in further and higher education (FHE), and academic and academic related staff in universities came under increasing pressure. In the first two sectors, school teaching and FHE, it was radically changed; in universities the negotiating machinery remained formally intact but by 1991 was probably under terminal strain. The abolition of the sixty-eight year-old Burnham Committees for negotiations on the pay of schoolteachers and FHE lecturers followed the breakdown on the Committee for schoolteachers of an informal concordat between the employers and the government under which no agreement would be reached against the Secretary of State's wishes. In 1986 the Labour-controlled employers' side was prepared to resolve a prolonged dispute over pay on terms which were unacceptable to the Secretary of State. The government's response to this and to a long-standing dissatisfaction with the Burnham machinery was the Teachers' Pay and Conditions Act 1987, which retained collective bargaining in the FHE sector, but empowered the Secretary of State to determine all conditions of employment for school teachers, subject only to taking the advice of an Interim Advisory Committee. Although the original intention had been to restore collective bargaining, the School Teachers' Pay and Conditions Act 1991 has created a Review Body to make recommendations to the Secretary of State on changes in teachers' pay and other conditions (see Fredman and Morris 1987, 1992).

These changes in industrial relations structures were accompanied by major changes in the overall framework for public-sector education in the second half of the 1980s. The Education (No. 2) Act 1986 allowed schools to opt out of Local Education Authority control in favour of grant-maintained status and direct funding from the DES. By July 1992 parents at 274 schools had voted in favour of this change and grant-maintained status for these schools had been approved. Under the Education Reform Act 1988 a new division of responsibility for managing schools and FE colleges is being phased in over the period up to 1993. In schools this is known as Local Management of Schools (LMS). This involves delegation of budgets to individual schools and colleges and a division of responsibilities including employment issues between LEAs and the individual institutions. This has important implications for the employment rights of teachers and lecturers not least relating to the legality of industrial action. In schools it also emphasises a divide between on the one hand heads – and in larger schools deputy heads – whose managerial function is increased and on the other hand, ordinary teachers. The Education Reform Act also took polytechnics out of LEA control and gave them independent status in 1989, but contrary to government expectations new institutions were established for national bargaining between National Association of Teachers in Further and Higher Education (NATFHE) and the Polytechnics and Colleges Employers Forum (PCEF) although one or two colleges have opted out of these.

In all three areas, pay was a frequent cause of disputes throughout the decade. Government cut-backs on local government finance provided the background to persistent failures by the Burnham Committees to reach agreements on pay. In FHE industrial action was regularly threatened and sometimes took place, though usually only on a limited scale. In both teaching and FHE the employers' sides were seeking radical changes in other conditions of service – which were then the subject of separate negotiations in national joint councils – and attempted to link progress on this to the annual pay negotiations. In schools, this resulted in extensive national industrial action organised by the National Union of Teachers (NUT) and National Association of Schoolmasters and Union of Women Teachers (NAS/UWT) in the period 1984–6. (A separate but similar sequence of events occurred in Scotland where there has always been separate negotiating machinery.) In universities a boycott of examinations preceded a delayed settlement of the annual pay claim in 1989. While pay dominated disputes in the education sector, the structural changes in schools, FE and HE exacerbated differences over other conditions of employment, issues that had already become an increasing source of disputes earlier in the 1980s, as well as introducing new causes of disputes over recognition and derogation from collectively agreed standards.

There were two main strands to the role of the law in disputes in the education sector in the 1980s. The first, and in retrospect probably the most important, was the decision of LEA employers to make deductions from the pay of teachers and lecturers who were taking action short of an all-out strike. In teaching this was an integral part of the employers' campaign to clarify teachers' conditions of employment in the face of increased use of the tactic of withdrawal from duties which teachers claimed were voluntary and not contractual obligations: supervision during the lunch break, cover for absent colleagues, attendance at parents' evenings, etc. The NUT's unsuccessful challenge to this practice in *Sim v Rotherham MDC*[16] provided some legal support for the management position. Similar deductions were threatened, and in three colleges made, against NATFHE members who took part in an examinations boycott as part of the dispute over negotiation of new conditions for HE lecturers in 1989. It seems clear from the *Sim* case and higher court decisions in cases arising elsewhere in the public sector that employers have a wide discretion over deductions from the pay of workers taking action short of a strike. Although universities did not threaten to make deductions from the pay of university lecturers in the 1989 exams boycott, a legally structured threat to reduce lecturers' pay which clearly reflected the developments in the case law in the employers' favour, was made in an attempt to influence the 1991 Association of University Teachers (AUT) ballot on an exams boycott.

The second main area of legal involvement centred on strike ballots. Most of the education unions already had a tradition of consulting the membership before authorising industrial action. In general, therefore, the need to hold strike ballots did not inject a new ingredient into their procedures. But after 1984 the way in which this consultation took place had to be changed in order to comply with the prescriptive directions of the new law. While some rule changes were clearly made with an eye to the legal provisions on balloting before industrial action, these were relatively minor developments. The changes that occurred were for the most part changes in procedures actually followed, rather than changes in the rules.[17] To this end many unions provided guidance for their officials on procedures to be followed where industrial action was contemplated. The most detailed guidance among the teaching unions was provided by the Assistant Masters and Mistresses Association (AMMA). This is perhaps ironic in the light of its history of not resorting to industrial action, although not ruling out the possibility of doing so. NATFHE, AMMA and the AUT went beyond their legal obligations in spelling out in some detail in the literature distributed with ballot papers precisely what action members would be asked to take in the event of majority support being obtained. The AUT had the benefit of experience of a consultation ballot in the late 1960s which canvassed views on a series of possible sanctions which members might take. The result, minority support for each option, was of little use to the union in its pay campaign.

The complexities of the law on strike ballots provide many opportunities for employers to threaten legal challenges to the validity of ballots held. Overall, however, compliance with the technical detail of the law did not create insuperable difficulties for the education unions in the disputes in which they were involved in the 1980s. Potential problems over, for example, reliance on earlier ballots to support a resumption of industrial action after school holidays or college vacations never gave rise to any legal challenge.[18] Both the NUT and NAS/UWT were challenged over failures to hold ballots in the 1984–6 period, but both unions quickly adjusted their stance to turn balloting to their advantage:

regular reballoting was used to demonstrate continued support for their campaign and thereby maintain the legitimacy and impetus for their action during this long period of dispute. For the NAS/UWT this meant reversing the 1985 conference decision not to hold ballots before industrial action. This change came after the union was sued for damages by Hereford and Worcester LEA for organising an unballoted half-day strike in protest at government proposals on teachers' pay and conditions in 1986. NATFHE also successfully adjusted its practices on balloting so as to avoid any legal challenge. But it is notable that in 1991 the Committee of Vice-Chancellors and Prinicipals (CVCP) alleged that the AUT's ballot was taking place before the negotiating process had been exhausted and thereby infringed a recommendation in the 1990 code of practice. The potential for ingenious legal challenges to any union decision on industrial action ballots was clearly increased after 1990, when the code took effect.

The other changes in the law relating to industrial action in the 1980s were not prominent in disputes in the education sector. The AUT was aware of the legal difficulties involved if it called for national action over redundancies at any one university, because of the more restricted definition of a trade dispute and constraints on lawful secondary action. As long as national bargaining remained intact in teaching and FHE neither the trade dispute definition nor the law on secondary action posed a threat to industrial action in these sectors over issues decided nationally. At the end of the decade, however, the structural changes in the schools and FHE sectors created new uncertainties in relation to the possibility of organising lawful industrial action extending beyond the boundaries of a single school or college. It remained to be seen how the vagaries of the definition of a trade dispute – a dispute between workers and *their* employer – the loss of immunity for secondary action, and the need for separate place of work ballots in some circumstances, would affect union dispute strategies in this new context. The extent to which industrial relations structures and established procedures were retained in the rapidly changing environment at all levels of the education sector was the key determinant of the range of legal constraints that could be imposed on the use of industrial action as a dispute tactic in the future.[19]

Other public services[20]

Education is only one part of the public sector. This sectoral report covers the other main public services: the civil service, local government and the National Health Service (NHS). It also makes some reference to the prison service. A distinctive feature of employment in the public services is the ambiguous role of the government. Only in the civil service and prison service is the government (technically the Crown) the actual employer and therefore necessarily involved in the process of making management decisions. The legal framework for administration of the NHS, however, also gives the government, through the Secretary of State for Health, considerable influence over management strategy (see Fredman and Morris 1989: 25–8). While local government enjoys greater autonomy, central government can influence the way that local management decision-making is exercised both through its control over local government finances and, if necessary, legislative changes which require local authorities to behave in a particular way. These powers and influences over management were particularly important to a government committed, as the Conservatives were when elected in 1979, to fundamental reform of the public services, including radical changes in established industrial relations practices.

Over the period from the 1920s to the 1970s, the public-services sector became highly unionised with well-developed, centralised collective bargaining arrangements. Union density was high among white-collar staff as well as manual workers, but only in the 1970s did the main white-collar organisations clearly emerge as trade unions from their origins as professional associations. This may partly explain the fact that for some white-collar unions, industrial action was virtually unknown before 1970. There was also a tradition of extensive involvement through at least joint consultation if not collective bargaining. Two key elements in the collective bargaining arrangements were the use of comparability with relevant parts of the private sector as the main criterion for pay determination for white-collar workers, and the availability of arbitration as the final stage in dispute solution. Among the general features of changes in the 1980s were the government's desire to end comparability as the basis for pay determination and its dislike of arbitration, which it consistently resisted as the means for solving major disputes. A more fundamental change was the introduction of Review Bodies to replace collective bargaining for some public-sector workgroups. The creation of a Review Body for Nursing Staff, Midwives, Health Visitors and Professions Allied to Medicine, for example, removed more than half of NHS staff from the scope of the collective bargaining machinery. Review Bodies, which are made up of government appointees, submit annual proposals for changes in pay to the government, having received evidence from interested parties.[21] Implementation of Review Body awards has in practice been difficult to reconcile with another objective of government policy which, while not peculiar to the 1980s, was a prominent feature of the decade. This was the control of public expenditure through keeping down the cost of pay settlements. Where collective bargaining has remained in place, unions have found that organisational changes have often meant an enhanced management prerogative in decision-making which has undermined joint regulation and consultation.

The most important organisational change in the civil service was the implementation of the proposals of the Ibbs Report of 1988 for transferring responsibility for the delivery of services from the civil service to executive agencies.[22] Forty-eight of these had been established by 1991. The underlying objective behind this development was to maximise management's independence within the parameters of given policy objectives and budgetary limits. Although HMSO, now an executive agency, announced in 1991 that it would be breaking away from the Civil Service pay structure, managerial independence has not yet led to the complete devolution of pay determination to agency level. One reason for this is the reluctance of the Treasury to loosen the controls which it has over civil service pay.

As already noted with reference to education, local government operated throughout the 1980s under increasing financial constraints imposed by central government. The introduction of Compulsory Competitive Tendering (CCT) for the provision of some local government services in 1981 and its extension to a wider range of services by the Local Government Act 1988 has changed the whole environment of local government industrial relations. Although a large majority of contracts are won by in-house tenders this has often been at the cost of job losses and terms and conditions below those in national agreements. The implementation of CCT for laundry, cleaning and catering services in the NHS from 1983 has had similar effects to those in local government. A large majority of contracts are won by in-house tenders, but at the expense of reduced staffing and overall worse terms and conditions of employment.[23] In the NHS at the beginning of the 1990s more radical structural reforms began to take effect with the transfer of a number of hospitals and other organisational units such as ambulance services to the management of self-governing trusts, with freedom to determine terms and conditions of employment outside the scope of national agreements. As in the civil service and local government, at the end of the 1980s the survival of national bargaining in the health service was in doubt. At the least it was contingent on modifications to allow sufficient flexibility for local variation.

The main issue giving rise to disputes in the civil service, NHS and local government in the 1980s was pay. The major disputes over pay were in the civil service in 1981, NHS in 1982, administrative, professional technical and clerical (APT & C) staff in local government in 1989 and ambulance workers in the NHS in 1989–90. The other major dispute in these areas in the 1980s was over the regrading exercise for nurses in 1988, a pay related issue. The industrial action in each case was prolonged. But it is important to appreciate a special characteristic of industrial action in the public services under review here. Public sector unions are well aware that indefinite strike action by many of the workgroups concerned is not really an option. Most of the services provided in these areas of the public sector particularly within the NHS, can be described as 'essential' in the sense that unacceptable consequences for the public would arise if they were deprived of access to the services for anything other than a short period of time – and in some cases if they were deprived of the services at all. Extensive industrial action in these services did occur in the early 1970s and again, in some of them, in the winter of discontent in 1978–9. This experience has conditioned unions' use of industrial action in disputes in two respects. First there is the risk that they will lose members to other organisations which do not take industrial action such as the Royal College of Nursing (RCN) in the case of nurses and Association of Professional Ambulance Personnel (APAP), a breakaway union of ambulance personnel formed as a result of the 1982 industrial action in the NHS. Second, unions need to confine their use of industrial action so that it has some impact on both management and the government, but does not cross the line which would lead to widespread loss of public support. There is therefore evidence that among white-collar public sector workers in particular there was more use of 'cut-price' industrial action – widespread short strike action or selective action in strategic workplaces – in the early 1980s. An additional factor is relevant in the case of the civil service. In 1984, workers at Government Communications Headquarters (GCHQ) were deprived of the right to belong to an independent trade union, even though the unions offered a 'no disruption' guarantee for essential security and intelligence services. This government action, allegedly in response to industrial action at GCHQ in the 1981 dispute, has left open the possibility that an effective ban on independent trade unions could be introduced into other areas of the civil service if industrial action were taken which went beyond the bounds of what the government would tolerate.

Against this background it is no surprise that in the major disputes referred to above the industrial action taken was strategically targeted. Inland Revenue Staff Federation (IRSF) members were called on to take the most extensive action in the 1981 civil service dispute in order to bring maximum pressure on the government by depriving it of tax revenue. National and Local Government Officers Association (NALGO)'s normal practice in major disputes has been to call for action by key workers in selected authorities and to pay them strike pay equal to their normal pay. In the 1989 APT & C dispute, after initially calling on all members to take part in one- to three-day stoppages, NALGO reverted to this practice. In the 1982 NHS dispute it has been suggested that the 'effectiveness' of industrial action was in part achieved through agreements with management that if reports of the impact of the action locally were exaggerated, unions would exercise restraint in the extent of action taken (Mailly *et al.* 1989: 146). However, in both this dispute and the 1981 civil service dispute government determination not to make any significant concessions meant that at the end of the disputes, little had been gained on the union side.

The introduction of CCT in the NHS and local government and agencies in the civil service might appear to be issues which would give rise to disputes. In the sense that unions have opposed these changes this is true. But the opposition has rarely taken the form of industrial action and then only at a local level. Well-publicised picketing in disputes over CCT at Addenbrooke's Hospital in Cambridge and in Barking and industrial action at Hammersmith Hospital in 1984 are examples of this. A more effective strategy for unions in the case of CCT was to concentrate on protecting jobs through supporting in-house tenders. In executive agencies in the civil service the priority for trade unions has been to retain recognition. So far agencies have continued to negotiate with trade unions although the possibility remains that here, as has already occurred in some of the new NHS self-governing trusts, they may find themselves faced with the threat of derecognition.

The trade union response to changes in the law was generally reflected in the procedures followed in practice rather than rule changes. As in education, the main legal pressure for change in union practices in disputes came from the law on strike ballots. Most unions had used ballots to consult members before 1984 – National Union of Public Employees (NUPE) was an important exception – and they did not find it difficult to adapt their procedures to accommodate the requirements of the law on strike ballots. There were considerable variations in the detailed procedures used, for example in relation to the amount of information included on the ballot paper, but on the whole no evident problems emerged in the 1980s, even over the potentially difficult requirement to hold separate place of work ballots in some disputes. In the public services as in other areas there is evidence that the need to ballot on industrial action encouraged the use of ballots on other issues; NUPE started to ballot on pay offers and the Prison Officers' Association

(POA) balloted on ending industrial action in 1989. The extent to which unions were prepared to use industrial action ballots varied considerably. Some unions, Institute of Professionals, Managers and Specialists (IPMS) for example, would not have balloted members unless they were sure that they would obtain a favourable result. Others balloted regularly, sometimes as a means of resolving political differences within the area concerned. NALGO lost important ballots of APT & C staff in 1986 and 1988. Ironically, the employers' confidence that it would lose again was in part responsible for the 1989 dispute which gave rise to prolonged industrial action.

Although there was a change in management attitudes in the 1980s with more emphasis on management prerogative and less on consultation and negotiation with trade unions, this was not accompanied by an increased willingness to resort to the law in the sense of pursuing available opportunities to seek labour injunctions or other remedies from the courts. The legal involvement of this sort in the main disputes referred to above was small. One idiosyncratic example was the decision by the government to pursue charges under the Conspiracy and Protection of Property Act 1875 against an IRSF official who followed two non-striking senior Inland Revenue officers along the motorway between Glasgow and Edinburgh after they had crossed picket lines to gain access to taxpayers' cheques. At the second time of asking, the Sheriff Court convicted the official of persistently following another person about from place to place and following another person 'with two or more persons in a disorderly manner in or through any street or road', but refused to impose any penalty having observed that no similar prosecution had been brought for sixty years. In fact, no previous case of any successful prosecution for this particular offence appears to have been brought since 1890.[24]

Several of the unions in the civil service, NHS and local government have been on the receiving end of labour injunctions in relation to local disputes. In some of these cases, the result would have been no different had the action been brought in the 1970s or an earlier period, e.g. cases relating to workplace occupations. The change identified by some of the unions was that they now found themselves operating in a climate where the threat of legal proceedings over industrial action was often felt to exist and occasionally realised. It is, however, clear that this was not a preferred management strategy. Although government support for local management to use legal remedies where appropriate is evident from Department of Health and Social Security (DHSS) circulars to health authorities after the 1979 dispute (see Morris with Rydzkowski 1984) and during the 1988 nurses regrading dispute, managers generally preferred not to do this – although politicians in local government may have had a different approach – and with good reason as alternative responses were usually available.

One option was to take disciplinary action against individual workers. This was often threatened and sometimes occurred where workers responded to union calls to show solidarity with other workgroups who were in dispute. An example was disciplinary action against civil servants who supported NHS workers during the 1982 dispute, which was limited to a first-stage warning in most cases. It would be accompanied by loss of pay and differences did arise over the amount of deductions made. A second type of response was, independent of any disciplinary action, to make deductions from pay of workers who had taken limited industrial action. This became an issue of considerable importance in these public services, as in education in the 1980s. In the NHS, the 1979 circular 'If Industrial Relations Break Down' advised health authorities that the normal course of action where workers did not perform the full range of their duties should be to offer them only a proportion of their pay and that as an *ex gratia* payment rather than a contractual entitlement. The authorities' response to this advice in the 1982 dispute varied considerably: some deducted pay, others sent workers home if they were not prepared to work normally, but most paid the workers in full. Pay deductions in respect of limited industrial action became a major issue in the second half of the 1980s. After the NUT took the initiative in challenging non-payment of teachers and deductions from pay in respect of their refusal to work normally (see above), NALGO was responsible for initiating the two actions which now provide the basis for the modern law. They confirmed a wide management prerogative to refuse to make any payment for less than normal performance of workers' duties.[25] In the light of the unions' necessary preference for limited industrial action in the public services, these decisions are of central importance in laying the ground for an effective management response.

A related, but rather different, issue was raised in the courts by the IRSF decision to challenge the right of the Inland Revenue to introduce new technology without reaching an agreement with the union. The Revenue had forced the union's hand by refusing to pay workers who would not work with the new technology, but remained willing to carry out their duties manually as before. The legal challenge, which was mounted on various different grounds, failed and the decision again reinforced an important management prerogative, in this case to impose changes in working practices.[26]

The most extreme management response to industrial action was the government's decision to ban trade union membership of GCHQ. In the domestic courts the unions ultimately lost their legal challenge to the ban on union membership but gained significant ground on the wider issue of the right to be consulted before changes were made in their conditions of employment.[27] Public sector unions have also challenged the contractual propriety of unilateral variations in terms of employment by local authorities (as a cost-cutting measure) and the rationality of the underlying policy decisions under public law.[28] The POA has been prominent in seeking public law remedies for workers subjected to disciplinary sanctions.[29] Those actions and, where possible, pursuit of related unfair dismissal cases where jobs are lost, are clear examples of unions wishing to be seen to be doing something about policies which they oppose but feel unable to stop. There is evidence that the extent of this sort of use of the law may have overstepped the limits of when resort to the law is appropriate from a trade union standpoint. Many trade union officials retain a sense that there are some disputes which are industrial relations issues and should be dealt with as such. Legal remedies may nevertheless be pursued because full-time officers feel compelled by membership pressure to assert their legal rights. Proactive use of the law by public service unions – including the education unions – was a feature of the decade, and from the union perspective it was not always a very productive one.

Printing and publishing[30]

The 1980s saw major changes in industrial relations in most of the printing and publishing sector. In 1980 there was national bargaining throughout the industry, although the coverage of the agreements between the Publishers Association and the National Union of Journalists (NUJ) representing editorial staff and Society of Graphical and Allied Trades (SOGAT) for warehouse employees was limited. By 1991 the only important national negotiations still taking place were between the British Printing Industries Federation (BPIF) on behalf of employers in general printing and the National Graphical Association (NGA) and SOGAT (now the Graphical, Paper and Media Union, GPMU). The national agreement for warehouse employees in publishing remains in place but far fewer employers participate in it. In both these remaining national negotiations the emphasis has increasingly been on agreeing enabling provisions which allow local productivity agreements to be made. The increased flexibility this has given to employers is seen by the BPIF to be an important strength of the national agreement. Both the provincial newspapers in 1987 (NUJ) and 1991 (NGA and SOGAT) and national newspapers in 1986 ended national bargaining and several of the companies and groups have either ceased to recognise one or more of the NUJ, NGA and SOGAT or limited their role to individual representation of members (see Smith and Morton 1990). As a result union membership has declined and workplace organisation has been weakened or even eliminated.

Although the period began with an eight-week campaign of industrial action by the NGA in the provincial press and general printing – who negotiated jointly up to the time of this dispute – over pay and hours, the single issue which dominated disputes in the 1980s was new technology.[31] The issue itself was not new. It lay behind the closure of *The Times* for eleven months in 1978–9. While the introduction of new machinery and working practices in general printing was managed through established procedures this was not achieved in either provincial or national newspapers. Pressure from the growth of 'free sheets' in the mid-1980s compelled the established 'paid-for' provincial press to force the issue. Shortly afterwards, the 'Wapping' dispute over the transfer of News Group's national titles from Fleet Street to premises where new production methods were used paved the way for all the national press to make changes which they had previously been unable to achieve by way of bargained agreements. In the later 1980s, while the moves made by employers towards derecognition were widely disputed by the unions in the provincial press in particular, there were only isolated examples of industrial action to try to prevent derecognition.[32]

The law had a high profile in two of the most publicised disputes of the 1980s: the Stockport *Messenger* dispute of 1983–4 and the Wapping dispute in 1986–7. It received less publicity in disputes which were at least as important over the introduction of new technology in the pre-press area in provincial newspapers in the mid-1980s. In the *Messenger* dispute a maverick employer, Eddie Shah, whose newspaper group was not affiliated to the Newspaper Society, the employers' association for the provincial press, had no attachment to the traditions of the industry to overcome as he pursued labour injunctions against both the NUJ and NGA. Disagreement over appropriate terms and conditions to be applied in new typesetting and printing operations had led Shah to refuse to recognise an NGA closed shop. NGA members were sacked and Shah's premises were extensively picketed. The NGA's then policy of boycotting labour injunction proceedings facilitated Shah's pressing for sanctions against the union for contempt of court in ignoring injunctions granted to him. In a manner reminiscent of the early 1970s, the dispute escalated out of the control of the parties as the NGA's assets were sequestrated for contempt of court after earlier fines imposed for contempt had failed to persuade the union to change its stance.[33] The industrial action failed to stop the production and distribution of Shah's newspaper. (On the *Messenger* dispute, see Gennard 1984.) This was not a new experience for the unions. A union campaign against the T. Bailey Forman Nottingham newspapers in the late 1970s over recognition had been similarly unsuccessful, and indeed also involved labour injunction proceedings, in this case brought by other newspaper groups.[34] But the manner in which Shah achieved his goal and the surrounding publicity was seen to demonstrate that existing labour practices in provincial newspapers could be changed and that industrial action to prevent this might be successfully overcome with the aid of the law. Few if any employers, though, would have then wanted to bring about change by going through a similar experience to Shah.

It was, ironically, pressure from 'free sheets' of the sort that Shah was producing that led the owners of the 'paid-for' provincial newspapers to press harder for changes in the pre-press production area which would involve greater task flexibility and loss of job control by the NGA. Attempts to reach a negotiated agreement on implementation of changes in pursuit of what the Newspaper Society described as 'Project Breakthrough' were unsuccessful. Thereafter individual companies or groups acted independently with varying degrees of assistance from the Newspaper Society. An agreement between Portsmouth and Sunderland Newspapers and the NGA led to a dispute between the employers and the NUJ and was in any event soon seen to achieve less than was desirable from the employers' perspective. The decisive disputes were at the Kent *Messenger* and the Wolverhampton *Express and Star*. In the latter management in effect locked out and then dismissed workers who would not agree to their proposal for new working arrangements which involved direct input of copy by journalists and advertising staff. The NGA saw the dispute as a crucial test of its influence over the introduction of new technology into the industry. It organised action not only by NGA members employed in the *Express and Star* group but also in other companies which supplied services to the *Express and Star*. Companies in the *Express and Star* group were able to secure a labour injunction against the NGA on the ground that it had not held a ballot. Attempts by some NGA officials to continue to organise industrial action in the face of this court order led to the NGA being fined for contempt.[35] The NGA's action failed to prevent the company from successfully introducing new work practices. The Wolverhampton *Express and Star* was assisted in this by inter-union difficulties which led the NUJ to reach an agreement with the company on the equipment over which the NGA was in dispute. More generally, provincial papers were considerably advantaged by the fact that they had reached a situation where they could continue to produce a paper without skilled NGA labour. The success of the Wolverhampton *Express and Star* set a precedent for other provincial newspapers to follow. Any workforce resistance was quickly overcome, with little significant industrial action.[36]

In the national press, change began with the meticulous planning by News Group Newspapers to move their whole operation from Fleet Street to the docks. The inevitable opposition of the print unions to this move was part of the companies' calculations. The NGA and SOGAT refused to sign the proposed agreement on new working arrangements at the new plant in Wapping and when they called their members out on strike they were all dismissed, a calculated move which enabled News Group to dispense with their services at no cost. The year-long industrial action which involved continuous picketing and regular demonstrations, gave rise to a number of applications for labour injunctions, most of which were successful. For its defiance of the first of these, SOGAT was found to be in contempt of court and, like the NGA in the Stockport *Messenger* dispute, lost control of its assets under the sequestration procedure for several months.[37] SOGAT's decision to end the dispute in 1987 was ostensibly taken because of fear that this process would be repeated.

To what extent did this use of labour injunctions and pursuit of sanctions for contempt of court where they were ignored derive from the legislative changes made in 1980, 1982 or 1984? Three of the provisions outlined above are relevant. The first is the narrowing of the right to picket peacefully to workers at or near their own place of work and removal of immunity from acts done in the course of picketing outside the ambit of this right. Very few of the pickets in either the *Messenger* or Wapping disputes could claim the protection of the right to picket peacefully, whether or not they were at their own place of work. (A large number of the demonstrators had nothing to do with the unions and were certainly outside their control.) The NGA and SOGAT therefore had no defence that could usefully be argued in the context of labour injunctions proceedings to any alleged tort liability for organising the picketing.

But the success of the print unions in defending their job territory up to the 1980s did not depend on effective picketing. It was rather the result of a network of union security arrangements which meant that work coming from or going to an employer in dispute would not be handled but would be 'blacked'. This practice was a principal target of the 1980 change in the law on secondary action. A number of the twenty-two labour injunctions relating to secondary action identified by Evans which were awarded between August 1980 and April 1987 were directed at blacking by the print unions (Evans 1985, 1987). From 1980 to 1990, however, secondary action taken against the immediate customers or suppliers of employers in dispute could in theory retain immunity. As was predicted at the time it could not do so in practice because the real world never complied with the detailed abstractions of the 'gateways to legality' in section 17 of the Employment Act 1980 (cf. Wedderburn 1981). To put the matter beyond any doubt, newspaper owners among others operated through a network of companies, so that any blacking was invariably not directed at the immediate customer or supplier of an employer in dispute, but rather a different company some way down the line in the chain of commercial contracts.[38]

The third relevant change in the law removed immunity from industrial action aimed at securing work for union members. This is an obscure and little appreciated provision, but it affected directly the practices by which the print unions – in particular the craft unions – could control jobs (see Lewis and Simpson 1982: 227–33). It was involved in the *Messenger* case which followed the dispute where Shah successfully claimed damages for commercial losses suffered during the period of the industrial action.

A distinctive characteristic of this sector in the 1980s was a greater willingness among employers not only to seek labour injunctions but go back to court to ask for sanctions to be imposed for contempt where injunctions were ignored. Shah and News Group were not unique among newspaper owners in this respect.[39] While the experience of fines and sequestration of assets was not a new one for trade unions – the 1972–3 period contained some celebrated examples of both – the severity of the fines and the way the sequestration process was handled did affect the unions' ability to run the relevant disputes effectively (see O'Regan 1991). This was the most public demonstration of a more general feature of disputes in the 1980s in newspapers; this was that the law came to play a much greater part in employers' strategies.

It might be concluded from this quite extensive resort to the courts and reliance on changes in the law made in the early 1980s that the law was a primary factor in the changes which occurred in the production process and industrial relations in both parts of the newspaper industry. On the union side there is a view that the coincidence of change in the law with management's ability to produce a paper without their skilled members reinforced the employer's determination to introduce changes in the production process and combined to put unions in a position where they were unable to protect the jobs of their members in the press. The view from the employers' side was rather different. One description of the role of the law in national newspapers was that it was 'background music' to the revolution in newspaper production. In the provincial press the *Messenger* dispute showed that even where unions were perceived to be in a strong position to defend labour practices, their resistance could be overcome. Once employers believed they could not survive new competition unless major changes in labour practices were made, they felt they had to press the matter to a conclusion. They were in a position to do this because technological advance had made the training of workers in new practices to replace traditional, but now redundant, skills relatively easy. The most important advantage which the law was seen to give employers was the right to dismiss workers who refused to accept proposed changes and took industrial action, cost-free.

This illustrates an important general point: employers in the print industry – and this is as true in general printing as it is in newspapers – became more aware of the law in the 1980s. The legal rights of workers who are dismissed while taking industrial action were little changed in the 1980s;[40] what did change was an awareness of them – or rather their absence. Employers increasingly used the services of employers' associations for advice on the law relating to industrial conflict over issues ranging from the consequences of dismissals to the details on strike ballots. As a result, while employers did not necessarily have a detailed understanding of the law, they were aware of a shift in the balance of the legal framework in their favour.

Engineering and construction[41]

At the beginning of the 1980s well-established national bargaining arrangements were in place across most of the engineering and construction sectors. Probably the best known of these was that in general engineering between the Engineering Employers' Federation (EEF) and Confederation of Shipbuilding and Engineering Unions (CSEU). Companies affiliated to the EEF employ just under half of the workers in the engineering industry with the core membership in aerospace, motor manufacture supply[42] and power generation. The CSEU is one of the most important joint union organisations and its membership includes all the main unions which organise in the engineering sector, covering both manual and white-collar workers. At the beginning of the period under review the national EEF-CSEU agreements covered national minimum pay rates together with other conditions including the length of the working week, notice, guaranteed week, overtime rates, holiday entitlement and principles covering payment by results; actual pay rates were negotiated at company or plant level. The main development in the 1980s was the ending of national bargaining in 1989.[43] This was a result of the failure of national bargaining to reach an agreement on the CSEU demand for a shorter working week, the issue that dominated industrial relations at both the beginning and end of the decade (see below). The nationally negotiated disputes procedures remained in force after the ending of national bargaining on substantive issues.

The National Engineering Construction Employers' Association (NECEA) is one of the fifteen constituent associations of the EEF but since 1981 it has also had its own autonomous policy making executive council.[44] In the same year the national agreement for the engineering construction industry agreement (NAECI) was concluded between employers' associations whose members are engaged in engineering construction, of which the NECEA is the largest, and a trade union side led by the Amalgamated Engineering Union (AEU) (Construction section). This was the solution to industrial relations problems throughout the 1960s and 1970s which were seen to result from the multiplicity of different arrangements then existing in the industry. The substantive terms and procedures established under this agreement proved to be successful in improving industrial relations in the 1980s, surviving their biggest test in the London steel erectors' dispute in 1989 (see below).

The NAECI was influenced by the similar, though by no means identical, agreement reached between the Electrical Contractors' Association (ECA) and Electronic, Telecommunication and Printing Union (EETPU) in the late 1960s. As in engineering construction, this followed a period of unsatisfactory industrial relations in electrical contracting characterised by frequent disputes. Under the ECA-EETPU agreement a Joint Industry Board has negotiated National Working Rule agreements for the electrical contracting industry since it was set up in 1968. The distinguishing features of the agreement reached are the highly prescriptive nature of their regulation of substantive issues and procedures which have proved to be very successful over nearly twenty-five years in resolving disputes, with only a relatively small number of issues being referred up to national level. In electrical contracting the industrial relations structures of the 1970s continued to operate in the 1980s.

There is a more direct link between the two other areas of the engineering and construction sectors which are under review. The Building and Civil Engineering Joint Board represents employers in both general construction and civil engineering in national negotiations on basic pay and other conditions of employment. Agreements reached at this level are then put to the separate national joint councils in the two sectors for ratification, and other items are resolved at this level. The union side in these negotiations is led by Union of Construction, Allied Trades and Technicians (UCATT) and also includes the Transport and General Workers' Union (TGWU), General Municipal and Boilermakers Union (GMB) and in general construction Furniture, Timber and Allied Trades' Union (FTATU).

An important characteristic of the construction industry is the high level of self-employment, especially on the building side; in civil engineering workers are relatively more likely to be directly employed. Self-employment and the use of subcontractors to supply labour are not recent developments but they reached a high point in the 1980s.[45] The long-standing policy of UCATT, whose membership is concentrated in this industry, not to recruit self-employed workers was changed in 1988. This change reflected a situation in which a majority of the workers in the industry were then believed to be self-employed. The inability of the unions to contain moves towards self-employment meant that collective bargaining came to have correspondingly reduced influence over actual terms and conditions on site.[46] Despite the decline in the level of unionisation, national bargaining survived. In the opinion of the Federation of Civil Engineering Contractors (FCEC), the procedural and substantive terms of the national agreement in civil engineering were perceived by members to provide a framework for stability in industrial relations. However, the Building Employers' Confederation (BEC), which carries out negotiations for employers in general construction, did come under pressure from its affiliates to move towards a simplified form of agreement at national level to which members could opt in or out.

The period under review was framed by disputes in the engineering industry over hours of work. The CSEU's 1979 claim for a reduction in the working week was settled by a nationally negotiated agreement for a one-hour reduction to thirty-nine with effect from 1981. This followed an eight-week period of industrial action consisting of an overtime ban punctuated by one- and two-day national strikes which received limited though significant support (see Meredeen 1988: ch. 6). The CSEU's 1983 claim for a further reduction in the working week to thirty-five hours led to a reported agreement in 1987 on a reduction to thirty-seven and a half hours, but with the unions refusing to agree to the employers' insistence that this should be conditional on locally negotiated productivity and cost offsets. The upshot was a carefully planned campaign of targeted strike ballots and industrial action by the CSEU unions over the period

October 1989–March 1991. This produced a number of local agreements on a thirty-seven-hour week in return for a range of union concessions (see Richardson and Rubin 1993).

These two disputes apart, the 1980s was a period in which disputes leading to industrial action in the engineering industry[47] were generally localised and often limited to working to rule or overtime bans. There were no major disputes over pay even in the upturn of the mid- to late 1980s. The recessions at the beginning and end of the period gave rise to many redundancies the size and extent of which acted as a constraint on industrial action as a form of resistance. There were significant local disputes over redundancies, such as the occupation of the Caterpillar plant in Glasgow in 1987 in opposition to its proposed closure (see Woolfson and Foster 1988), changes in working practices and flexibility requirements. But overall there was a significant decline in industrial action in the industry from the levels of the 1960s and 1970s.[48]

The construction industry also experienced fluctuating economic fortunes. A general depression in demand after the early 1970s and again after the 1979–81 recession was followed by a recovery in the private commercial sector up to the late 1980s and then another recession which had a particularly heavy impact in construction.[49] The absence of any major national dispute in construction for the two decades after 1972, however, reflects a decline in trade union influence over this period, a development which was linked to the growth in self-employment already noted. The 1981 national negotiations over pay did raise a serious possibility of industrial action before a negotiated agreement was eventually reached. But the industrial action which did take place in building and civil engineering was confined to local disputes, one or two of which received some publicity which was generally focused, as has often been the case in construction, on incidents occurring during picketing.

The tightly drawn procedures in electrical contracting and engineering construction generally proved successful in resolving those disputes that arose in the 1980s. That is not to say that there was no industrial action in these areas. Most of the large-scale projects in which engineering construction is involved experienced some – usually unofficial – industrial action, but this tended not to be protracted and was usually resolved by the procedures, frequently at site level.[50] A major dispute in engineering construction at the Isle of Grain refinery predated the 1981 NAECI and was indeed one source of the impetus for that agreement. The strength of the new procedures was seriously tested by an unofficial six-week strike of steel erectors in London in 1989. At the time it was feared that this might necessitate changes in the agreement, but in the event the dispute was ended through joint pressure from the employers and union full-time officers and the NAECI remained intact.

The overall picture is therefore of disputes arising mainly at plant or site level over local issues with the national hours disputes in engineering being very much an exception to the general trend. It is difficult to measure the full extent and importance of these local disputes, but it would be a mistake to regard them and the threat or use of industrial action as unimportant. From a union perspective it is clear that a large amount of time and other resources is devoted to the resolution of these issues.

The legal involvement in disputes over this period only rarely took the form of labour injunction proceedings. One of the best known of these was the unsuccessful attempt by British Aerospace to prevent Manufacturing, Science and Finance (MSF) from organising industrial action at its Preston factory in the 1989–91 hours dispute on the ground that it did not have the support of a valid ballot.[51] Publicity was also given to some legal actions brought to try to end workplace occupations, a tactic which workers continue to use even though there has never been any way in which it can be done lawfully. In addition there were occasions on which injunctions were sought and granted against pickets.[52]

The full extent of the impact of the law is found rather in the way in which it influenced the strategies of employers and unions both in general and in particular disputes. All parties were aware that changes in the law had opened up new possibilities for employers to seek legal restraints on the organisation of industrial action. As a result, in the words of a senior official of one employers' association, 'industrial relations is increasingly conducted with an eye to the law'. In construction, the emphasis on subcontracting on the commercial side of the industry means that any industrial action which does occur is frequently if not inevitably secondary action in the legal sense of the term – some or all of the workers called on to take part will not be in dispute with their employer – and whether or not that could have passed through one of the gateways to legality for secondary action in the 1980–90 period was not a relevant issue in the real world.[53] Of equal importance was the virtual impossibility of UCATT's – and that of other unions in respect of their construction industry membership – holding a lawful ballot in the light of membership records that were almost certainly inadequate. This was not so much a reflection on the efficiency of the unions' organisation as on the nature of employment in the industry. While the law on balloting may have facilitated the organisation of industrial action for some unions, for those in the construction industry it made it effectively impossible to do so lawfully.

As in other sectors, in engineering the law on strike ballots was the most important influence among the 1980–90 changes in the law on industrial action. The near impossibility of meeting the requirements of the balloting law in construction was most probably one factor which explains the apparent failure of the unions there to address this issue. In engineering, union responses to the changes concentrated on industrial action ballots. For the AEU this meant a reversal of existing practice, which was not to hold ballots on industrial action. The union's position had been that the election of all officials meant that they were already sufficiently answerable to the members for their decisions. The EETPU, by contrast, had more experience of balloting members, by post, on whether to accept or reject pay offers, if not expressly on whether they were prepared to take industrial action (see Undy and Martin 1984: ch. 3). The impact of the law was not necessarily a negative one from a union perspective. It was a crucial factor in the nature of the campaign pursued by the CSEU in the 1989–91 hours dispute, the outcome of which was seen by the unions to have been successful. Legal advice to the CSEU not only indicated legal difficulties in the way of holding a national ballot: it also pointed up the likelihood of site ballots producing a sufficient number of 'yes' votes among the different unions to make the threats of industrial action real and a valuable part of CSEU strategy in the dispute. More generally head office guidance to union full-time officers invariably included – and sometimes seemed to be dominated by – the question of balloting and, since 1991, authorisation of industrial action. Whether this concern with formal procedures in the conduct of disputes was overall advantageous to trade unions is a matter for debate.

In the mid-1980s, the EEF did not regard a legal obligation on unions to hold ballots before industrial action as a priority for labour law reform. After it was introduced, however, it was active in pressing for a code of practice on how balloting should be carried out in practice (see EEF 1987). No other employers' association in the engineering and construction sector showed such detailed concern over the way in which strike ballots are used in practice. Employers' associations in construction were more involved in pressing for changes in the law to restrict the conditions which could be attached to tendering for commercial contracts – in their case for building and allied work such as property management. The outlawing of 'union-only' and 'recognition-only' clauses in commercial contracts by the Employment Act 1982 and related withdrawal of immunity from industrial action over these issues was in part a response to this pressure. So too was the elimination of non-commercial considerations from the conditions for tendering for local government contracts by the Local Government Act 1988 (see generally Evans and Lewis 1988). While the ECA and NECEA expressed faith in the effectiveness of their procedures as a means of dispute solution and the ECA in particular was sceptical of the value of new legal rights for employers in disputes, there was a general belief on the employers' side that the changed legal environment was a beneficial development. Indeed on occasion, albeit rarely, employers in the ECA made the union aware that they were prepared to look to legal redress if irregularities in balloting or picketing were not put right.

The heightened awareness of the law was also reflected in greater concern over the legal implications of dismissing workers during disputes, especially those who were taking industrial action and, after 1990 in particular, unofficial strikers. Union support for legal action to contest some of these dismissals, where appropriate, was evident in engineering and construction as elsewhere. This was especially likely to be provided where employers implemented redundancies without regard to the rights of unions and workers over consultation and observance of procedures.[54] As elsewhere, however, this use of the law by trade unions met with only varying degrees of success.

CONCLUSIONS

It is clear that the law was an important factor in some disputes in the 1980s, influencing the strategies adopted by both employers and trade unions. It is equally clear that simplistic generalisations as to the effect of the labour legislation of the decade in reducing the number of strikes such as those made in government Green Papers are at best misleading. Our research would suggest that a belief in the existence of some unarticulated process whereby the policy underlying legislation is automatically translated into reality by the actions of the parties whose behaviour the legislation is intended to affect, is without foundation. Two interlinked observations may be made on the basis of our work. The first is that the law has in general become a more important factor across the spectrum of industrial relations. The 1980s underlined a trend which emerged in the 1960s and probably became entrenched and irreversible by the second half of the 1970s. The second observation is that to understand the impact of the law it is essential to locate it in the context in which it operates and this varies considerably between different sectors. Organisation of our information in terms of different sectors is not merely a convenient way of presenting the material. It points up important variations both in those aspects of the law which have an impact and the way in which they take effect.

It is the particular sectoral context which explains how and why the law has become an important influence on industrial relations. Recent experience in the education sector provides a very clear illustration of this. Traditionally the workforce across this sector has not been associated with industrial action at anything but a local level. While there are some famous examples of strike action by schoolteachers in local disputes in the late nineteenth and early twentieth centuries (see Seifert 1987: ch. 2) the nature of the teaching unions and national bargaining machinery established in 1919 were such that differences did not give rise to widespread conflict. Yet the 1980s saw more industrial action in this sector generally and schools in particular than any earlier period. In school teaching this contributed to the termination of collective bargaining in 1987. The explanations for this open conflict go back into the 1960s and 1970s and the vulnerability of this group of public-sector workers to pressures from government pay policies (which, it can be argued, were equally a feature of the 1980s, albeit in a different guise).

The legal component of disputes in school teaching, FHE and to a lesser extent, universities, was significant. Some of it related to the labour legislation of the 1980s. But an equally important part of it did not. It followed from the decision of the Local Education Authorities, as employers, to try to put an end to the unions' use of action short of a strike at no cost to their members by withholding pay and challenging the unions or individual workers to use the law to put limits on this assertion of management prerogative. The failure of the challenges made in court cases has its legacy in the tight definitions of the contractual duties of schoolteachers in the Teachers' Pay and Conditions Act 1987 and arguably also the terms of recent agreements for lecturers in FE and HE.

We would therefore draw the following qualified conclusions on the basis of these two interlinked observations. Overall, the importance of the law as a factor influencing industrial disputes has increased. But this is part of a continuing process of a strengthening legal input to industrial relations which began in the two preceding decades and the degree of importance of the law varied considerably between different sectors. In some sectors it was, if not totally absent, negligible. In the footwear industry, for example, a large part of the industry is covered by national bargaining between the employers' association and a trade union side which is dominated by the specialist union for the industry. It is a contracting industry subject to intense competition from imports, with the consequential pressures on industrial relations which that imposes. Disputes have almost always been contained and solved within the framework of a long-established disputes procedure. Ironically, perhaps, this procedure has been agreed for nearly a hundred years in the form of a Trust Deed, but the nature of the legal constraints which this imposes has never been clear either to the parties themselves or to outside commentators. Both sides reported that the law had not been an influence on developments in general or disputes in particular in the 1980s. The same is true of electrical contracting, where the distinctive features of industrial relations include tight regulation by industry-wide substantive and procedural agreements which have now been in place for nearly twenty-five years. The procedures are seen by the parties to have been relatively successful in containing and resolving both collective and individual disputes.

Against the background of these observations and this conclusion, it is possible to identify the principal elements of the legal influence where it occurred. One aspect of the law stands out. It is the need for trade unions to hold a ballot before calling on workers to take industrial action. This has influenced trade union practices in relation to organising industrial action in different ways which depend on the nature of trade union organisation and the workgroups concerned. The objectives and effects of this change in the law in 1984 and the subsequent amendments in 1988 and 1990 have generated considerable debate. We would offer the following observations with regard to its effects on the basis of our research.[55]

First, there is little evidence that decision-making bodies within trade unions are reluctant to hold industrial action ballots for fear that members will vote against taking action. There are occasions when officials ballot expecting a 'no' vote in order to diffuse pressures from the workers and maybe vindicate union strategy – e.g. in accepting a pay offer in the belief that at that time, no better offer can be secured. It is also the case that some unions have learned the lesson of the importance of consultation and campaigning for support in ballots as a result of 'no' votes in industrial action ballots which they wanted to win. The experience of the National Union of Railwaymen (NUR) in losing ballots in 1985, when guards were balloted on industrial action over Driver Only Operations and in 1986 in BREL, illustrates this point. A very effective campaign was successfully mounted to secure ballot support in disputes over pay and bargaining arrangements in 1989.

Second, some unions have been able to use balloting on industrial action positively to structure their strategies in the conduct of disputes. In 1985 the NUT conducted no fewer than eleven ballots in the prolonged dispute over pay and conditions, not only to ensure that its actions remained within the law, but also to maintain the momentum of support for its campaign. Both sides in the engineering hours dispute recognised the importance of the CSEU strategy in targeting selected companies for ballots and then, where necessary (which it often was not) strike action. On the union side it was confirmed that the introduction of a legal obligation to ballot and uncertainty over whether a national ballot would be successful in securing legal immunity were important factors in shaping the CSEU's campaign.

Third, against this positive and successful side to the law from a union perspective may be set the obstacle which the need to ballot imposes where the issue in dispute demands an immediate response to have any chance of making an impact. Where the issue is local, the result may be unballoted and unofficial action, which could cause separate legal difficulties for the union, but might lead to speedy resolution of the dispute. In many cases this represents no change to established practice. But where the issue is larger, a perceived inability to respond without securing ballot support – because it is believed that to do so would lead to the employer(s) seeking a labour injunction – may prove fatal to any possibility of an effective response. The campaign of the TGWU and dockers against the abolition of the National Dock Labour Scheme in 1989 provides a notable example of this.

Fourth, it is tentatively suggested that if ballots do have the effect of reducing the incidence of industrial action, this is not the result of either a large number of ballots leading to 'no' votes in situations where previously industrial action would probably have taken place, or a reluctance by unions to call ballots. It has been suggested that ballots can provide information to negotiators which assists them in resolving disputes by agreement. This was one reason for employers' support for ballots. There are some examples of both management and unions misjudging the outcome of ballots, for example the NUR in 1985 and 1986 and local authorities in 1989. It would, however, be overstating the case to conclude that ballots generally provide at least one side with information that it would not otherwise have had. Another way in which ballots could lead to less industrial action would be through a more subtle effect on the nature of trade union organisation over a period of time. This would come about through organisational changes leading to greater centralisation and formalisation; over time this could lead to modification of the substantive policies adopted on industrial action. While there is some evidence that there is a trend towards more centralisation and formalisation within some trade unions, there is also evidence of the opposite effect arising from other developments. The introduction of LMS in schools and executive agencies in the civil service are examples of pressures on unions to develop strong branch organisation. It is, therefore, too soon to see whether balloting is generally leading to a greater centralisation of union organisation.

A fifth effect of the introduction of the legal obligation to ballot in order to secure legal immunity for organising industrial action is that balloting has become far more widespread than the law requires. Balloting on employers' offers and even proposed settlements now takes place where previously it would not have happened. This may delay the resolution of disputes. There may also be some confusion as to whether ballots held are over employers' offers, industrial action or both.

Finally it may be noted that the complexity of the law, particularly if taken together with the glosses on it in the 1990 Code of Practice, gives considerable opportunities to employers who are so inclined to challenge the validity of ballots held in labour injunction proceedings. It is clear that employers who do this may be adopting a high-risk strategy. Successful legal challenges may contribute to settlement of disputes without industrial action taking place. But they may be technical victories having no apparent effect, as in the teachers' dispute in 1985[56] and London Underground in 1989.[57] Equally they may fail and point up an evident weakness in the employer's stance in the dispute as in the challenge by British Aerospace to ballots held in the hours dispute in 1989 and the British Rail challenge to the NUR in the 1989 dispute where in the light of the majority in favour of industrial action the technical nature of the employers' claim made its action look distinctly unmeritorious.[58]

No one other aspect of the law stands out as having had the same general influence as the law on strike ballots. Of the other areas of law which had an important impact in more than one sector we would argue that of at least equal importance to the restriction of the immunities in the 1980s labour legislation is the law on employees' right to be paid when taking action short of a strike. In 1980 the law on this point was unclear. By 1990 the courts had confirmed the existence of a wide management prerogative to withhold pay from workers who refuse to work normally. Employers may exercise the right to make deductions from pay as a means of securing compensation for the workers' breaches of contract or they may refuse to make any payment for work done short of normal performance of the workers' duties as in some local government disputes. When combined with the apparent existence of an equally wide prerogative to change working practices, these rights for employers have altered the balance of bargaining power between employers and unions in areas where effective industrial action has hitherto only been in the form of limited and selective action short of a strike, and either the workers' right to be paid was in practice unaffected or there had been an expectation of payment of a proportion of normal pay for the work actually performed. In the education sector and the white-collar areas of the civil service and local government the impact of this legal development has been considerable.

A related strand in the influence of the law is partly, but only partly, attributable to the changes made by the labour legislation of the 1980s. It is an increased awareness among employers and managers of the complete vulnerability of the individual worker who takes industrial action to disciplinary sanctions, including stopping pay and, most important, summary dismissal. A worker who goes on strike or, in most if not all cases, takes action short of a strike, can be dismissed without notice or pay in lieu of notice and, in virtually all cases, without the right to bring an action for unfair dismissal either. The publicity given to the solicitors' letter to News Group Newspapers advising on the best time to provoke a strike to lay the foundation for cost-free dismissals in the Wapping dispute[59] probably contributed as much to the heightened awareness of this state of affairs as the legislative modifications to the law on unfair dismissal of workers taking industrial action in 1982 and 1990. The short point is that English law does not recognise an individual right to strike (see generally Ewing 1991). In the 1980s employers began to appreciate the freedom which this gave them to carry out threats to dismiss workers taking industrial action. Of course this freedom remains limited if the workers concerned are not replaceable. But where, as in the newspaper industry, disputes were over employers' demands for task flexibility linked to the introduction of new technology, awareness of this legal weapon in their armoury reinforced employers' resolve to achieve their goals in full.

The significance of the other changes made by the 1980s labour legislation was generally more limited. Taken as a whole these changes were far from being irrelevant. There was a widespread feeling among both unions and employers' associations that they contributed to a climate where there was a general awareness of a continuing shift in the balance of bargaining power. But they were for the most part far from crucial to the way in which disputes were resolved. For some trade unions, particular changes have had a seminal influence. The removal of immunity from secondary action meant that general unions which have traditionally called on one group of members to support others involved in disputes – e.g. transport workers to stop supplies going in and coming out of the premises of employers with whom workers are in dispute – became widely exposed to the risk of labour injunctions if they continued this practice. As a rule unions do not now call for action of this sort. In some, though by no means all, cases, they may be happy to attribute this change to the law although the reality may be rather that the action is not called for because unions are aware that the support of members concerned would not necessarily be forthcoming. Equally the ending of some of the union security practices which included controls over the labour used on work supplied to or services provided for their employer may have been as much because of changes in commercial and labour practices which made them impossible to defend, as because of the unlawful nature of the practices after 1982 and the removal of immunity from industrial action taken to defend them. There is evidence that others survive because they can be defended and all the parties concerned are content to preserve them. Legal prohibition cannot guarantee the ending of practices which do not owe their existence to the law.

While strike ballots have had a universal impact, the other 1980s labour legislation restrictions on the immunities for organising industrial action have not made such a general impression. They have, however, contributed to a climate of opinion about a decline in union bargaining power. Some have had a more specific and narrowly focused impact, but their general contribution to the influence of the law on industrial action has probably been less than the development and increased awareness of the sanctions that could be imposed at an individual level. This is part of the much wider growth in the influence of the law in industrial relations and, as with strike ballots, is likely to remain important unless and until legislation is passed to curtail employers' powers or to put it another way, an attempt is made to create a legal individual 'right to strike'.

NOTES

1 For statistics on strike activity for the period 1893–1989 see Milner and Metcalf (1993).
2 *Taff Vale Railway Co v Amalgamated Society of Railway Servants* [1901] AC 426.
3 Individuals such as union officials who organised industrial action were given only a limited degree of immunity from some tort liabilities where they acted 'in contemplation of furtherance of a trade dispute'. On the enactment of the Trade Disputes Act 1906 see Kidner (1982).
4 See too the uncertain attribution of the increase in industrial action after 1906 to the liberalisation of the law and the economic climate in Pelling (1987: 122–3).
5 The classic exposition of the abstentionist role of the law is Kahn Freund (1954). On voluntarism see Flanders (1970).
6 For a survey of the evidence see Simpson and Wood (1973: 37–42).
7 See ibid., ch.10.
8 *NWL Ltd v Woods* [1979] ICR 867, 886.

9 Some of these cases are reported. See *Beaverbrook Newspapers Ltd v Keys* [1978] ICR 582 and *Associated Newspapers Group Ltd v Wade* [1979] ICR 664.

10 Cf. the analysis of the influence of changes in the law on union membership by Freeman and Pelletier (1990).

11 See Donovan (1968: ch. VIII). On the evidence available in the early 1980s, the introduction of a legal remedy for unfair dismissal had not reduced the level of strikes over dismissal, see Dickens *et al.* (1985: 224–32).

12 For more detailed analysis of the changes made by the 1980, 1982 and 1984 Acts, see Wedderburn (1986: 68–96 and ch. 8); Lewis (1986: chs 6, 7 and 9); Hepple and Fredman (1986: Part II, ch. 5). On the Employment Act 1988, see McKendrick (1988). On the Employment Act 1990, see Simpson (1991).

13 The amount of damages that may be awarded is limited by section 16 of the Employment Act 1982 by reference to the size of the union. For unions with more than 100,000 members a maximum of £250,000 may be awarded to any one plaintiff.

14 In the 1980s the courts continued the expansion of the 'economic tort liabilities' that began in the 1960s and 1970s. Most of the relevant case law arose out of labour disputes. An important characteristic of the reported decisions is that since they concern 'interlocutory' proceedings, they do not generally provide a clear view of what the law is but only a view on whether it is arguable that the law is what the employers (or other parties) who initiated the proceedings allege it to be. The decision of the Court of Appeal in the case arising out of industrial action threatened by the TGWU in the docks dispute in 1989 was a particularly clear example of the judiciary accepting that there might exist a form of tort liability which would outflank the whole system of immunities in a wide range of circumstances. The House of Lords reversed the Court of Appeal decision without having to discuss this issue. *Associated British Ports v TGWU* [1989] ICR 557. See Simpson (1989).

15 See generally Fredman and Morris (1989); Kelly (1991); Meredeen (1988: ch. 9); and Seifert (1987, 1989).

16 [1986] ICR 897. See Morris (1987).

17 None of the legislative changes in the 1980–90 period required unions to make any changes in their rules relating to industrial action. Rule changes might have been seen as advisable in order to clarify where authority to call for industrial action lay but in practice this was not a major problem either for unions in general or for unions in the education sector in particular.

18 This issue has been the subject of two decisions in the Court of Appeal. In *Monsanto plc v TGWU* [1987] ICR 269, where industrial action was suspended for two weeks pending negotiations which failed to resolve the dispute it was held that no further ballot was required to preserve the union's immunity. By contrast in *Post Office v UCW* [1990] ICR 258 the resumption of a campaign of selective twenty-four hour stoppages after a period of nine months in which no stoppages were called for was held not to be protected by the authority of the earlier ballot. See Auerbach (1990).

19 Cf. the view of Fredman and Morris (1992: 44) that 'the government has imposed a non-statutory "no-strike" condition upon teachers', with the changes made by the School Teachers' Pay and Conditions Act 1991.

20 See generally Beaumont (1992), Fredman and Morris (1989), Kelly (1991), and Mailly *et al.* (1989).

21 The other Review Bodies cover judges, senior civil servants and senior officers in the armed forces; the rest of the armed forces; doctors and dentists; and now schoolteachers. Only the schoolteachers' Review Body was set up by statute and makes recommendations on conditions other than pay. See generally Fredman and Morris (1989: 184–6).

22 Ibbs (1988). See Baldwin (1988). Earlier organisational changes followed the Financial Management Initiative in 1983, which aimed at decentralising operational decisions and control of resources to line management whilst tightening up and strengthening strategic departmental management within strict budgetary constraints, and the contracting out of a number of support services such as cleaning in the mid-1980s. The latter caused major redundancies among NUCPS members in particular. At the same time the transfer of some organisations including the Royal Dockyards and Royal Ordnance out of the civil service into private ownership meant that some unions, notably IPMS, had to adapt to working in a completely new environment.

23 Workers who remain in the NHS are still engaged on Whitley terms and conditions of employment: but employers can make changes to working practices which serve to undermine them to some extent, for example demanding a greater amount of work within a shorter period of time.

24 See the *Financial Times*, 14, 19 and 22 December 1981, and the *Guardian*, 14 and 22 December 1981. An appeal against the conviction was dismissed: *Elsey v Smith* [1983] IRLR 292.

25 *Miles v Wakefield Metropolitan District Council* [1987] ICR 368, and *Wiluzinski v Tower Hamlets London Borough Council* [1989] ICR 493. See Morris (1987), and Shrubsall (1989).

26 *Creswell v Board of Inland Revenue* [1984] ICR 508. See Fentiman (1985).

27 *Council of Civil Service Unions v Minister for the Civil Service* [1985] ICR 14. See Fredman (1985).

28 See e.g. in respect of the changes in the terms of employment of school 'dinner ladies', which involved departing from national agreements. *Burdett-Coutts v Hertfordshire County Council* [1984] IRLR 91, *R v Hertfordshire County Council ex parte NUPE*, 16 April 1984 and *R v Birmingham City Council ex parte NUPE*, 16 April 1984. See Fredman (1984).

29 *R v Secretary of State for the Home Department, ex parte Benwell* [1984] ICR 723; *R v Secretary of State for the Home Department, ex parte Broom* [1985] ICR 766.

30 For the background to one part of this sector, see Sisson (1975); Meredeen (1988: ch. 5). On developments in the 1980s see generally Gennard (1990).

31 'New technology' is a convenient shorthand expression for a number of developments arising from changes in available printing technologies. New technology disputes may, therefore, concern one or more of a range of issues: opposition to the introduction of new equipment; disagreement over payment for operating this equipment; related changes in working practices; and reductions in staffing. The issue which was central to disputes in the 1980s was the elimination of 'double key stroking' in the typesetting of advertising and editorial copy; new equipment enabled this to be done directly by journalists and advertising staff – 'single key stroking' – removing the need for a separate composing room where copy was typeset by compositors who were usually NGA members. This revolutionised the pre-production process for the national and provincial newspapers.

32 One of the most extended disputes involved widely supported industrial action by journalists at the Aberdeen *Press and Journal* in 1990. This was not successful in preventing derecognition of the NUJ although some concessions were made by the management over job losses. See the *Financial Times* 6 and 24 November 1989, 24 February and 16 September 1990.

33 *Messenger Newspapers Group v NGA* 14 October, 17 and 25 November 1983, [1984] ICR 345. The company also successfully pursued a claim for damages: *Messenger Newspapers Group Ltd v NGA* [1984] IRLR 397.

34 *Associated Newspapers Group Ltd v Wade* [1979] ICR 664.

35 See *Express and Star Ltd v NGA* [1986] ICR 589.

36 For an account of these developments see Gennard (1990: 493–501), where the Kent *Messenger* dispute is described as the more important in the light of the differences in the nature of the NGA membership and organisation in the relevant companies in the two disputes. The failure of the NGA, SOGAT and NUJ to provide a co-ordinated response is seen as a crucial weakness in the trade unions' response.

37 *News Group Newspapers Ltd v SOGAT* 10 February 1986 and 4 March 1986, both unreported, and [1986] ICR 716.

38 See the corporate structure of News Group Newspapers which is described in *News Group Newspapers Ltd v SOGAT* [1987] ICR 181 and also the rather different structures in *Dimbleby and Sons Ltd v NUJ* [1984] ICR 386.

39 Other instances include *Express Newspapers Ltd v Mitchell* [1982] IRLR 465; *Express and Star Ltd v NGA* [1986] ICR 589; *Mirror Group Newspapers (1966) Ltd v Harrison* 7 November 1986, and *Kent Free Press Ltd v NGA* [1987] IRLR 267.

40 This is not to underrate the importance of the changes made in 1982 and 1990 to the law of unfair dismissal as it applies to workers who are dismissed while taking part in industrial action. These changes reflect significant strands in government policy on the law of industrial conflict. See Wallington (1983) and Simpson (1991: 435–8).

41 For background information on engineering see Marsh *et al.* (1971, 1981). On construction see generally Evans and Lewis (1989).

42 The major motor manufacturers are not affiliated to the EEF.

43 Prior to this happening, the EEF was already considering allowing affiliates to opt out of the national agreement and become non-conforming members.

44 The NECEA had previously operated as an antonomous body for a period in the 1920s.

45 For the historical background see Clark (1967). For more recent developments see Evans and Lewis (1989).

46 On the attempts to maintain some control through what is now National Working Rule 27 of the Working Rule Agreement of the National Joint Council for the Building industry, see Evans and Lewis (1988: 210–13). NWR27 requires employers 'to take all reasonable steps to ensure that all building trade operatives are in the direct employment of the company and its sub-contractors and in either case are employed under terms and conditions laid down by the Council or, if not directly employed . . . are engaged under terms and conditions which, overall, are no less favourable to the operative'.

47 This does not include motor manufacturing.

48 It is notable that there was a general decline in the total numbers employed in engineering over the decade, even during the upturn of the mid-late 1980s,

although there were some variations within the sector – e.g. employment in metal goods increased between 1985 and 1989 before declining in the next two years. See EEF (1992: 9).

49 See e.g. statements by the BEC chairman and president reported in the *Financial Times* 5 August and 26 November 1991, 4, 28 and 30 January 1992.

50 The most important body for (*inter alia*) dispute resolution on site is the Project Joint Council. See NAECI, Section 13.5 and Appendix B. On the experience of disputes in engineering construction see 'British Success in Engineering Construction, The Project Record' National Economic Development Office and National Joint Council for the Engineering Construction Industry (n.d.).

51 As the case did not give rise to a reported judgment the exact nature of the legal issues raised is not entirely clear. From newspaper reports it appears that British Aerospace raised two separate issues: whether the CSEU unions had secured the necessary degree of support under the CSEU constitution for its affiliates to take industrial action, and whether MSF could disaggregate the votes of different occupational groups of its members. The attempt to secure labour injunctions ultimately failed on both grounds, see the *Financial Times* 27, 28 and 31 October and 1 November 1989. The locus standi of an employer on the first issue is clearly open to question.

52 One unreported case which received some publicity because it involved picketing at, inter alia, the new British Libary site was *Laing Homes Ltd v Higgins* in February 1986.

53 The legal position in any particular dispute would in all probability be fairly complex. For example, where workers engaged by a labour only subcontractor are not paid because the subcontractor has become insolvent, it is not uncommon for them to stop work and maybe picket an entrance to the site. Attempts by these pickets to persuade other workers not to come on site could in theory pass through the gateway to legality for peaceful picketing (see Wedderburn 1981: 117) but in practice the picket would probably fall outside the narrow bounds of the legal right to picket peacefully and so the legal immunity from civil liability for inducing breach of contract would be lost. Organising supportive action by other workers on site would clearly be secondary action outside the protection of the immunities.

54 It may be noted, however, that the law has not developed in a way that would enable redundancies implemented in breach of agreed procedures to be successfully challenged by way of an action based on breach of the redundant employees' contracts of employment. See *Alexander v Standard Telephones & Cables plc* [1990] ICR 291; (No 2) [1991] IRLR 286.

55 For a different perspective on the effect of the introduction of the law on strike ballots see Manning (1993).

56 *Solihull Metropolitan Borough Council v NUT* [1985] IRLR 211.

57 *London Underground Ltd v NUR* [1989] IRLR 341; (No. 2) 343.

58 *British Railways Board v NUR* [1989] ICR 678. See generally Simpson (1989).

59 See the *Morning Star*, 4 February 1986.

REFERENCES

Auerbach, S. (1988) 'Injunction procedure in the seafarers' dispute', *Industrial Law Journal*, 17 (December): 227–38.

—— (1990) 'The wording of balloting requirements', *Industrial Law Journal*, 19 (June): 120–4.

Baldwin, R. (1988) ' "The next steps": ministerial responsibility and government by agency', *Modern Law Review*, 51 (September): 622–8.

Beaumont, P.B. (1992) *Public Sector Industrial Relations*, London: Routledge.

Clark, G. de N. (1967) 'Industrial law and the labour-only sub-contract' *Modern Law Review*, 30 (January): 6–24.

Clegg, H.A., Fox, A. and Thompson, A.F. (1964) *A History of British Trade Unions since 1889*, Volume I, 1889–1910, Oxford: Clarendon Press.

Conservative Party (1968) *Fair Deal at Work: the Conservative Approach to Modern Industrial Relations*, London: Conservative Political Centre.

Daniel, W.W. (1985) 'The United Kingdom', in M. Cross (ed.) *Managing Workforce Reduction: an International Survey*, London: Croom Helm: 67–90.

Department of Employment (DE) (1970) *Industrial Relations Bill: Consultative Document*, London: DE.

—— (1989) *Removing Barriers to Employment*, Cm 665, London: HMSO.

—— (1991) *Industrial Relations in the 1990s*, Cm 1602, London: HMSO.

Dickens, L., Jones, M., Weekes, B. and Hart, M. (1985) *Dismissed: a Study of Unfair Dismissal and the Industrial Tribunal System*, Oxford: Blackwell.

Donovan Commission (1968) *Royal Commission on Trade Unions and Employers' Associations 1965–1968, Report*, Cmnd 3623, London: HMSO.

Engineering Employers' Federation (EEF) (1992) *Economic Trends*, (Spring).

Evans, S. (1985) 'The use of injunctions in industrial disputes', *British Journal of Industrial Relations*, 23 (March): 133–7.

—— (1987) 'The use of injunctions in industrial disputes, May 1984–April 1987', *British Journal of Industrial Relations*, 25 (November): 419–35.

Evans, S. and Lewis, R. (1988) 'Labour clauses: from voluntarism to regulation', *Industrial Law Journal*, 17 (December): 209–26.

—— (1989) 'Destructuring and deregulation in the construction industry', in S. Tailby and C. Whitson (eds) *Manufacturing Change: Industrial Relations and Restructuring*, Oxford: Blackwell: 60–93.

Ewing, K.D. (1991) *The Right to Strike*, Oxford: Clarendon Press.

Ewing, K.D. and Napier, B.W. (1986) 'The Wapping dispute and labour law', *Cambridge Law Journal*, 45 (July): 285–304.

Fentiman, R. (1985) 'Contracts of employment and technological change', *Industrial Law Journal*, 14 (March): 51–3.

Flanders, A. (1970) 'Trade unions and the force of tradition', in *Management and Unions. The Theory and Reform of Industrial Relations*, London: Faber.

Fredman, S. (1984) 'Contractual and public law remedies in respect of unilateral alterations', *Industrial Law Journal*, 13 (September): 177–81.

—— (1985) 'Crown employment, prerogative powers and national security', *Industrial Law Journal*, 14 (March): 41–6.

Fredman, S. and Morris, G. (1987) 'Teachers' Pay and Conditions Act 1987', *Industrial Law Journal*, 16 (June): 107–10.

—— (1989) *The State as Employer*, London: Mansell.

—— (1992) 'School Teachers' Pay and Conditions Act 1991', *Industrial Law Journal*, 21 (March): 44–7.

Freeman, R. and Pelletier, J. (1990) 'The impact of industrial relations legislation on British union density', *British Journal of Industrial Relations*, 28 (July): 141–64.

Gennard, J. (1984) 'The implications of the Messenger Newspaper Group Dispute', *Industrial Relations Journal*, 15 (No. 3): 7–20.
—— (1990) *A History of the National Graphical Association*, London: Unwin Hyman.
Hepple, B. and Fredman, S. (1986) *Labour Law and Industrial Relations in Great Britain*, Deventer: Kluwer.
Ibbs (1988) Prime Minister's Efficiency Unit Report, *Improving Management in Government: The Next Steps*, London: HMSO.
Industrial Law Journal (*ILJ*) (1985) special issue: 'The Miners' dispute and the law', 14 (September): 145–214.
Kahn-Freund, O. (1954) 'Legal framework', in A.D. Flanders and H.A. Clegg (eds) *The System of Industrial Relations in Great Britain*, Oxford: Blackwell: 42–127.
Kelly, G. (1991) *A History of the Local Authorities' Conditions of Service Advisory Board 1947 to 1991: Industrial Relations in Local Government*, London: Centurion.
Kidner, R. (1982) 'Lessons in trade union law reform: the origins and passage of the Trade Disputes Act 1906', *Legal Studies*, 2 (March): 34–52.
Lewis, R. (ed.) (1986) *Labour Law in Britain*, Oxford: Blackwell.
Lewis, R. (1991) 'Reforming industrial relations: law, politics and power', *Oxford Review of Economic Policy*, 7 (1): 60–75.
Lewis, R. and Simpson, R. (1982) 'Disorganising industrial relations: an analysis of sections 2–8 and 10–4 of the Employment Act 1982', *Industrial Law Journal*, 11 (December): 227–44.
Mailly, R., Dimmock, S.J. and Sethi, A.S. (eds) (1989) *Industrial Relations in the Public Services*, London: Routledge.
Manning, A. (1993) 'An economic analysis of the effects of pre-strike ballots', Chapter 6 of this volume.
Marsh, A., Evans, E.O. and Garcia, P. (1971) *Workplace Industrial Relations in Engineering*, London: Kogan Page.
Marsh, A., Hackmann, M. and Miller, D. (1981) *Workplace Relations in the Engineering Industry in the United Kingdom and Federal Republic of Germany*, London: Anglo-German Foundation.
McKendrick, E. (1988) 'The rights of trade union members – part I of the Employment Act 1988', *Industrial Law Journal*, 17 (September): 141–61.
Meredeen, S. (1988) *Managing Industrial Conflict*, London: Century Hutchinson.
Millward, N. and Stevens, M. (1986) *British Workplace Industrial Relations 1980–1984: the DE/ESRC/PSI/ACAS Surveys*, Aldershot: Gower.
Milner, S. and Metcalf, D. (1993) 'A century of UK strike activity: an alternative perspective', Chapter 11 of this volume.
Morris, G. (1987) 'Deductions from pay for industrial action', *Industrial Law Journal*, 16 (September): 185–8.
Morris, G. and Rydzkowski, S. (1984) 'Approaches to industrial action in the National Health Service', *Industrial Law Journal*, 13 (September): 153–64.
O'Regan, C. (1991) 'Contempt of court and the enforcement of labour injunctions', *Modern Law Review*, 54 (May): 385–407.
Parker, S.R., Thomas, C.G., Ellis, N.D. and McCarthy, W.E.J. (1971) *Effects of the Redundancy Payments Act*, London: HMSO.
Pelling, H. (1987) *A History of British Trade Unionism*, 4th edition, Harmondsworth: Penguin.

Phelps Brown, E.H. (1959) *The Growth of British Industrial Relations: a Study from the Standpoint of 1906–14*, London: Macmillan.
Richardson, R. and Rubin, M. (1993) 'The shorter working week in engineering: surrender without sacrifice?', Chapter 10 of this volume.
Shrubsall, V. (1989) 'Limited industrial action and entitlement to pay', *Industrial Law Journal*, 18 (December): 241–4.
Seifert, R.V. (1987) *Teacher Militancy. A History of Teacher Strikes 1896–1987*, London: Falmer.
—— (1989) 'Industrial relations in the school sector', in R. Mailly, S.J. Dimmock and A.S. Sethi (eds) *Industrial Relations in the Public Services*, London: Routledge: 199–258.
Simpson, R. (1989) 'The summer of discontent and the law', *Industrial Law Journal*, 18 (December): 234–41.
—— (1991) 'The Employment Act 1990 in context', *Modern Law Review*, 54 (May): 418–38.
Simpson, R. and Wood, J. (1973) *Industrial Relations and the 1971 Act*, London: Pitman.
Sisson, K. (1975) *Industrial Relations in Fleet Street*, Oxford: Blackwell.
Smith, P. and Morton, G. (1990) 'A change of heart: union exclusion in the provincial newspaper sector', *Work, Employment and Society*, 4 (March): 105–24.
Undy, R. and Martin, R. (1984) *Ballots and Trade Union Democracy*, Oxford: Blackwell.
Wallington, P. (1983) 'The Employment Act 1982 s 9 – a recipe for victimisation?', *Modern Law Review*, 46 (May): 310–17.
Wedderburn, Lord (1981) 'Secondary action and gateways to legality: a note', *Industrial Law Journal*, 10 (June): 113–18.
—— (1986) *The Worker and the Law*, 3rd edition, Harmondsworth: Penguin.
—— (1991) *Employment Rights in Britain and Europe*, London: Lawrence and Wishart.
Weekes, B., Mellish, M., Dickens, L. and Lloyd, J. (1975) *Industrial Relations and the Limits of Law: the Industrial Effects of the Industrial Relations Act 1971*, Oxford: Blackwell.
Woolfson, C. and Foster, J. (1988) *Track Record: The Story of the Caterpillar Occupation*, London: Verso.

6 An economic analysis of the effects of pre-strike ballots

Alan Manning

The Trade Union Act 1984 removed immunity from industrial action authorised or endorsed by a trade union which had not previously conducted a secret ballot on the issue and had not received a majority vote in favour of it. In effect, this made compulsory the holding of a strike ballot before any form of official industrial action. This is the piece of 1980s trade union legislation which has almost certainly directly affected the largest number of workers so it has at least the potential to have the biggest impact on the economy (see Elgar and Simpson 1993). The aim of this chapter is to consider what economic theory might predict to be the effects of pre-strike ballots on economic outcomes. As economic theory tends to use very stylised models to address issues, it is quite possible that this type of approach is misleading and other forms of analysis might be more rewarding. This chapter makes no attempt to evaluate the usefulness of economic theory relative to other approaches.

To start, it is worth considering what the originators of the legislation thought its effects were going to be. At the time, the reasons given for the legislation were firstly to make trade unions more representative of their members and, secondly, to reduce the incidence of strike activity. For example, in April 1983, Norman Tebbit, then Employment Secretary, said that 'if all trade unions were to take the views of their members through secret ballot before embarking on industrial action, many unnecessary and damaging strikes could be avoided'.[1] And Alan Clark, then an Employment Minister, said that 'what really undermines the [trade union] movement in the eyes of the public is when they see on their television sets the car-park mass meeting at which crucial strike decisions are taken by a show of hands amidst jeers and catcalls'.[2] At the time there was probably thought to be no conflict between the twin objectives of increasing the power of union members relative to their leaders and negotiators, and reducing strike activity, perhaps because many trade unionists had voted Conservative in the general elections of

1979 and 1983 in spite of the fact that its proposals for trade union law were opposed by union leaders. Some conflict emerged later; the Employment Act 1990 took steps to restrain unofficial strike action, suggesting that the aim of reducing strikes had priority over giving power to the rank-and-file. It is also quite likely that reducing strike activity was seen not just as an end in itself but as the means to the end of reducing union power which, the government argued, would reduce wages and increase employment.

So, if we want to look at the effects of strike ballots, we should examine the likely impact of their introduction on union democracy, strike activity, wages and employment. This is what we will attempt in this chapter. It would be nice to have some empirical test of the hypotheses presented here but that is likely to be very difficult to provide. For example, McConnell and Takla (1990) use industry-level panel data for the period 1970–87 to look at the effects of legislation on strike activity. But, while this study is the most careful for this country, the fact that the legislation was introduced in all industries at the same time means that it is hard to disentangle the effects of legislation from the effects of other aggregate factors that are varying over time. What is needed is something like the study of Gunderson, Kervin and Reid (1989) who use panel data on Canadian provinces, which has the advantage that the legislative framework has changed both over time and across provinces. They find that mandatory strike ballots significantly reduce strike incidence.

The plan of the chapter is as follows. In the next section, we examine economic models of representative democracy to consider the likely effect of strike ballots on the relationship between union leaders and their members. The second section then considers an asymmetric information model to look at the likely effect of pre-strike ballots on strike activity. The third section considers possible effects of the ballots on union bargaining power.

BALLOTS AND TRADE UNION DEMOCRACY

Where one has to choose a delegate or leader to make decisions that affect one's welfare, it is natural to think that it would be best to choose someone who has preferences close to one's own. If the leader is being elected by majority vote by an electorate with conflicting preferences, then one would, in some crude sense, expect the person elected to have the preferences of the 'average' voter (the most famous result of this type is the median voter result, that, under certain conditions, the median voter effectively gets to choose the leader). In this case any divergence between the views of union leaders and members (such as allegedly existed in the late 1970s in Britain) could be taken as evidence of imperfections in the democratic process of the institutions concerned.

But, in recent years there has been a fashion in economics for looking at models where it is not in people's self-interest to vote for people with identical preferences to themselves, so that a divergence of views between members and leaders cannot necessarily be interpreted as imperfections in the democratic process. Most of this research has been in the context of choosing a country's leader (see Persson and Tabellini 1991, for a good survey of this) but the underlying principles can also be applied to the analysis of trade unions. Let us first consider the two main reasons why one may choose to be represented by someone with views different from your own.

First, there is what is called the time consistency problem. In some situations, one would like to commit oneself *ex ante* to follow a course of action that it is not in your interest to follow *ex post*. In this case, it may be better to delegate decision-making to someone who does not suffer from the same temptations. An example in the political sphere is that a country may want to promise not to appropriate foreign capital investment in order to encourage it. But, once the investment has taken place, it may be difficult to resist the temptation to extract rents from it. In the context of trade union models, an example of the time consistency problem is the model of van der Ploeg (1987). There, workers want to promise future wage moderation in order to encourage the firm to invest. But, the temptation is to raise wages after the investment is locked-in. There is an incentive for workers to find ways of making their promises of wage moderation credible. In van der Ploeg (1987) it is suggested that unions could sign binding long-term wage contracts to achieve this aim, but an alternative would be to delegate wage bargaining to a union representative who is less militant than the average union member. In this case, there would be a divergence in views between leaders and members but it is not a signal of flawed democracy. Of course, in this case, the leadership is more moderate than the rank-and-file, which was not the diagnosis of the unions provided by the Conservative party in the late 1970s. But, an example of this type of problem might be where a union has signed a greenfield agreement which promises moderation in return for investment and then finds it difficult to deliver the membership.

However, union leaders might be expected to be more militant than their members if we consider the other main motive for being represented by someone different from oneself. This is the strategic motive. In situations where bargaining determines outcomes the incentive is to pretend to be more aggressive than one really is in order to

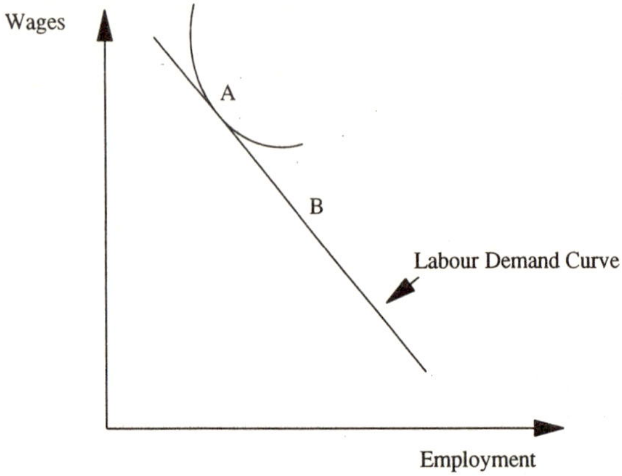

Figure 6.1 Delegation in the Labour Demand Curve model

frighten the other party into giving concessions. This type of idea has been presented in the context of oligopoly theory by Vickers (1985) and in union models by Jones (1989) and Szymanski (1991). Their argument is the following. Consider a labour demand curve model in which the wage is determined by bargaining but employment is controlled unilaterally by employers. If the union has the power to dictate the wage it will choose a point where the labour demand curve is tangential to their indifference curve. This is represented by point A in Figure 6.1. However, if the employer has some power in wage bargaining, the wage will be lower, e.g. we will end up at point B. Obviously the union members would like to move up the labour demand curve towards point A. One way to do this is to delegate bargaining to a union leader who is more militant than the members. Formally, one could model this as assuming the leader cares less about employment than the membership or has a higher reservation wage. The incentive to elect a more militant leader is increased as the union's power in wage bargaining is weaker. In this case, union leaders would tend to be more militant than the rank-and-file.

It should also be noted that the incentives are much less clear if we have other models of trade union behaviour. For example, if we have an efficient bargain, then electing a leader who cares less about employment will tend to raise wages, which is good for union members but will also tend to move the agreement away from the true contract curve, which is inefficient.

So far, we have argued that a divergence in views between union members and leaders should not necessarily be seen as a failure of internal democracy within unions, although it is not clear *a priori* whether we would expect leaders to be more or less militant than their members. This means that one of the main justifications for the introduction of pre-strike ballots is not necessarily valid. This does not mean, however, that the introduction of ballots will have no effect.

The introduction of pre-strike ballots will reduce the ability of trade union members to commit themselves to following a leader whose objectives differ from their own. For example, the strategic motive for electing a militant leader who threatens strike action is to induce the employer to make a high initial wage offer that the members can accept without having to go on a strike for which they are not really prepared. Without ballots, the strike threat may be credible because the union leader has been given the authority to call for a strike and has the ability to discipline those members who do not obey. However, with ballots the leaders' authority is undermined as they must seek a mandate for any strike action from their members so the credibility of a leader's negotiating posture becomes of less importance. So, the incentives for electing a leader with views different from one's own is likely to be reduced by the introduction of strike ballots as the government predicted, but for completely different reasons.

However, one can also argue that strike ballots act as much more of a constraint on leaders who are more militant than their members than on those who are more moderate. This is because the law does not require negotiated agreements to be ratified by the membership if the leaders want to accept the deal (although it should be noted that many unions do seek such ratification). So, a moderate union leader can accept a deal the membership would like to reject. However, a militant leader who wants to reject an offer and to take industrial action in pursuit of a better one, has to have this course of action ratified in a ballot. So, one could argue that after the introduction of pre-strike ballots we would expect to see union leaders becoming more moderate with a consequent reduction in wages.

This section has used economic models of representative government to consider the likely effect of the introduction of ballots on trade unions. It has been argued that ballots may mean we are less likely to see militant union leaders but this does not necessarily imply any 'improvement' in the democratic process within unions. However, the models we have considered here are not suitable to considering the effects of ballots on strikes; this is the purpose of the next section.

BALLOTS AND THE INCIDENCE OF STRIKES

Recent economic models of strikes have rested on some kind of asymmetry in information between union and employer. Models in the literature have tended to focus on the case where the union is uncertain about the profitability of the firm, e.g. Hayes (1984). Although, some empirical support has been claimed for this model (e.g. McConnell 1989, for US data) this assumption is probably more for analytical convenience than realism. The fact that employer's offers are generally rejected when ballots are held strongly suggests that there is some asymmetric information about, for example, the militancy of workers. Indeed, Card, in a study of Canadian data, concluded that 'it may be that a richer model of strikes, allowing for asymmetries on both sides of the bargaining table, is needed to fully describe the data' (1990: 654). However, theoretical models with two-sided asymmetric information are notoriously difficult to handle (e.g. see Cramton 1984).

So, in this section (where we are simply concerned with the likely effect of pre-strike ballots) we consider a simple model in which all the asymmetric information is about the reservation wage of workers and the employer makes a series of wage offers which the union decides whether to accept or reject. We abstract from the delegation issues discussed in the previous section by assuming that the union makes decisions by majority vote, which means that the median voter will be decisive.[3]

How, in this framework, can we model the impact of ballots? A natural assumption is that the result of the ballot gives information about the militancy of workers and hence some useful information about what is the minimum wage offer that is acceptable to workers. If the vote against the initial offer is 50.1 per cent then the employer may reasonably conclude that a small improvement will be acceptable; if the vote is 99.9 per cent against then a much larger increase may be necessary. In contrast, without ballots the employer only has the information that more than 50 per cent of workers rejected the offer and is unable to 'fine-tune' subsequent wage offers.[4]

This information-revealing aspect of ballots has been emphasised by others. For example, Brown and Wadhwani wrote that 'balloting improves the information available to each side about their relative bargaining strength, and in this sense is likely to increase the efficiency of bargaining' (1990: 61). Elgar and Simpson (1993) also say there is some evidence for this view but emphasise that often ballots provide information that is available to the parties concerned anyway. But, there are at least two reasons why it is not altogether clear that bargaining efficiency will be increased by the extra information provided by ballots.

First, the amount of information revealed by ballots is endogenous to the behaviour of the parties involved. If workers realise that employers will raise their wage offer if there is a large vote against the initial offer, they may be encouraged to vote for a strike even if they are not very militant. Then the amount of information conveyed by a rejection may be very small. Secondly, for the information of a strike ballot to be useful to the employer the initial offer must be rejected. This encourages employers to make a lower initial wage offer then they otherwise would. This would inevitably make bargaining more drawn out, which is not obviously efficient.

These issues were investigated using the simplest possible model of wage bargaining with asymmetric information. The employer is assumed not to know about the reservation wage of its workers. There are three workers (the smallest number to make the problem interesting) each of whom knows only his own reservation wage. The employer makes an initial wage offer which the workers decide to accept or reject by majority vote. If rejected the employer makes a second offer and again the workers use a majority vote to decide whether to accept it. The incentive to reach agreement quickly arises because agents discount the future. The difference between the situation with and without ballots is that with ballots the employer's second period offer will depend on whether rejection of the first offer was unanimous or not.

There are a number of ways to compare the equilibrium with and without ballots. First we might be interested in the probability of the initial offer's being rejected (which we will call a one-period strike) or of both offers being rejected (which we will call a two-period strike). We might also be interested in the wage outcomes in the two equilibria. Are wages higher or lower with ballots? Finally, we might be interested in whether expected profits are increased by the introduction of balloting. Details of the equilibrium for the two models are contained in a Technical Appendix to this chapter. Here, we will provide some intuition for some of the results.

First, an individual worker's strategy is to vote against an offer if their reservation wage exceeds some cut-off level b* (which will be increasing in the wage offer). First, let us assume that workers use the same cut-off rule in deciding to accept or reject the initial wage offer both with and without ballots. We want to compare the second period wage offers. With ballots the second period wage offer will be higher if the rejection was unanimous than if it was only a majority decision. Without ballots, the second period wage offer will be somewhere in between. This is shown in Table 6.1.

This has the implication that workers will benefit from strike ballots when there is a large majority in favour of rejection. Such an argument is often put forward as a reason why balloting may be to the advantage of unions. But, in the model presented here, such a conclusion is too glib as

Table 6.1 Comparison of second period outcomes

	Cut-off reservation wage used by workers in first period		
	0.5	*0.7*	*0.9*
Second period wages			
No ballots	0.864	0.936	0.991
Ballots (majority)	0.833	0.926	0.990
Ballots (unanimity)	0.920	0.969	1.000
Second period strike incidence (%)			
No ballots	10.03	5.64	0.91
Ballots	5.51	0.89	0.24
Initial wage required to achieve cut-off rule			
No ballots	0.827	0.912	0.982
Ballots	0.851	0.914	0.982

Note

1 These simulations were done for a value $y = 1.5$.

there is also a downside for the union: if the majority in favour of rejection is small then the wage offer will be lower than it would be in the absence of balloting. A correct analysis of the effect of balloting on unions should focus on *ex ante* expected utility and it is much less clear then that balloting favours unions.

We might also be interested in the effect of balloting on the probability of a strike in the second period. As Brown and Wadhwani (1990) predict, the effect is likely to be a reduction in strike probability as the information available to the employer is better. This is confirmed by Table 6.1. Finally, we should note that, because of the improved information, expected second period profits are higher with balloting than without.

So far, we have assumed that workers use the same rule in deciding whether to accept or reject the initial offer with or without balloting. But, there is no reason to believe that this is the case. In fact, we would expect that, for a given initial wage offer workers are more likely to vote for rejection with balloting than without. This is because voting for rejection increases the probability of there being a unanimous rejection and this increases the probability of getting a higher wage offer in the second period. So, for a given initial wage offer the model presented here would predict that we are more likely to observe rejection with balloting.

But, there is also no reason to believe that the initial wage offer will be the same with balloting. As the probability of rejection for a given wage offer is higher we would expect the employer to respond by making a higher initial offer. This is confirmed by Table 6.2. Whether this higher initial offer ends up increasing the probability of acceptance is unclear

Table 6.2 Comparison of first period wages

Output	*Discount factor*		
	0.1	*0.5*	*0.9*
$y=1.0$			
No ballots	0.589	0.615	0.604
Ballots	0.591	0.636	0.709
$y=1.5$			
No ballots	0.761	0.811	0.798
Ballots	0.761	0.819	0.847
$y=2.0$			
No ballots	0.855	0.903	0.908
Ballots	0.855	0.903	0.916

Table 6.3 Comparison of strike incidence

Output	*Discount factor*					
	0.1		*0.5*		*0.9*	
	p1	*p2*	*p1*	*p2*	*p1*	*p2*
$y=1.0$						
No ballots	25.5	14.1	32.0	18.0	49.9	29.7
Ballots	26.1	13.5	31.8	16.7	50.6	27.8
$y=1.5$						
No ballots	16.0	0.8	21.6	1.3	53.5	6.9
Ballots	16.0	0.8	20.4	1.2	47.5	5.5
$y=2.0$						
No ballots	6.9	0.0	8.4	0.1	25.7	9.5
Ballots	6.9	0.0	8.4	0.1	23.6	8.7

Note

1 p1 is the percentage incidence of one period strikes; p2 is percentage incidence of two period strikes.

but for the models considered by us it does. The probabilities of any strike at all and the probability of a two period strike are presented in Table 6.3.

It is also worth noting that the effect with balloting that it is harder to get initial agreement is bad for profits. In fact, this effect can outweigh the positive effect on profits of the improved information in the second period as shown in Table 6.4. One should not necessarily conclude that balloting is good for employers.

In the model presented above we have assumed that if the employer's initial offer is rejected in a ballot then there is automatically a strike of at least one period. But, as Brown and Wadhwani (1990) emphasise,

Table 6.4 Comparison of expected profits

Output	*Discount factor*		
	0.1	*0.5*	*0.9*
$y=1.0$			
No ballots	0.254	0.236	0.242
Ballots	0.253	0.229	0.226
$y=1.5$			
No ballots	0.624	0.592	0.596
Ballots	0.624	0.592	0.585
$y=2.0$			
No ballots	1.073	1.046	1.033
Ballots	1.073	1.046	1.033

employers generally make concessions after rejection of their initial offer and settlement normally occurs without a strike. What would we expect to happen if employers can make a second offer before there is any risk of a strike happening? Then, the employer does not really want their initial offer to be accepted. Acceptance of the first offer would imply that they could have successfully offered a lower wage. Employers would want to use the first offer as an information-gathering device so we would expect to see a low initial wage offer. But, workers would also realise that there is no cost to voting against the initial offer. There will not be an immediate strike and, if anything, the employer's second offer will be higher, the larger the majority in favour of strike action. In this case, balloting may simply become a ritual; employers routinely make an offer they do not expect workers to accept and workers routinely vote against it. Little or no information is conveyed by this process, and the real process of bargaining begins only after the ritual ballot has been conducted. Ballots would then have no effects on outcomes and would simply be a waste of time. The fact that such a high proportion of ballots are in favour of strike action could perhaps be taken as evidence in favour of the ritualisation hypothesis.

In this section, we have used a very simple asymmetric information model to look at the likely effect of balloting where balloting has been seen as a means by which the employer gathers information about the militancy of workers. The model is highly stylised and ignores many features of bargaining that are in reality important, but we would argue that such an approach can be useful in clarifying one's views about the likely effects of ballots. For example, we have emphasised how conclusions like 'employers have better information with balloting so it is to their advantage' are probably too simplistic because they ignore the endogenous nature of the information extraction process. In the model here, strikes are reduced by the introduction of balloting but there is a suspicion that this is not a general result.

BALLOTS AND TRADE UNION BARGAINING POWER

In both the delegation and asymmetric information models presented above, the introduction of ballots was predicted to have an effect on wages even though this was not the main focus of interest. But, there may be other, more direct, ways in which ballots may affect the level of trade union bargaining power and hence wages. As economic models of bargaining power are rudimentary to say the least, this analysis is even more speculative than what has gone before.

First, ballots may have an effect on the fragmentation of bargaining. If workers largely vote in line with their self-interest, employers may be able to make offers that benefit a majority of workers at the expense of a minority. The opportunities for exploiting divisions among workers would seem to be greater with balloting. This is even more likely to be the case when one takes account of other pieces of legislation that restrict the electorate in ballots to those who are directly in dispute with their employer and which restrict secondary action. Gregg and Machin (1992) found that decentralisation of wage bargaining was associated with slower wage growth and balloting may have been a factor in making such decentralisation easier and more profitable for employers. Some indirect evidence for this view is provided by Undy and Martin, who in a study of the uses of balloting in the British trade union movement before it was compulsory, concluded that 'balloting . . . is also unlikely when an agreement affects separate groups differently, since it is regarded as unfair' (1984: 160).

Second, and along somewhat similar lines, Manning (1993) argued that the introduction of ballots is likely to reduce union influence over employment decisions much more than their influence over wages. There, the traditional union structure of a union leader capable of unilaterally calling strikes and disciplining those who do not obey was seen as a way of workers offering to each other a system of mutual support if their jobs were threatened. *Ex ante*, workers will support such a system of insurance even if, *ex post*, workers whose jobs turn out to be safe would not want to go on strike. But, introducing ballots destroys the credibility of this mechanism. Once it is clear whose jobs are threatened, self-interested workers whose jobs are safe are unlikely to vote for strike action over the issue. This means that unions are likely to lose influence over employment. However, as workers' interests are generally more closely aligned in wage disputes, we might expect these effect of ballots on union influence in wage bargaining are likely to be much smaller. Given that, in most economic models, union influence over employment is desirable while union influence over wages is not, this argument suggests that balloting may have adverse effects on efficiency.

Third, balloting takes time and delay in organising industrial action may give opportunities for both sides to make preparations to strengthen their bargaining positions. Given that, in the absence of ballots, many strikes were initiated very rapidly, the presumption must be that the delay is generally to the advantage of the employer.

Fourth, balloting may have shifted the balance of power towards shopfloor activists and away from leaders as ballots act as a constraint more on official strike action than on unofficial strike action. There was some evidence for this in, for example, the series of strikes on London Underground in the spring and summer of 1989. The government responded in the Employment Act 1990 by allowing dismissal of unofficial strikers and forcing union leaders to disown unofficial strikes if they wanted to retain immunity. Hence, it is unclear whether this acts to increase or reduce trade union bargaining power.

CONCLUSION

This chapter has looked at some simple economic models of the likely effect of the introduction of pre-strike ballots in the Trade Union Act of 1984. We have concentrated attention on whether the ballots are likely to improve union democracy or reduce the incidence of strikes which were the stated justifications for the legislation, but we have also paid attention to possible effects on wages and employment which there is good reason to believe were also regarded as important. What has emerged is that it is quite likely that the effect of ballots is very complex, with different consequences in different situations. What is needed is some way of evaluating the relative and absolute importance of the different effects. But, as suggested in the introduction, it is likely to be hard if not impossible to provide convincing empirical evidence on the effects of pre-strike ballots because their introduction was a one-off change applying across the whole economy at a time when many other substantial changes were taking place. And, conclusions from a case-study approach, while informative about that particular case, are difficult to generalise. This probably means that any analysis of the effects of ballots is likely to remain largely speculative.

TECHNICAL APPENDIX

In this section, we present a simple bargaining model designed to capture the information-revealing aspects of pre-strike ballots.

Assume that, to be productive, a firm requires the presence of three workers. If the workers are employed, the output per worker is y. We assume that the reservation wage, b, of each individual worker is an independent draw from a distribution function $G(b)$ which is common knowledge. Each worker knows their own reservation wage but not that of anyone else.

The process of wage determination is assumed to be the following. There are two periods. In the first period, the employer offers a wage to the workers. They decide by majority voting whether to accept or reject this offer. If accepted, all workers are employed (even if for one individual the wage may be below their reservation wage[5]) and production takes place immediately. If rejected, the employer makes another wage offer in the second period and, again, the workers decide by majority vote to accept or reject this offer. If accepted, production takes place. If rejected, the game ends. The discount rate is assumed to be δ so there is an incentive to come to an early agreement.

The difference between the situation with and without pre-strike ballots is assumed to be the following. Without pre-strike ballots the employer only has the information at the second period that a rejection has occurred but not the strength of that rejection. They do not know whether the rejection was unanimous or a majority decision. In contrast, we assume that this information is available with ballots so that the employer's second period wage offer can be contingent on this information. Let us consider equilibrium in the two cases.

Without ballots

An equilibrium in this case is characterised by a pair (w_1, w_2) denoting the first and second period wage offers respectively and a cut-off level of the reservation wage b_1 such that workers vote to reject w_1 if their reservation wage exceeds b_1 and vote to accept otherwise. Let us consider what conditions must be satisfied by the equilibrium.

First, we need to derive the distribution function for the median reservation wage which we will denote by $F(b)$. As the individual workers' reservation wages are assumed to be iid we have:

$$F(b) = 3[G(b)]^2 - 2[G(b)]^3 \tag{1}$$

Consider the optimal second period wage offer w_2. If the employer believes that the median reservation wage is above b_1 because the initial offer was rejected, then the distribution function of the median reservation wage conditional on this information is given by:

$$F_2(b) = \frac{F(b) - F(b_1)}{1 - F(b_1)} \quad \text{for } b \, \varepsilon \, [b_1, \bar{b}] \tag{2}$$

A second period offer w_2 will only be rejected if the median reservation wage exceeds it which happens with probability $[1 - F_2(w_2)]$. w_2 will be chosen to maximise expected second period profits i.e. we have:

$$w_2(b_1) = argmax_w \, (y - w).F_2(w) \tag{3}$$

where the notation denotes that fact that the optimal w_2 will, in general, depend on b_1.

Now consider what determines b_1. Without balloting, an individual will decide to accept or reject the initial offer solely on the basis of whether he or she prefers it to the discounted value of the second period offer. A person with reservation wage b_1 will be indifferent between the two options, i.e. we will have:

$$w_1 - b_1 = \delta.(w_2(b_1) - b_1) \tag{4}$$

Finally, w_1 will be chosen to maximise expected profits which are given by:

$$E\Pi = (y - w_1).F(b_1) + \delta.(y - w_2).[F(w_2) - F(b_1)] \tag{5}$$

subject to (3) and (4). The solution to this problem is well known, e.g. see Sobel and Takahashi (1983), so we will not discuss it here.

With ballots

The difference now is that if w_1 is rejected the employer also has information about the strength of that rejection, i.e. whether it was unanimous of a majority decision. This information is useful to the employer in deciding on their second period wage offer and this offer will generally depend on the result of the ballot. Denote by w_2^u and w_2^m the wage offers corresponding to a unanimous and majority decision respectively.

As before, we can show that, in equilibrium, the optimal pure strategy for workers is to vote against the initial offer if their reservation wage exceeds some cut-off level b_1 (although this will generally be a point different from the previous case). We need to work out the distribution function for the median reservation wage conditional on rejection of the initial offer.

If a worker votes to reject the initial offer, the distribution function for their reservation wage conditional on this information is given by:

$$G_2(b) = \frac{G(b) - G(b_1)}{1 - G(b_1)} \quad \text{for } b \,\varepsilon\, [b_1, \bar{b}] \tag{6}$$

If rejection of w_1 was unanimous the employer knows that every worker's reservation wage is above b_1. By analogy with (1), the distribution function of the median reservation wage, conditional on this information, will be given by:

$$F_2^u(b) = 3.[G_2(b)]^2 - 2.[G_2(b)]^3 \tag{7}$$

However, if rejection of w_1 was by a majority vote, then the employer knows that one worker has a reservation wage below b_1 and two have reservation wages above it. The distribution function of the median reservation wage, conditional on this information is given b:

$$F_2^m(b) = 2.G_2(b) - [G_2(b)]^2 \tag{8}$$

The second period wage offers (w_2^u, w_2^m) will be chosen to maximise expected second period profits i.e we have:

$$w_2^i = argmax_w \, (y - w).F_2^i(w) \; i = U,M \tag{9}$$

Now consider the determination of b_1. This is more complicated than in the previous case because, for example, a vote for rejection makes it more likely that there will be a unanimous rejection and hence this increases the expected second period wage.

Let us consider an individual with reservation wage b. Suppose the other two workers are following the proposed equilibrium strategy, i.e. reject w_1 if $b > b_1$. Then, the probability of the other two workers voting for rejection of the initial offer is given by:

$$p_{RR} = [1 - G(b_1)]^2 \tag{10}$$

The probability of one other vote for acceptance and one for rejection is given by:

$$p_{RA} = 2.G(b_1).[1 - G(b_1)] \tag{11}$$

and the probability of two other votes for acceptance is given by:

$$p_{AA} = [G(b_1)]^2 \tag{12}$$

If this worker votes for acceptance then, with probability $(p_{AA} + p_{AR})$ there will be a majority for acceptance and the worker will receive w_1 today. However, with probability p_{RR} there will be a majority for rejection. The second period wage offer will then be w_2^m. A worker on the margin of accepting w_1 will certainly accept w_2^m but with probability $[1 - G_2(w_2^m)]^2$ the other workers will vote to reject the second period offer as well in which case this worker will receive nothing. So, the expected utility from voting for the initial offer is:

$$EU^A = (p_{AA} + p_{RA}).(w_1 - b) + p_{RR}.\{2.G_2(w_2^m) - [G_2(w_2^m)]^2\}.\delta.(w_2^m - b) \quad (13)$$

Now consider what happens if this worker votes for rejection of the initial offer. With probability p_{AA} a majority will vote for acceptance giving pay-off w_1. With probability p_{RA} there will be a majority rejection. In this case, the worker who voted for acceptance of the initial offer has a reservation wage below b_1, so will definitely vote for acceptance of w_2^m. Similarly, this worker when on the margin of accepting w_1 will certainly accept w_2^m so this offer will be accepted with certainty. Finally, with probability p_{RR} there will be a unanimous rejection of w_1 leading to a second period offer of w_2^u which will be rejected with probability $[1 - G_2(w_2^u)]^2$. Putting this together, the expected utility from voting for rejection if your reservation wage is b is given by:

$$\begin{aligned} EU^R = {} & p_{AA}.(w_1 - b) + p_{RA}.\delta.(w_2^m - b) \\ & + p_{RR}.\{2.G_2(w_2^u) - [G_2(w_2^u]^2\}.\delta.(w_2^u - b) \end{aligned} \quad (14)$$

b_1 is simply that value of b for which $EU^A = EU^R$. Using (13) and (14) we can write this as:

$$\begin{aligned} w_1 = {} & b_1 + \delta.(w_2^m - b_1) + \delta.(p_{RR}/p_{RA}).[[2.G(w_2^m) - [G(w_2^m)^2].(w_2^m - b_1) \\ & - [2.G(w_2^u) - [G(w_2^u)]^2].(w_2^u - b_1)] \end{aligned} \quad (15)$$

Note, although (15) is written with w_1 as the dependent variable and associates a unique value of w_1 with a given value of b, (15) should really be thought of as giving b as a function of w_1. This relationship is not generally unique. In the simulations we assume that, for a given value of w_1, the value of b that is best for workers is chosen.

The aim of the employer is to choose w_1 to maximise expected profits which are given by:

$$\begin{aligned} E\Pi = {} & (y - w_1).F(b_1) + [1 - G(b_1)]^3.F_2^u(w_2^u).\delta.(y - w_2^u) \\ & + 3.[1 - G(b_1)]^2.G(b_1).F_2^m(w_2^m).\delta.(y - w_2^m) \end{aligned} \quad (16)$$

subject to (9) and (15).

Simulations

In all the simulations described in the text, we assumed that the individual reservation wages were uniformly distributed on the unit interval, i.e. $G(b) = b$. The values of y and δ are given in the tables.

NOTES

I would like to thank Paul Gregg and other participants at the conference for their comments.

1 *Employment Gazette*, January 1983: 3.
2 Quoted in *Employment Gazette*. December 1983: 499.
3 This is because the assumption that workers differ only in their reservation wage means that preferences are single-peaked.
4 We are assuming that the introduction of balloting has no effect on the information about workers' militancy available to union leaders; it is arguable whether this is reasonable.
5 We assume that workers commit themselves to abide by the majority decision because the presence of all three is required for the firm to be productive.

REFERENCES

Brown, W. and Wadhwani, S. (1990) 'The Economic Effects of Industrial Relations Legislation since 1979', *National Institute Economic Review*, February: 57–70.

Card, D. (1990) 'Strikes and Wages: A Test of an Asymmetric Information Model', *Quarterly Journal of Economics*, 55: 625–60.

Cramton, P. (1984) 'Bargaining with Incomplete Information: An Infinite Horizon Model with Two-Sided Uncertainty', *Review of Economic Studies*, 51: 577–93.

Elgar, J. and Simpson, R. (1993) 'The Impact of the Law on Industrial Disputes in the 1980s', Chapter 5 of this volume.

Gregg, P. and Machin, S. (1992) 'Pay Bargaining down the Line: The Economic Impact of Decentralisation in UK Firms in the 1980s', unpublished mimeo University College London.

Gunderson, M., Kervin, J. and Reid, F. (1989) 'The Effect of Labour Relations on Strike Incidence', *Canadian Journal of Economics*, 22: 779–94.

Hayes, B. (1984) 'Unions and Strikes and Asymmetric Information', *Journal of Labor Economics*, 2: 57–83.

Jones, S.R.G. (1989) 'The Role of Negotiators in Union-Firm Bargaining', *Canadian Journal of Economics*, 22: 630–42.

McConnell, S. (1989) 'Strikes, Wages and Private Information', *American Economic Review*, 79: 801–15.

McConnell, S. and Takla, L. (1992) 'Mrs Thatcher's Trade Union Legislation: Has it Reduced Strikes?', unpublished mimeo, LSE.

Manning, A. (1993) 'Pre-Strike Ballots and Wage-Employment Bargaining', Oxford, Economic Papers, forthcoming.

Persson, T. and Tabellini, G. (1990) *Macroeconomic Policy, Credibility and Politics*, Chur, Switzerland: Harwood.

Sobel, J. and Takahashi, I. (1983) 'A Multistage Model of Bargaining', *Review of Economic Studies*, 50: 411–26.

Szymanski, S. (1991) 'Median Voter Militants', unpublished mimeo, London Business School.

Undy, R. and Martin, R. (1984) *Ballots and Trade Union Democracy*, Oxford: Blackwell.

van der Ploeg, R. (1987) 'Trade Unions, Investment and Employment: A Non-Cooperative Approach', *European Economic Review*, 31: 1465–92.

Vickers, J. (1985) 'Delegation and the Theory of the Firm', *Economic Journal Conference Papers*, 95: 138–47.

7 Dispute deterrence: evidence on final-offer arbitration

Simon Milner

INTRODUCTION

Final-offer arbitration (FOA) is a disputes procedure which compels an arbitrator to decide wholly for one side or the other in a dispute. By definition there is no compromise option, in direct contrast to conventional arbitration where the decision criteria of the arbitrator are not so constrained. Stevens (1966) first set out the theory associated with FOA, arguing that in contrast to conventional arbitration, which encouraged disputes, FOA would promote more genuine bargaining and would specifically deter disputes. The theory behind Stevens's argument and critiques of it are discussed below.

The theoretical and practical debate about the relative merits of FOA compared to conventional arbitration has been conducted primarily in the US, where there is considerable experience with such procedures in the public sector. A brief summary and assessment of the US evidence is provided.

During the 1980s a number of UK private-sector plants signed new collective agreements which included FOA. Data from bargaining rounds in these, and comparison plants with conventional procedures, provide the first UK evidence on the issue of FOA and dispute deterrence. The UK sample is described below and the evidence is presented and analysed in subsequent sections.

It is important to be aware of the different contexts of FOA in the US and UK before analysing the theory and evidence, because these suggest that we should not necessarily expect the same results for FOA in the UK as in the US. Apart from concerning professional baseball players' negotiations, FOA in the US is an overwhelmingly public-sector phenomenon, introduced as a alternative to allowing public employees a right to strike, (see Lester (1984) and Kearney (1984) for descriptions of various states' disputes procedures). It has been introduced through legislation for a particular group of workers and is usually a compulsory procedure – once the parties have reached a certain stage in their negotiations without agreement, they are compelled to use FOA to resolve the dispute.

The recent UK examples of FOA are wholly in the private sector, occurring in plants which form some of the so-called 'new style deals'. The plants with such deals have been characterised as predominantly greenfield, often Japanese hi-tech companies (Bassett 1986, Rico 1987). Co-signatory to many of these agreements is the Electrical, Electronic, Telecommunication and Plumbing Union (EETPU). Typically the agreements have also incorporated single-union recognition, strike-avoidance clauses, task flexibility and single status for white- and blue-collar employees. FOA has therefore usually only been one element in a package of unusual components in the agreement.

Three significant differences between the US and UK contexts of FOA stand out. The private sector, public sector backdrop is prominent. Second, all the UK examples are part of voluntarily signed collective agreements, rather than imposed through legislation. Finally, UK collective agreements are not usually legal contracts, unlike in the US, such that a no-strike clause in a UK agreement is only morally binding on the parties, therefore industrial action is not legally ruled out even after arbitration.

THEORY

Introduction

The theory behind FOA has evolved primarily in North America, mainly stemming from arguments in favour of FOA in a seminal article by Stevens (1966). At its most basic the theory runs that because the parties are uncertain about the arbitrator's behaviour under FOA if the dispute goes to arbitration, a contract zone of more favourable (and negotiable) solutions to the dispute is created. This incentive effect was directly contrasted by Stevens to the 'chilling effect' of conventional arbitration: because the parties believe that the arbitrator will compromise between the two final offers, they always have an incentive to maintain an extreme position in the face of arbitration, actually increasing the probability of arbitration taking place.

A negotiated outcome is said to be Pareto-superior to an arbitrated settlement for three reasons: because it is assumed that the parties are bargaining over the distribution of a fixed pie and that the costs of arbitration reduce the size of the divided pie (Farber and Katz 1979); because agents are more likely to know about their own and each other's preferences than the arbitrator does (Crawford 1979); and it is more likely that agents will accept a negotiated settlement and make it work (Crawford 1979). A repeated reliance on arbitrated decisions (known as the 'narcotic effect', or recurring chilling) is also said to undermine stable bargaining relationships (Anderson and Kochan 1977).

Costs of disagreement and uncertainty

The debate regarding the relative merits of FOA and conventional arbitration has moved on considerably since 1966, and there is a strong analogy with theories of strike incidence. Essentially the debate now revolves around two central questions: what factors determine the probability of disagreement in bargaining?; and what impact, if any, do alternative forms of arbitration have on these factors?

Starting from first principles, the probability of disagreement is said to depend upon the potential cost of disagreement, which has two elements – direct costs and potential costs of losing. This is similar to the joint cost theory of strikes, which argues that the probability of a strike occurring is inversely related to the joint costs of such a strike (Kennan 1986).

Direct costs of arbitration (in the US) include arbitrator's and lawyers' fees and costs incurred because of a delayed settlement. Bloom (1981) particularly emphasises the role of these costs, to argue that there may be substantial negotiation costs which encourage arbitrated settlements. Direct costs do not have a significant bearing on the FOA versus conventional arbitration debate, however, since there is no reason to expect these costs to differ across type of procedure.

More central to the FOA versus conventional arbitration debate is the role of potential costs of losing, which is determined by the uncertainty surrounding the award which would result if the parties go to arbitration. This is the key element in Stevens's argument. Farber and Katz (1979) assert that uncertainty is the crucial element for the deterrence of disputes. What FOA does is make the potential cost of the uncertain outcome greater because of the either-or mechanism.

Their argument has been criticised, however, on a number of levels. First, there are circumstances in which conventional arbitration can induce the same level of uncertainty and potential cost as FOA – if the variance of past arbitrator decisions is the equivalent of them acting as final-offer arbitrators (Ashenfelter *et al.* 1992). Restated, this suggests that if conventional arbitrators have produced awards in the past sufficiently far removed from the split-the-difference notion, and parties are aware of this, then conventional arbitration can produce the same potential costs of losing incentive as FOA.

Crawford (1979) has a more fundamental objection to the Farber-Katz model, by arguing that in fact uncertainty is minimal for most arbitration regimes because parties learn about arbitrator preferences over time. One of the key assumptions of his model is that parties are certain about what the arbitrator's decision will be before arbitration takes place.

Crawford's objection seems unrealistic unless parties have had considerable experience of arbitration and arbitrators are interchangeable. Certainly in the UK where there is relatively little experience with arbitration compared to North America, it would be difficult to support his objection. The Ashenfelter *et al.* (1992) caveat seems plausible – challenging the split-the-difference assumption of Stevens's theory. However, their argument also rests on some unrealistic assumptions – that conventional arbitrators behave as if they were final-offer arbitrators and that parties are fully informed about past arbitrator behaviour. Although there is some evidence from the UK of conventional arbitrators on occasion acting as final-offer arbitrators (Brown 1986), this concerns only a minority of awards. In the UK, it would be surprising to find that parties had full or even partial knowledge of past arbitrator behaviour because ACAS arbitration awards are unpublished and unavailable except with the consent of both parties. When an arbitrator is suggested to disputants by ACAS, the parties are not provided with a list of past decisions by that arbitrator, so it would be very difficult for the parties to acquire such information. Therefore on potential costs of disagreement, FOA does score better than conventional arbitration and consequently it should be associated with a lower probability of disagreement.

Countervailing factors

Another strand of the debate focuses on the issue of whether uncertainty and high potential costs of disagreement are sufficient to prevent disputes. Five possible explanations have been offered for why disputes might occur even if the costs of disagreement are high.

If the parties have unrealistic and optimistic expectations or differing beliefs regarding arbitrator behaviour then disputes could arise (Stevens 1966, Farber 1980, Farber and Bazerman 1989). This argument rests on the idea that even though in theory FOA produces more uncertainty, parties' estimation of the level of uncertainty may be flawed, so they have a 'false certainty'. Another way of describing this is to state that the parties may be over-optimistic about their chances of winning the award and therefore do not compromise beyond a certain point, preventing the establishment of a contract zone.

Second, Crawford (1979) has argued that a contract zone may not exist because negotiators commit themselves to irreversible positions in order to appear tough in bargaining. If the positions are close enough then a negotiated solution may be possible, but if they are irreconcilable then a dispute will occur. Even if a dispute is imminent, parties may not want to undermine the credibility of their toughness in bargaining because the exercise will be repeated in succeeding rounds. Bloom and Cavanagh (1987) support Crawford's argument and suggest that commitment to irreconcilable bargaining positions may occur because of the principal–agent relationship.

The latter explanation has been considered more fully by McCall (1990), who argues that especially on the union side, principal–agent problems may nullify the incentives FOA creates to avoid disputes. McCall provides a similar explanation, though with a slight twist, for the use of arbitration as Ashenfelter and Johnson (1969) proposed for the occurrence of strikes. Assuming that the union negotiator is more informed about the ability to pay of the employer than the members, and the members believe that their agent has been shirking in negotiations, then the members may audit the negotiator by forcing the latter to take a pay claim to arbitration.

Principal–agent problems could in theory also occur on the side of management, especially in multi-establishment firms. A plant manager may be under pressure to commit himself or herself to a low offer, which will probably entail the need for arbitration, in order to appear tough to higher level management and to prove that he or she is not selling themselves short in negotiations.

Overall it is important to be aware of the signals which bargaining positions create, both to a negotiator's 'opponent' and to their constituency. Signalling credibility or toughness may be more important than achieving a solution without an impasse even in the uncertain environment of FOA.

Farber and Katz (1979) argue that even when the potential costs of disagreement are prohibitive, if the parties are risk-neutral or risk-loving then disagreements will occur. This possible explanation for FOA failure has also been suggested by Minford and Peel (1983). Even if the parties do not believe that their offer has a greater chance of selection than the other side's, they may prefer the uncertainty of winning (losing) a potentially higher (lower) arbitration award to the relative certainty of a negotiated settlement.

Finally, DeNisi and Dworkin (1981), drawing on some comments by Grodin (1972) suggest that if the parties are relatively naive negotiators then they may not fully comprehend the uncertainty and potential costs of losing under FOA. Minford and Peel (1983) express a related argument, that under the first few years of an FOA procedure the parties may be more likely to experience the problem of over-optimistic expectations.

Stevens's original theory in favour of FOA has therefore been criticised on a number of levels – first on the central question of whether or not FOA does entail more uncertainty than conventional arbitration. However, a more significant line of argument has been that even if the potential costs of disagreement are high there are a range of reasons why FOA may still get invoked. The crucial issue then becomes whether or not the 'potential cost of losing' effect (if it exists) can and does outweigh the countervailing effects. Is FOA a strong enough incentive mechanism to counteract the other causes of disputes more effectively than conventional arbitration? Despite the fact that there is a substantial body of empirical work in the US on dispute procedure effectiveness, so far no study using non-experimental data has tackled this fundamental question.

US EVIDENCE

Although both FOA and conventional arbitration are fairly widespread in the US public sector, no US study has so far been able properly to compare the impact of these alternative procedures using evidence from the real world. This is partly because there are no examples of legislated procedures which provide for conventional arbitration for one section of public employees and FOA for another within the same state.[1] But there have also been very few interstate comparison studies, and none which attempt to control for other state level effects. On the whole the non-experimental studies of dispute deterrence and arbitration mechanisms are therefore disappointing. In general they only examine the experience of one jurisdiction, have little or no comparative element, cover too few bargaining rounds and make inadequate attempts to control for other possible influences on the impasse rate. Rather than attempt interstate comparisons researchers have increasingly turned to the social science laboratory, using students as negotiators, to test impasse procedure effectiveness. This is partly because even if rigorous interstate comparisons were possible, i.e. controlling for tangible factors such as structural and economic factors, it would be very difficult to control for factors such as risk aversion or over-optimistic bargainers, singled out as important in the theoretical literature.

There are considerable problems of external validity and therefore applicability over experimental results. It is by no means clear that we would expect students of industrial relations, dispute resolution or any other subject to be adequate substitutes for real world negotiators. Experimenters have attempted to replicate the threats and incentives of the real world through performance-related cash and grade point bonuses. However, these are probably insufficient to replicate the social and other non-pecuniary pressures which exist in the real world.

Therefore this new UK evidence is relatively novel. It provides the first opportunity correctly to test FOA against conventional arbitration, i.e. within the same jurisdiction, in similar workplaces and with the inclusion of control variables, using real world data.

One North American study does deserve a more detailed mention, even though it is not ostensibly concerned with measuring the chilling effect, because it is probably the only one which attempts to test the alternative theories of disagreement. Currie (1989), using data from teacher negotiations in British Columbia which are covered by a compulsory conventional arbitration statute, sets out to assess the relative merits of the following theories:

'Attitudes towards risk' Currie interprets the Farber and Katz (1979) theory as that over time parties will become less risk-averse about using a disputes procedure because the uncertainty surrounding it will decline with experience. This theory is therefore tested on the prediction that parties which have more experience with a procedure would be more likely to have an impasse.

'Differing beliefs' This hypothesis of why disputes occur despite the uncertainty of arbitration, is tested in two ways by Currie. She argues that beliefs are more likely to differ in times of economic uncertainty, and therefore includes the volatility of macroeconomic variables in the model. Further, she argues that parties may be less likely to make mistakes when such mistakes are costly. If the direct costs of arbitration are relatively fixed, the per capita cost of arbitration decreases with the size of the bargaining unit (assuming similar union density across units). So arbitration should be more common in larger units.

'Principal–agent models' Currie tests the McCall (1990) hypothesis concerning agents being forced to go to arbitration by the principal to check that the agent is not 'shirking' in negotiations. She argues that an agent is more likely to be 'audited' in this way if there has been a string of relatively low settlements (union side) or high settlements (management side) in the past. Therefore relative wages in the two previous bargaining periods are included in the Currie model to test the McCall theory.

The results of Currie's work are somewhat less interesting, because there is no comparison of conventional arbitration to FOA, than the variables she uses to test these alternative theories. For the record she finds that none of the theories provides a particularly satisfactory explanation for the incidence of arbitration; rather it appears that state dependence, or the narcotic effect, is the crucial factor. A bargaining unit that had used arbitration in one period was at least 10 per cent more likely to use arbitration in the following round than one that had not. Currie's study cannot tell us anything about whether or not FOA would have produced similar results but at the very least it provides an example of how to test for the various factors which might affect the impasse rate other than the dispute procedure itself.

THE UK SAMPLE

Collective agreements incorporating an FOA procedure have been signed in a number of British private-sector plants in the 1980s, forming some of the so-called 'new style deals'. Information on the extent of FOA agreements in the UK is therefore immersed in more general studies of new style, no-strike or single union deals signed in the 1980s. This helped to provide a ready-made comparison group for the FOA plants. The non-FOA but no-strike or single union establishments are a convenient and appropriate control group for their counterparts with FOA, since this lessens the potential difficulty of confusing an FOA effect with a general cooperative industrial relations effect. It must be acknowledged, however, that because both the FOA and control groups comprise part of the new style consensual industrial relations sector, this research may tell us little about the effect of putting FOA into old style non-cooperative bargaining structures.

Plants with new style deals were identified from surveys which provide the names and some details of these companies.[2] In sum the reports record twenty-seven different FOA agreements in a total of eighty-four new style deals. Trade unions involved in these deals were contacted both to clarify the status of existing agreements and to supply details of any new agreements or any agreements not specified in the available reports. After trawling all the available sources the final list consisted of 101 different workplaces having either FOA or non-FOA new style deals.

Data gathering was structured into two phases. First, a postal survey of the 101 workplaces was undertaken to obtain substantive information on plant characteristics, the impasse procedure and three outcome measures: use of impasse procedure; incidence of industrial action; and pay settlements, over the preceding five years. Second, long detailed interviews were undertaken at eight of the FOA plants where an impasse was reached in at least one year, to try to obtain more detailed empirical and attitudinal information about FOA effectiveness generally and in particular bargaining rounds in these workplaces.

The postal survey examining the last five annual bargaining rounds was sent in February 1991 to the 101 plants. Of the seventy-five plants which responded, three did not actually recognise a trade union for bargaining and therefore must have either derecognised a union or were incorrectly identified in the trawl of sources. These three responses were therefore rejected from the sample on the grounds that collective bargaining over pay did not actually take place.[3]

The basic characteristics of the seventy-two valid respondents are summarised in Table 7.1. The sample shows a preponderance of plants which employ more than 250 workers, have high union density, are either UK- or Japanese-owned, operate in the electronics or engineering industries and were established on their present site in the 1980s.

Forty-four of the plants have provision for arbitration, of which twenty-seven provide for FOA and seventeen have conventional arbitration arrangements. There are also ten plants which provide for conciliation and/or mediation but not arbitration. Furthermore there is variety in the arbitration arrangements because some provide for pre-arbitration stages of conciliation and/or mediation and others stand alone. The configurations of disputes procedures are illustrated in Figure 7.1.

Two data sets were constructed from the responses: one comprising the seventy-two plants which recognise a union for bargaining; and one in which each bargaining round is a separate case. The latter file of 297 bargaining rounds (some respondents did not supply a full five years' data) contains information on pay settlements, use of disputes procedure and industrial action.

EVIDENCE FROM THE POSTAL SURVEY

Introduction

The variety of dispute procedures within the sample provide both complexity and depth for an analysis of FOA and impasse rates. The taxonomy of procedures (represented in Figure 7.1) is repeated in a similar flow chart form for impasse rates in Figure 7.2. Figure 7.2 shows that of the 212 wage rounds where a dispute procedure was available,[4] twenty-seven went to impasse, an overall impasse rate of 12.7 per cent. This compares with national private-sector impasse rates of 12 per cent and 17 per cent, for 1980 and 1984 respectively, for pay and conditions disputes (Millward and Stevens 1986: Table 7.5).[5]

Figure 7.2 also illustrates the complexity within the impasse rate measure. Of the twenty-seven impasses, ten involved rounds where there was no provision for arbitration (box h), six where there was no

Table 7.1 Characteristics of the sample

Characteristics	*Number*	*%*	*Characteristics*	*Number*	*%*
1. Employment by size band			5. Location by region		
<25	1	1.4	North	12	16.7
25–99	8	11.1	Yorks and Humberside	5	6.9
100–249	26	36.1	East Anglia	2	2.8
250–499	13	18.1	South-East	11	15.3
500+	24	33.3	South-West	2	2.8
			Wales	28	38.9
2. Country of HQ			Scotland	1	1.4
UK	25	34.7	Northern Ireland	3	4.2
Other EEC	7	9.7			
Europe non-EEC	3	4.2	6. Industrial sector		
Japan	24	33.3	Metals	4	5.6
USA	12	16.7	Mechanical engineering	9	12.5
Other	1	1.4	Electronics	31	43.1
			Vehicles	4	5.6
3. Union recognised			Food and drink	6	8.3
AEU	18	25.0	Plastics	8	11.1
EETPU	36	50.0	Other	10	13.8
ISTC	1	1.4			
GMB	5	6.9	7. Plant vintage: date established		
TGWU	8	11.1	Pre-1980	24	33.3
Multi-union	4	5.6	1980–5	15	20.8
			1986	8	11.1
4. Union density			1987	6	8.3
0–24%	8	11.1	1988	9	12.5
25–49%	12	16.7	1989	7	9.7
50–74%	31	43.1	1990	3	4.2
75–100%	18	25.0			
Don't know	3	4.2	Total	72	100.0

Source: LSE 'New Style' Industrial Relations Survey

Notes

AEU Amalgamated Engineering Union
EETPU Electrical, Engineering, Telecommunication and Plumbing Union
ISTC Iron and Steel Trades Confederation
GMB General, Municipal, Boilermakers and Allied Trades Union
TGWU Transport and General Workers' Union

provision for mediation/conciliation (box g), and eleven where there was provision for both (box f). Of these eleven, only four involved the use of arbitration (box j) as the other seven were settled either during or after pre-arbitration meetings (box i).

Impasse rate models

This complexity provides five different impasse rate models on which to test the impact of FOA:

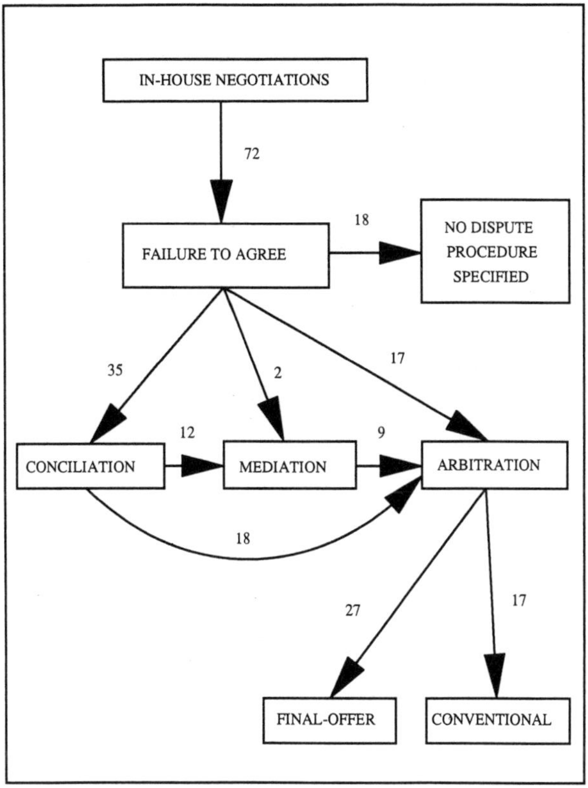

Figure 7.1 Dispute procedures in 72 new style agreements

1 Model A. Overall impasse rate: using all 212 rounds and not distinguishing the degree of impasse (Table 7.2, Columns I and II).
2 Model B. Overall impasse rate within arbitration available rounds: a sub-sample of 170 rounds (b), looking at all seventeen impasses in these rounds (f + g) (Table 7.2, Columns III and IV).
3 Model C. The use of arbitration within arbitration available rounds: the same sub-sample as (2), but looking at the ten impasses involving the use of arbitration (g + j) (Table 7.2, Columns V and VI).
4 Model D. Overall impasse rate in the mediation/conciliation available rounds: sub-sample of 144 rounds (c + d), looking at all twenty-one impasses (f + h) (Table 7.3, Columns I and II).
5 Model E. Use of mediation/conciliation only: sub-sample of 140 rounds, i.e. same as (4) but excluding the four rounds where

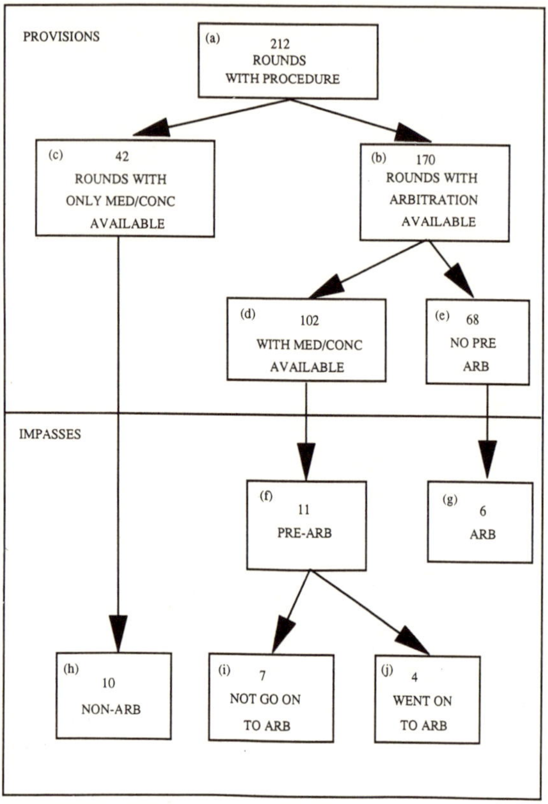

Figure 7.2 Impasses per bargaining round

arbitration is also used, and looking at the remaining seventeen impasses (h + i) (Table 7.3, columns III and IV).

The hypothesis tested for each model is that bargaining rounds where FOA is available should be associated with a lower impasse rate, controlling for other potential determinants.

The controls

Following the example of Currie's (1989) study (see the third section of this chapter) a number of variables were included in the models to test for other factors which various theories suggest are causes of disagreement in bargaining.

To recap, one theory holds that the parties must be risk-averse about using their dispute procedure. The risk aversion level of the parties was

Table 7.2 Logit regressions on impasse rates: Models A, B and C

Variables	*Model A* (*I*)	(*II*)	*Model B* (*III*)	(*IV*)	*Model C* (*V*)	(*VI*)
1. Dispute procedure						
FOA available	−0.211	0.125	−0.004	0.46	0.998	7.79
t	(0.396)	(0.197)	(0.005)	(0.493)	(0.814)	(0.223)
Conciliation available	−ve*	0	0	0	−ve**	0
Mediation available	+ve*	+ve**	0	+ve*	0	0
2. Risk aversion						
Plant established pre-1980	+ve**	0	0	0	0	0
UK-owned plant	0	+ve*	0	0	0	0
Multi-unionism	+ve**	+ve*	+ve**	+ve**	+ve**	+ve**
3. Differing beliefs						
Year dummies						
1987	–	0	–	0	–	0
1988	–	0	–	0	–	0
1989	–	0	–	0	–	0
1990	–	0	–	0	–	0
4. Principal–agent						
Part of larger enterprise	–	0	–	0	–	0
5. Costs of disputes						
Plant size dummies						
100–249 employees	–	−ve**	–	0	–	0
250–499 employees	–	0	–	0	–	0
500+ employees	–	0	–	0	–	0
Constant	−ve***	0	−ve***	0	−ve***	0
Impasse rate	0.127	0.127	0.100	0.100	0.059	0.059
Sample size	212	212	170	170	170	170
Chi-squared (d.f.)	27.0 (6)	35.9 (14)	16.5 (6)	26.8 (14)	19.8 (6)	30.9 (14)
% correct predictions	90.09	89.62	90.59	90.59	94.12	95.29

Notes
Significant at *** 1%, ** 5%, * 10%.
1 Dependent variable: Columns I–IV = any failure to agree, Yes (1) No (0). Columns V–VI = use of arbitration, Yes (1) No (0).
2 Samples: Column I–II = all 212 rounds with impasse procedure. Columns III–VI = all 170 rounds with arbitration available.
3 Defaults: Year dummies = 1986
Size dummies = 25–99 employees
4 '0' indicates that variable was included in model but was not significant.
5 '–' indicates that variable was not included in model.

Table 7.3 Logit regressions on impasse rates in rounds with mediation and/or conciliation available: Models D and E

Variables	*Model D*		*Model E*	
	(I)	*(II)*	*(III)*	*(IV)*
1. Dispute procedure				
FOA available	−1.750	−1.919	−1.768	−2.252
t	(1.875)*	(1.704)*	(1.917)*	(1.855)*
Mediation available	0	+ve*	0	0
2. Risk aversion				
Plant established pre-1980	+ve**	0	+ve**	0
UK-owned plant	+ve**	+ve***	+ve**	+ve***
Multi-unionism	+ve**	+ve**	0	0
3. Differing beliefs				
Year dummies				
1987	–	0	–	0
1988	–	0	–	0
1989	–	0	–	0
1990	–	0	–	0
4. Principal–agent				
Part of larger enterprise	–	0	–	0
5. Costs of disputes				
Plant size dummies				
100–249 employees	–	−ve**	–	−ve**
250–499 employees	–	0	–	0
500+ employees	–	0	–	0
Constant	−ve***	0	−ve***	0
Impasse rate	0.149	0.149	0.121	0.121
Sample size	144	144	140	140
Chi-squared (d.f.)	26.58 (5)	41.70 (13)	16.24 (5)	35.84 (13)
% correct predictions	89.58	89.58	91.43	90.71

Notes
Significant at *** 1%, ** 5%, * 10%.
1 Dependent variable: Columns I–II = any failure to agree, Yes (1) No (0). Columns III–IV = use of mediation and/or conciliation, Yes (1) No (0).
2 Sample: Columns I–II = all rounds with mediation and/or conciliation available. Columns III–IV = all rounds with mediation and/or conciliation which did not use.
3 Defaults: Year dummies = 1986
Size dummies = 25–99 employees
4 '0' indicates that variable was included in model but was not significant.
5 '–' indicates that variable was not included in model.

controlled for through two separate 'experience' measures; whether or not the plant was established before 1980 and; how long (in years) the parties had their current dispute procedure. The hypothesis concerning these variables suggests that as parties become more familiar with each other and their dispute procedure, their risk aversity concerning disputes will decline. Therefore, if this theory has some substance both variables should be positively associated with the impasse rate.

The risk-aversity theory was also tested through a multi-unionism variable with the hypothesis that groups may be more likely to take risks, because they can defer blame for losses to other members of the group. The multi-unionism variable was also included in the light of recent UK evidence showing an association between multi-unionism and strike incidence (Metcalf, Wadsworth and Ingram 1993, Machin, Stewart and Van Reenan 1992). Both studies report that if there is more than one union recognised in the plant, and they bargain separately, then the probability of a strike is significantly higher. Presumably this should also be the case with disputes not involving industrial action. Note, however, that in our sample it is not possible to distinguish whether or not multiple unions bargain separately or jointly.

A UK-owned variable was also included in the models to test the risk aversion theory on the basis that UK firms may have more experience with ACAS[6] intervention in disputes and therefore may be less risk averse about the use of ACAS.

Two alternative theories suggest, contrary to the risk aversion theory, that in fact experience will induce fewer rather than more disputes. The naive negotiators hypothesis of DeNisi and Dworkin (1981) suggests that more experienced bargainers will be less likely to reach impasse than the less experienced because they are more fully aware of the consequences of their actions. The over-optimistic or differing beliefs hypothesis might also predict a similar result to the naive negotiator hypothesis. As parties become more familiar with each other and the dispute procedure, they may be less likely to make mistakes concerning the expected outcome of a dispute. Therefore it is not clear in which direction the experience variables might be expected to function.

The differing beliefs hypothesis was further tested by Currie using the volatility of macroeconomic variables (the coefficient of variation of the Consumer Price Index in her study). For the UK sample because only the year of the settlement (not the month) is known, year dummies were included in one model as a crude approximation of macroeconomic factors.

Bargaining unit size was included to test the hypothesis that the costs per union member of impasses might be a factor. There is somewhat of a worry here, though, because impasses are not generally that expensive in the UK as ACAS services are free and lawyers' fees do not feature to anything like the same extent as in North America. So even if a size effect is apparent it is not clear that this would support the direct cost of impasse hypothesis.

The principal–agent hypothesis is tested using two variables, the previous real pay settlement (following the Currie example) and whether or not the workplace is part of a larger enterprise. These two variables should provide evidence of principal–agent problems on either union or management side.

If lower previous settlements are associated with an increase in the incidence of impasse in the following round this might suggest a principal–agent problem on the union side. On the other hand, if non-independent plants are associated with a higher incidence of disputes, this might suggest that plant management feels forced to go to impasse to indicate that they are not shirking in negotiations to enterprise-level management.

Results on final-offer arbitration theory

Different specifications of models A to E are shown in Tables 7.2 and 7.3. For each model the coefficient and *t* statistic of the FOA variable is shown at the top of every column. For all other variables the significance, or non-significance, and the sign on the coefficient are indicated. The tables provide two specifications of each model, the first including FOA and variables designed to control for risk aversion and the second including variables covering differing beliefs, principal–agent problems and the costs of disputes.[7]

The impact of FOA on 'the overall impasse rate' (Model A) is shown in Table 7.2, columns I and II. The sample consists of all 212 rounds with some form of dispute procedure and the dependent variable records any failure to agree (the use of any form of third party intervention) as an impasse. Therefore the model does not differentiate the degree of dispute. FOA has a negative coefficient in one of the equations and is positive in the other, but in neither is it significant. Therefore, using the crudest measure of impasse rate, FOA does not out-perform conventional procedures in deterring disputes, holding all else equal.

The sample is narrowed down in columns III–IV (Model B) to exclude all forty-two rounds where there is no provision for arbitration. Therefore if rounds are not covered by FOA, then conventional arbitration is the final stage in the procedure. The dependent variable remains any failure to agree. Again FOA rounds are not associated with a significantly different probability of impasse compared to conventional arbitration rounds.

In columns V and VI the sample used is the same as for columns III and IV, but the dependent variable is the use of arbitration – which is probably the most important test of FOA theory – rather than any failure to agree (Model C). FOA was specifically advocated to deter the use of and reliance on arbitration, which is where conventional arbitration was held to be at fault. The results do not support the hypothesis that FOA is more effective at deterring its own use than conventional arbitration. In fact in both equations the FOA coefficient is positive, although in neither is the coefficient significant.

When the sample is recast to concentrate on rounds with mediation and/or conciliation (i.e. boxes c and d in Figure 7.2), there seems to be some evidence in support of the deterrent power of FOA. Table 7.3 shows that the availability of FOA is associated with a significantly lower impasse rate in rounds where mediation and/or conciliation is provided (Models D and E). The only difference between the two sets of columns is that the sample in columns III and IV excludes the four rounds where arbitration as well as pre-arbitration procedure was used. So whereas columns I and II measure any failure to agree at an impasse, columns III and IV just count the use of non-arbitration procedures.

It is not surprising that FOA deters disputes more effectively compared to where no arbitration provision exists (in forty-two of the comparative rounds, i.e. comparing box d to box c). But it must be emphasised that it is FOA which is the key element here, because it performs better than other measures of arbitration.

Table 7.4 shows results when models D and E are re-estimated using all arbitration and conventional arbitration instead of FOA (the FOA estimations are reproduced for ease of comparison). Of the three arbitration variables, only FOA is significant in both models.

The results therefore support the idea that it is the interaction of FOA with mediation and/or conciliation that deters disputes. This does not mean that an FOA procedure not accompanied by pre-arbitration stages will be made more effective by the inclusion of pre-arbitration stages, but rather that an unaccompanied mediation/conciliation procedure will be made more effective through the addition of FOA than of conventional arbitration. This can be concluded because using only the 114 rounds where FOA was available (not reported in the Tables) did not indicate that either mediation and/or conciliation had any impact on the impasse rate. It seems safe to conclude therefore that in this sample the existence of FOA in a multi-stage procedure deters impasses more effectively than conventional arbitration.

Of the other dispute procedure variables, mediation was significantly associated with a higher incidence of disputes and conciliation with a

Table 7.4 Logit regressions on impasse rates in rounds with mediation and/or conciliation available using different arbitration variables

Variables	*All arbitration*		*Conventional arbitration*		*Final-offer arbitration*	
	(I)	*(II)*	*(III)*	*(IV)*	*(V)*	*(VI)*
1. Dispute procedure						
Arbitration coefficient	−1.249	−1.292	0.008	0.298	−1.844	−2.194
t	(1.543)	(1.504)	(0.009)	(0.323)	(1.710)*	(1.883)*
Mediation available	+ve**	+ve*	+ve**	+ve*	+ve**	0
2. Risk aversion						
Plant established pre-1980	0	0	0	0	0	0
UK-owned plant	+ve**	+ve**	+ve**	+ve**	+ve***	+ve***
Multi-unionism	+ve**	0	+ve*	0	0	0
3. Costs of disputes						
Plant size dummies						
100–249 employees	−ve**	−ve**	−ve**	−ve**	−ve**	−ve***
250–499 employees	0	0	0	0	0	0
500+ employees	0	0	0	0	0	0
Constant	0	0	−ve**	−ve**	0	0
Impasse rate	0.149	0.121	0.149	0.121	0.149	0.121
Sample size	144	140	144	140	144	140
Chi-squared	37.67	30.08	35.25	27.85	38.66	32.18
d.f.	8	8	8	8	8	8
% correct predictions	89.58	91.43	89.58	91.43	89.58	91.43

Notes
Significant at *** 1%, ** 5%, * 10%.
1 Dependent variables; Columns I, III and V – any failure to agree, Yes (1) No (0). Columns II, IV and VI = use of mediation and/or conciliation only, Yes (1) No (0).
2 Sample: Columns I, III and V = all rounds with mediation and/or conciliation available. Columns II, IV and VI = all rounds with mediation and/or conciliation available which did not use arbitration.
3 Defaults: Year dummies = 1986
Size dummies = 25–99 employees
4 '0' indicates that variable was included in model but was not significant.

lower incidence in some models, which is somewhat against expectations. One possible explanation may be that under mediation at least the parties know that a possible solution to the dispute will be suggested by the third party and may prefer this to the continuance of negotiations under a conciliator. So it may not be that conciliation deters disputes but rather that it is more likely to be available in plants with low dispute rates anyway. Perhaps mediation and arbitration feature in the procedures of plants which are potentially more likely to have disputes because the parties prefer procedures which have more bite.

Results of other theories

Acknowledging the caveat that small sample sizes make it unlikely that all influential variables will prove statistically significant, the results concerning the alternative theories of disputes deserve some comment. Most striking is the fact that the variables estimating levels of risk aversion perform better than all three other theories tested. Plants established before 1980, those UK-owned and those with more than one union are more likely to have reached impasse than their respective counterparts (though not significantly so in every model). The number of years with a dispute procedure is not significant (not reported in the Tables), however, which implies that the Farber and Katz (1979) explanation of why risk aversity may be lower in some bargaining units is not correct for this sample.

The plant vintage result suggests that it is the parties' experience of bargaining with each other, rather than under a particular disputes procedure, which reduces risk aversion. An alternative explanation of this particular result could be that it is related to the life cycle of the product; older plants may have more disputes because their profit rate is declining compared to newer plants.

The multi-union finding is the most consistently significant result in the various models and supports previous findings about the importance of multi-unionism in estimations of strike incidence.

Of the other theories tested only the per capita costs of disputes shows any indication of being significant; smaller plants are significantly less likely to reach impasse than larger ones. However, it is not clear that this variable is necessarily supporting that particular theory – it could also be interpreted as providing support for the risk aversion hypothesis, if larger groups are more likely to take risks because they can spread the consequences of losing over a larger constituency.

The naive negotiator, differing beliefs and principal–agent theories are not supported by the results, although again the variables employed may not provide the best means of estimating these effects. For instance, the year dummies, used as an approximation of the volatility of macroeconomic factors and the differing beliefs theory, are probably too imprecise to capture the essence of the theory. Furthermore, analysis of the principal–agent theory was hampered by the absence of data on the pay settlement at t-1 for a large proportion of rounds which cut the sample size considerably. Therefore the results concerning these models (not reported) must be treated with some caution. The impact of the plant's being part of a larger enterprise was tested separately from the previous pay settlement variable on the full sample, but was found to be non-significant.

Summary

The postal survey data therefore provide a fairly extensive body of information about the impact of FOA and other dispute procedures on impasse rates, as well as results concerning other theories of impasse. Overall it appears that even after controlling for other potential causes of impasses, FOA does not in general deter disputes more effectively than conventional arbitration – except in the case of multi-stage dispute procedures. However, the survey cannot answer the crucial question of why FOA has not deterred disputes particularly effectively in the UK. This lower than expected impasse deterrence effect of FOA was investigated in the interview stage of the research and is reported in the following section.

EVIDENCE FROM THE INTERVIEWS

The interview panel consisted of eight plants which satisfied the following criteria: a disputes procedure which included FOA; an impasse (though in two cases no actual arbitration) in at least one year; and a willingness to be approached for further information indicated on the survey reply. Apart from these factors the interview panel was fairly varied. There was some geographical concentration, with three plants in the South-East, only one in the North-East, two in North-West England, one in North Wales and one in East Anglia. Only two of the plants were greenfield sites when the deal was signed. Three of the plants were multi-union and the remainder had single-union recognition with the EETPU. All the plants were in manufacturing, with four in electronics or electrical engineering, one in the food industry, one paper producer and two vehicle manufacturers.

The interviews covered a range of issues including those relating to why FOA does not appear to have performed as well at deterring disputes as theory might predict.[8] The various alternative theories which aim to explain disagreement in bargaining despite uncertainty were also assessed.

One possible explanation for the relative 'failure' of FOA is that parties signing agreements incorporating FOA have not done so with the intention of deterring disputes, but instead just view FOA as a novel way of resolving disputes. In theory even if parties did sign FOA agreements in that frame of mind, there is no reason to suspect that this would necessarily undermine the deterrent power of FOA. However, in the early years of bargaining under FOA one might expect that this attitude towards FOA would encourage its use, perhaps for the novelty value.

In fact, when asked what attracted them to FOA, the majority of interviewees produced answers which are very much in line with FOA theory. Responses included the following:

'it [FOA] really makes you consider your position';
'it makes you try harder in negotiations';
'it makes people more reasonable and it means that you are more in control';
'the fact of potentially going to pendulum arbitration will often lead to the resolution of disputes'.

In a couple of cases the interviewees specifically contrasted the merits of FOA with conventional arbitration by saying that the latter allowed the parties to 'get off the hook' at the end of negotiations and that 'splitting the difference is too easy for the arbitrators'. This second point illustrates an important adjunct to the argument that because arbitrators usually do not split the difference, then conventional arbitration has been unfairly characterised in the arguments in favour of FOA (Kessler 1987, Lewis 1990). In fact the crucial issue is not what the arbitrators actually do but rather what the parties expect the arbitrator to do. If they anticipate that the arbitrator will split the difference then negotiations are likely to chill.

Some of the interviewees' justifications for the FOA procedure, however, do not have a similar academic rationale. These include the 'finality' of the process, its 'straightforwardness and formality', and its role as a 'final court of appeal' for a dispute. All three of these arguments could equally be used concerning a conventional arbitration procedure. In general, however, the parties' explanations of the anticipated merits of FOA at the time the deal was signed fit closely with the academic arguments. This suggests that the naive negotiator argument postulated by DeNisi and Dworkin (1981) may not be an apposite description of the real world.

For each dispute the interviewees were asked why the dispute was allowed by both sides to get to arbitration rather than settled in-house. Virtually all the responses fit into one or more of four alternative explanations of why disagreements in bargaining may occur despite the uncertainty of FOA.

Naive negotiators Naivety did figure in the explanation for some of the disputes but not naivety about the process of FOA itself, as hypothesised by DeNisi and Dworkin (1981). In one instance naivety about each other and simply how to bargain caused the failure to settle in-house (although the dispute was resolved in conciliation). In another naivety, or perhaps confusion, caused the dispute to be referred to a third party – the 1985 mediated settlement at Sanyo (see Kessler 1987 for details). However, the confusion in this case actually arose over a preliminary stage in the procedure rather than the final-offer mechanism itself. Other than these two disputes it seems quite clear that the parties knew what they were doing and what FOA entailed.

In one interview the personnel manager stated that there were some 'problems' at first with FOA because the employees considered adopting a policy of always going to arbitration on the basis that at the very least they would get management's final offer and might possibly get their claim. The employees recognised the incentive FOA creates to 'cheat' in the sense of allowing the other side to bargain with the intention of settling the dispute whilst yourself holding on for arbitration. Management persuaded the employees that this would be a myopic tactic in that the following year management would also have an incentive to chill, therefore undermining the whole procedure. The employees were in some sense naive regarding the notion of bargaining under FOA as a repeated rather than a one-off game. Having said this there was no evidence in this plant of FOA being invoked because of such naivety.

Differing beliefs To recap, this explanation rests on how realistic the parties' different expectations of winning the arbitration hearing are. If they have sufficiently divergent expectations then they will prefer to take the dispute to arbitration, because both sides are sure that they will win, than negotiate a settlement.

The interviews revealed two cases of FOA being invoked when management was sure it would win in arbitration and yet it lost. In one case our interviewees stated that they had three reasons for believing their case was cast-iron safe: their rates were competitive in the local labour market; and compared to their previous parent company's rates for the same jobs; and that the low employee turnover indicated satisfaction with the rate. They were 'very, very confident' that their final offer would be selected and that the arbitration award would reinforce management's prerogative on pay.

In the another dispute management similarly felt that it was bound to win the hearing such that even if the dispute had involved more employees, and therefore had been for higher stakes, they would still have allowed the dispute to go to arbitration because they were so sure of winning.

These two cases seem to provide strong support for the differing beliefs explanation of 'FOA failure'. However, there is something of a problem here because we do not know how 'reasonable' the arbitrator's choice of final offer was. In other words, there needs to be some evidence that the arbitrator's choice would have been made by the 'average' arbitrator. Bearing in mind this caveat, the fact that in other cases the interviewees did not suggest that they were completely sure of winning at arbitration provides some justification for the differing beliefs explanation for these two cases.

Risk-loving parties In some senses, whenever parties allow a dispute to get to arbitration under FOA, they are committing the act of a risk-loving party. They are preferring the risk of a possibly better arbitrated outcome to the certainty of a negotiated settlement. However, in only one case did management indicate that it thought this was the explanation for the dispute reaching arbitration.

The interviewee argued that management knew that it would win the award and that the union side probably knew that it would lose but that they [the union] 'took a long shot'. The union took the slim chance of possibly winning in arbitration rather than reduce their claim in negotiations, and achieve a possibly better outcome.

Principal–agent problems Negotiators may take a dispute as far as arbitration, knowing they will lose, because of pressure from their constituents – other managers in the case of management negotiators and members in the case of union negotiators. There were two cases of FOA use and one of near-use which could be explained in terms of principal–agent problems.

In one case the 'problem' was on management side. A new managing director was determined to be tough in negotiations because his predecessor had been and he wanted to impress senior management at the company's headquarters. Therefore he refused to compromise on a low offer to the employees even though he and the rest of the plant's management knew that they would lose at arbitration with such a low offer. The personnel manager at this plant stated that management did not even want to win at arbitration because they would have lost in the long run due to subsequent staff turnover problems. This is a clear case of a party behaving irrationally in the face of FOA because of pressure from constituents.

In two cases the principal–agent difficulty was on the union side, although in one the dispute was settled before arbitration. In one case, the union regional official gave up pursuing the workers' claim early on in negotiations, because it went directly against the official national union policy. However, because the members at the plant threatened the union's position by inviting a rival union to recruit outside the factory gates, a national official was compelled to take up the case once more.

Having done this, the official was virtually bound to take the dispute 'all the way' to arbitration in order to show the union's commitment to its members in the plant. So considerations of the likelihood of winning were of secondary importance to being seen to be pursuing the claim to the hilt.

In the second case, the union negotiator was very inexperienced and having promised too much to the members was not able to back down in negotiations for fear of 'losing face', according to the personnel manager. This dispute was actually settled in conciliation mainly through the role of the national union official who 'imposed some reality' on the union position.

The most apposite of the four explanations for 'FOA failure' in these cases are therefore differing beliefs and principal–agent problems. Negotiators did not seem to be naive about FOA itself, although they may have been naive about each other, nor did they seem to be particularly risk-loving gamblers.

These findings are therefore somewhat at odds with the explanations suggested by the data – that low risk aversion is the principal explanation for the incidence of impasses despite the presence of FOA. However, the results may be consistent because essentially the interviews measure very different factors from the survey. The interviews provide qualitative, attitudinal data which is subject to the interviewer's interpretation, and therefore it would be surprising to see these data mirroring the quantitative information from the postal survey. For instance, concerning principal–agent theory, the variables used to test it statistically (previous pay settlement and part of larger enterprise) may not have registered the three cases for which it seems to be relevant from the interviews. Even in the case where a plant manager pursued a dispute to arbitration because of perceived pressure from higher level management, an important factor, other than the multi-establishment enterprise, was the previous manager's reputation which could not have been captured using the survey data.

Furthermore, analysis of the survey concentrates on differences between plants which are associated with different levels of disputes, whereas the case studies highlight contingent factors which caused (or failed to prevent disputes) within a particular plant or bargaining round.

CONCLUSIONS

Although the UK evidence on final-offer arbitration is still quite sparse, the bargaining experience of plants with FOA and similar non-FOA plants over recent years provides the first environment in which to test properly the theory of FOA and dispute deterrence. So far the evidence provides only quite weak support for FOA theory. On the whole FOA does not significantly deter disputes compared to conventional arbitration except in multi-stage procedures. This result is consistent even after controlling for other potential causes of disputes, which does suggest that the incentives to avoid disputes under FOA are not more powerful than those under conventional arbitration.

What is unclear, however, is whether or not this means that both FOA and conventional arbitration have a chilling effect or whether both deter disputes. Without a yardstick of the level of disputes, including *ad hoc* referral of disputes to third parties and industrial action, in plants without a written disputes procedure including arbitration, it is not possible to determine what is the correct interpretation.

NOTES

Colleagues who have provided helpful comments on the work include Bill Hawes, John Kelly, Sid Kessler, David Metcalf, Andrew Oswald, Marcus Rubin, Jonathon Wadsworth and Andrew Wilkinson. The usual disclaimers apply.

1 Note that in some states, Minnesota and New Jersey (Freeman 1986), there are laws which allow the parties to choose, at the time of impasse, to use either conventional or final-offer arbitration. However, the parties do not know which procedure will be used prior to or during negotiations, therefore these statutes do not permit a proper test of the relative deterrent power of FOA.

2 Income Data Services (IDS) 1987, Trades Union Congress (TUC) 1988, Industrial Relations Review and Report (IRRR) 1989, and Labour Research (LR) 1989. These reports do not all concur on the details of the agreements. The number of agreements listed and discrepancies in the number of FOA deals is indicated in Milner (1993).

3 See Milner (1993) for further discussion of the sample. The non-respondents were not biased in any way which discredits the representativeness of the sample.

4 In other words, eighty-five bargaining rounds are in plants with no dispute procedure in their collective agreement. Note that this does not necessarily mean that they did not reach impasse. There may have been *ad hoc* referral of disputes to third parties. Data from a survey of ACAS arbitrations for the period 1988–9 reveal that about 20 per cent of cases occurred in plants with no provision for ACAS intervention in their collective agreement (Brown 1989).

5 However, the two measures are not quite compatible since the national figures include interventions which would not figure in our sample, for example by senior management. Also our sample covers just manufacturing plants whereas the WIRS figures include the private service sector.

6 The publicly funded but independent Advisory, Conciliation and Arbitration Service established in 1974, which is the principal body for dispute resolution in industrial relations in the UK.

7 Four previous versions of each model are not reported in Tables 7.2 and 7.3, for reasons of space. In particular the models including the other 'experience' variable (number of years with procedure) and the previous real wage variable are excluded. Both variables were non-significant. Note, however,

that the lagged real wage was not observed for a large number of bargaining rounds; therefore sample size was restricted for model specifications including this variable.

8 See Milner (1993: ch. 6) for a full discussion of the interviews.

REFERENCES

Anderson, J.C. and Kochan, T.A. (1977) 'Impasse procedures in the Canadian federal service: Effects on the bargaining process', *Industrial and Labor Relations Review*, 30, (3): 283–301.

Ashenfelter, O. and Johnson, G. (1969) 'Bargaining theory, trade unions and industrial strike activity', *American Economic Review*, 59, (1): 35–49.

Ashenfelter, O. and Layard, R. (eds) (1986) *Handbook of Labor Economics*, North-Holland: Elsevier.

Ashenfelter O., Currie J., Farber, H.S. and Speigel, M. (1992) 'An experimental comparison of dispute rates in alternative arbitration systems', Working Paper No. 237, Industrial Relations Section, Princeton University, forthcoming in *Econometrica*.

Bassett, P. (1986) *Strike Free: New Industrial Relations in Britain*, London: Macmillan.

Bloom, D.E. (1981) 'Is arbitration really compatible with bargaining?', *Industrial Relations*, 20, (3): 233–44.

Bloom, D.E. and Cavanagh, C.L. (1987) 'Negotiator behaviour under arbitration', *American Economic Review*, Papers and Proceedings, 77, (2): 353–8.

Brown, A. (1986) 'Survey of arbitration and mediation procedures', ACAS, mimeo, September.

—— (1989) 'Survey of ACAS arbitration 1988–89: Preliminary results', ACAS, mimeo, October.

Crawford, V.P. (1979) 'On compulsory-arbitration schemes', *Journal of Political Economy*, 87, (1): 131–59.

Currie, J. (1989) 'Who uses interest arbitration? The case of British Columbia's teachers, 1947–1981', *Industrial and Labor Relations Review*, 42, (3): 363–79.

DeNisi, A.S. and Dworkin, J.B. (1981) 'Final-offer arbitration and the naive negotiator', *Industrial and Labor Relations Review*, 35, (1): 78–87.

Farber, H.S. (1980) 'An analysis of final-offer arbitration', *Journal of Conflict Resolution*, 24, (4): 683–705.

Farber, H.S. and Bazerman, M.H. (1989) 'Divergent expectations as a cause of disagreement in bargaining: Evidence from a comparison of arbitration schemes', *Quarterly Journal of Economics*, 106, (1): 99–120.

Farber, H.S. and Katz, H.C. (1979) 'Interest arbitration, outcomes and the incentive to bargain', *Industrial and Labor Relations Review*, 33, (1): 55–63.

Freeman, R. (1986) 'Unionism comes to the public sector', *Journal of Economic Literature*, 24: 41–86.

Grodin, J.R. (1972) 'Either-or arbitration for public employee disputes', *Industrial Relations*, 11, (2): 260–6.

Income Data Services (IDS) (1987) 'Single union deals and disputes procedures', *IDS Report*, No. 509.

Industrial Relations Review and Report (IRRR) (1989) 'Single union deals', 442, 27 June.

Kearney, R.C. (1984) *Labor Relations in the Public Sector*, New York: Dekker.
Kennan, J. (1986) 'The economics of strikes', in O. Ashenfelter and R. Layard (eds) *Handbook of Labor Economics*, North-Holland: Elsevier.
Kessler, S. (1987) 'The swings and roundabouts of pendulum arbitration', *Personnel Management*, December: 38–42.
Labour Research Department (1989) 'Are single-union deals on their way out?', *Labour Research*, November: 9–11.
Lester, R.A. (1984) *Labor Arbitration in State and Local Government*, Princeton: Princeton University.
Lewis, R. (1990) 'Strike-free deals and pendulum arbitration', *British Journal of Industrial Relations*, 28, (1): 32–56.
McCall, B.P. (1990) 'Interest arbitration and the incentive to bargain: A principal–agent approach', *Journal of Conflict Resolution*, 34, (1): 151–67.
Machin, S., Stewart, M. and Van Reenen, J. (1992) 'The economic effects of multiple unionism: evidence from the 1984 Workplace Industrial Relations Survey', CEP Discussion Paper No. 66.
Metcalf, D., Wadsworth, J. and Ingram, P. (1993) 'Multi-unionism, size of bargaining group, and strike incidence: evidence from British manufacturing in the 1980s', *Industrial Relations Journal*, 24, (1): 3–13.
Millward, N. and Stevens, M. (1986) *British Workplace Industrial Relations 1980–1984: The DE/ESRC/PSI/ACAS Surveys*, Aldershot: Gower.
Milner, S. (1993) 'Final-offer arbitration in the UK: Incidence, processes and outcomes', London: Department of Employment, Research Paper No. 7, February.
Minford, P. and Peel, D. (1983) 'Compulsory arbitration procedures and incomes policy', *Three Banks Review*, 137: 3–16.
Rico, L. (1987) 'The new industrial relations: British electricians' new-style deals', *Industrial and Labor Relations Review*, 41, (1): 63–78.
Stevens, C.M. (1966) 'Is compulsory arbitration compatible with bargaining?', *Industrial Relations*, 5: 38–52.
Trades Union Congress (TUC) (1988) *Meeting the Challenge; First Report of the Special Review Body*, London: TUC.

8 North American research on interest arbitration

Craig Olson

Collective bargaining in the US public sector is a recent phenomenon. In 1959 the state of Wisconsin passed the nation's first public-sector bargaining law, giving state public-sector workers the right to join unions (Saltzman 1986). Since then, a majority of states have passed collective bargaining enabling laws for at least some state and local government employees. In the 1960s and early 1970s unionization and collective bargaining contract coverage expanded rapidly in the public sector, a trend that contrasts sharply with the decline of unionization in the US private sector.[1]

While a single national law (e.g. the Wagner Act, as amended) provides bargaining rights to most private-sector workers, laws governing state and local government workers remain the responsibility of individual states and these policies differ significantly across states. Despite this diversity, most state legislatures have chosen to use the Wagner Act as a template for developing state policies and this framework has produced certain similarities across states. Union representation rights are typically secured through a state-supervised election that is preceded by the determination of the 'appropriate bargaining unit'. Comprehensive bargaining laws usually prohibit certain employer and union activities (e.g. unfair labour practices) and require that the parties bargain in good faith in an attempt to reach an agreement. The outcome of these negotiations is a written, fixed-term agreement lasting from one to three years and there is usually a neutral state agency established to administer and interpret the law.[2]

The most important area where states differ among themselves and the Wagner Act is with respect to strike policies and the resolution of disputes that arise when the parties negotiate new contract terms. While the Wagner Act provides private-sector workers with the 'right' to strike, with a few notable exceptions (e.g. Hawaii, Pennsylvania) strikes by public-sector employees are illegal and public-sector strikers may be subject to substantial penalties. The major example of a state law with substantial *and* enforced strike policies is the Taylor law in New York; striking workers are penalised one day's pay (in addition to the pay lost for being on strike) for each day of the strike. This penalty is collected and kept by the struck government and has been consistently enforced (Olson 1986). A substantial number of jurisdictions have paired the strike prohibition with strike alternatives designed to help the parties achieve a timely and equitable settlement. These policies include the use of an outside neutral as a mediator, factfinder or arbitrator. In 1984, seventeen states had compulsory arbitration for at least one employee group and thirteen states had no third party procedure or simply prohibited public-sector strikes by state and local government employees (Valletta and Freeman 1988).[3]

Unlike arbitration, mediation and factfinding do not provide the neutral with the authority to settle the dispute with a binding decision. Because mediators and factfinders lack the authority to issue a binding award or impose other costs on the parties, these procedures are widely viewed as poor substitutes for the right to strike because they do not provide the parties with sufficient incentives to reach an agreement. On the other hand, it is argued that uncertainty about the binding outcome from arbitration may impose sufficient pressure on the parties to encourage negotiated settlements. In 1984, seventeen states provided compulsory interest arbitration for protective service employees (e.g. police and firefighters) and six states extended this procedure to other 'less essential' workers (e.g. teachers).

The widespread use of arbitration has produced a substantial body of research evaluating the operation and effect of interest arbitration. In this chapter I would like to provide a summary and evaluation of this research. I have divided the chapter into five sections. In the next section I describe the different forms of arbitration and the key research questions. In the subsequent three sections I review the theoretical and empirical research that address three important research topics. The last section discusses future research needs.

AN OVERVIEW OF ARBITRATION

The first major distinction between arbitration systems in the US is whether the arbitrated dispute is over the interpretation of language in the current contract or a dispute about the terms of a renegotiated agreement. The former type of arbitration is referred to as rights or grievance arbitration while the latter category is referred to as interest arbitration. The decision to use either form of arbitration if an impasse is reached may be voluntarily agreed to by *both* parties on either an *ad hoc* basis or through prior written agreement, or the state may compel the parties to use arbitration when *either* side requests arbitration. The former type of arbitration is referred to as voluntary while the latter is compulsory arbitration. In the private sector under the Wagner Act, when labour and management agree to use either grievance or interest arbitration the decision is voluntarily agreed to by the two sides and cannot be imposed on the parties by the state. Voluntary grievance arbitration is almost universal among private-sector union workers while voluntary interest arbitration is rarely used. In the public sector most states permit the parties to agree voluntarily to use either grievance or interest arbitration and, as noted above, seventeen states have passed compulsory interest arbitration laws for some public employees.[4] Interest arbitration is further classified into the type of constraints placed on the decision-making process of the arbitrator. Here the major distinction is between conventional and final-offer arbitration. Under conventional arbitration the neutral can make any award to settle the dispute and under final-offer arbitration each side submits a final offer to the arbitrator and the arbitrator is then constrained to select one of the offers as his or her award.

US and Canadian research on interest arbitration completed over the last fifteen years has focused on three major issues:

1 How is the behaviour of negotiators affected by different forms of arbitration (e.g. conventional versus final-offer)?
2 How do arbitrators make decisions?
3 What is the effect of arbitration on wages and benefits?

A long-standing criticism of interest arbitration is that the availability of arbitration may 'chill' negotiations and discourage the parties from reaching a bilateral settlement. To avoid this effect Stevens (1966) proposed final-offer arbitration and argued this procedure would encourage bilateral agreements because each side would be willing to concede more than might otherwise be the case because of the risk that the other side's offer might be chosen by the arbitrator. Significant theoretical and empirical work has been devoted to evaluating this prediction.

How arbitrators make decisions is closely related to the concern over the chilling effect of arbitration. Conventional arbitration may chill negotiations because arbitrators may 'split the difference' and make a compromise award equal to the average of the two parties' positions. Such a decision model may reduce the incentives the parties have to make concession because more extreme positions before the arbitrator will result in more favourable arbitration outcomes. Farber (1981) notes this model cannot be entirely correct because it implies that the positions of the parties should be dramatically different (plus/minus infinity in a formal model). On the other hand, if *some* weight is given to the positions of the parties then conventional arbitration may discourage negotiations relative to final-offer arbitration. This issue has produced several notable papers on arbitrator decision-making and studies of several closely related issues, including the process the parties use to select arbitrators.

The last topic to receive considerable attention is the impact of arbitration on wages. This research has been motivated by two concerns. First, since interest arbitration has been quite successful in reducing the incidence of public-sector strikes, research has focused on the cost of this outcome to taxpayers as measured by the wages and benefits paid to workers under contracts written under the threat of compulsory interest arbitration. To evaluate this question researchers have relied on either comparisons within or across states where there has also been variation in compulsory arbitration coverage. There has also been some research looking at settlements *within* jurisdictions that provide arbitration by comparing arbitration awards with negotiated settlements. This comparison may provide important insight into how the bargaining behaviour of the parties is affected by arbitration.

THE IMPACT OF ARBITRATION ON BARGAINING BEHAVIOUR

Early studies investigating the relative benefits of final offer and conventional arbitration compared dispute rates in different jurisdictions under conventional and final-offer arbitration (e.g. Stern *et al.* 1975). Unfortunately, the relative efficacy of the procedures has not been convincingly established because of the difficulty of attributing differences between states in dispute rates to differences in the arbitration procedures. Inferences are also difficult to make because of slight variations in dispute settlement procedures, and because similar procedures may be used at different points in time. Thus, other bargaining law, economic and political differences that might plausibly affect disputes also differ across jurisdictions (Olson 1988).[5] As a result, in my opinion existing research using field data has not been very useful in evaluating the relative efficacy of different arbitration systems.

As an alternative to investigating arbitration using field data, researchers have turned to laboratory studies to compare different arbitration systems. One recent and noteworthy study was done by Ashenfelter *et al.* (1992). This study, which was conducted in an experimental lab using student subjects, compared conventional arbitration under three conditions and contrasted conventional and final-offer arbitration. While there have been other lab studies on different arbitration systems, none of the previous studies have explicitly controlled for the uncertainty the parties face when they negotiated under the threat of arbitration. Theoretically (Farber and Katz 1979, Farber 1980), we know that the concession each side is willing to make to in order to avoid arbitration is a function of the risk aversion of the parties and the parties' uncertainty about the arbitration outcome. These concessions define the size and position of the contract zone; if the parties are risk-neutral or if there is no uncertainty about the arbitration award the contract zone shrinks to zero. Since the probability of a negotiated settlement may be a function of the size of the contract zone, it is important to control for the uncertainty faced by negotiators when evaluating conventional and final-offer arbitration.

In the Ashenfelter *et al.* study subjects were given the task of negotiating over the division of a 400 point pie and the payment each subject received was a function of the negotiated split. Each bargaining pair negotiated over the division of the pie twenty times. In the first ten rounds the parties received nothing if an agreement was not reached after negotiating 5.5 minutes. Bargaining pairs were randomly assigned to use either conventional arbitration or final-offer arbitration to settle the dispute if no agreement was reached in 5.5 minutes in rounds 11–20.[6] Subjects in the final-offer treatment were shown a set of offers and a final-offer selection where the award was based on the offers and a random draw from an $N(350,50^2)$ distribution. Subjects assigned to the conventional arbitration treatment were also randomly assigned to one of three levels of underlying arbitrator uncertainty In the conventional arbitration cells the decision of the arbitrator and the award was equal to a random draw from a normal distribution with a mean of 350 and an S.D. of either 12.5, 25 or 50. The parties were shown a sample of draws from their distribution to help the parties form their expectations about arbitration outcome. The underlying level of arbitrator uncertainty matched the high-variance conventional arbitration treatment subjects assigned to the FOA treatment.

This design permitted the authors to investigate conventional arbitration dispute rates under different levels of arbitrator uncertainty and differences between conventional and final-offer arbitration controlling for the underlying uncertainty in the arbitration process.

Briefly, Ashenfelter *et al.* found no significant difference in the dispute rates between the final offer and the high-variance conventional arbitration treatments. In the final-offer arbitration treatment the offers of the subjects were not significantly different from the offers predicted for risk-neutral negotiators. They also found settlement rates in the three conventional arbitration cells was lowest in the low-variance treatment. This suggests the parties were risk-averse and uncertainty about the arbitration outcome did have a modest effect on settlements.

The results from this experiment suggest that the relative efficacy of final-offer and conventional arbitration as measured by dispute rates remains an open question. Of course, one may be sceptical of these results because they may not generalise to the field because the subjects (students) and lab environment differ in important respects from the 'real world'. While this may be a valid criticism, it is doubtful whether more definitive results can be generated from the field unless researchers can combine the realism of actual negotiations with the control possible in an experiment.

Closely related to the impact of different forms of arbitration on average arbitration usage rates is whether or not the use of arbitration changes the probability that the parties will use arbitration in later bargaining rounds. 'Addiction' to arbitration has been identified as a potential drawback of arbitration because the parties should be better able to negotiate. Borrowing from the labour economics literature, this 'addiction' effect has also been referred to as positive state dependence because the use of arbitration increases the probability that the parties will be observed in the arbitration 'state' in a later bargaining round. The possibility of state dependence in the use of arbitration means that even if average dispute rates were similar under conventional and final-offer arbitration, one system might be viewed as less desirable if it led to usage concentrated in a small number of jurisdictions.

Identifying whether or not there is state dependence in the use of arbitration has been an elusive task. The basic problem is that repeated use of arbitration among some bargaining pairs may reflect either state dependence or the fact that some bargaining pairs, for reasons unobserved by the researcher, are simply more prone to have disputes. The latter factor is referred to as unobserved heterogeneity in dispute-proneness and was introduced into the arbitration literature by Butler and Ehrenberg (1981). While they propose a particular statistical strategy for distinguishing between state dependence and unobserved heterogeneity, different assumptions about the structure of the unobserved heterogeneity require different statistical techniques and may yield different conclusions (Babcock 1988). Currie and Farber (1992) have recently revisited this issue using the experimental data from the Ashenfelter *et al.* experiment and arbitration data from teacher disputes in British Columbia. They find no evidence of addiction or state dependence in the experimental data but do find significant state dependence in the British Columbia data and modest evidence favouring positive state dependence. This result is consistent with Currie's (1989) earlier analysis of the British Columbia data.

ARBITRATOR DECISION MAKING

While it has been very difficult to determine empirically if the use of arbitration varies significantly between conventional and final-offer arbitration, progress has been made testing one of the key assumptions that has led to the different predicted effects of the two procedures. As noted above, conventional arbitration is criticised because it allows arbitrators to 'split the difference' between the parties' positions and this decision rule discourages compromise settlements. Several studies have focused on this issue and the more general issue of how arbitrators make decisions.

The basic model used in these studies begins with the idea that the fair wage belief of the arbitrator is a weighted average of a set of observable facts that describe the dispute and a component that is unobserved to both the parties and the researcher. This fair wage belief, W_{ARB}, is equal to $Z + \varepsilon$ where Z summarises the observed facts and $\varepsilon \sim N(0,\sigma_3^2)$ is unobserved. The variance of ε reflects the parties' uncertainty about the arbitrator's fair wage belief and this uncertainty provides risk averse parties with an incentive to negotiate a settlement.

In final-offer arbitration the probability that the employer's final offer is chosen is the probability that W_e is closer than W_u to W_{ARB}. If the final offers of the parties are equal to W_u and W_e where $W_u > W_e$ and W_{ARB} is $N(Z,\sigma_\varepsilon^2)$, this probability is

$$Pr(\text{employer's offer is chosen}) = \Phi(1/\sigma_\varepsilon((W_u + W_e)/2 - Z)) \quad (1)$$

where $\Phi(.)$ is the CDF for a standard normal variable.

In conventional arbitration the arbitrator can impose any award to settle the dispute. Two 'extreme' models of arbitrator decision-making under conventional arbitration have been proposed that differ in the relative weight arbitrators place on the exogenous facts of the dispute (e.g. $Z+\varepsilon$) and the positions of the parties (e.g. W_u and W_e) when reaching a decision. In one model the arbitration award is simply equal to $Z+\varepsilon$ and the arbitrator is not influenced by the positions of the parties at the arbitration hearing. In the other model an arbitrator places no weight on the exogenous facts of the case and simply 'splits the difference' between the positions of the parties and makes an award equal to $(W_u + W_e)/2$. Neither of these models is likely to be correct. The latter model implies the parties should take infinitely extreme positions at the arbitration hearing. This model cannot be correct because we do not observe these extreme positions. Similarly, the model where the arbitrator ignores the positions of the parties is inconsistent with the effort and resources the parties spent developing a position and trying to convince the arbitrator of the appropriateness of their position.

A compromise model is supported the two empirical studies (Bazerman and Farber 1986, Bloom 1986). These studies basically estimate a model where the fair wage belief is defined as a weighted average of $Z+\varepsilon$ and $(W_u + W_e)$ or

$$W_{ARB} = \alpha(Z+\varepsilon) + (1-\alpha)(W_A + W_B)/2 \qquad (2)$$

where α is the weight placed on the exogenous facts of the case and $(1-\alpha)$ is the weight placed on the average offers of the parties. This specification nests the two extreme versions of the model; if $\alpha = 1$ then the offers are irrelevant to the arbitrator and if $\alpha = 0$ then arbitrators simply award the mean of the final offers, regardless of the facts. Bazerman and Farber and Bloom use similar research designs to identify α. Each study uses a 'policy capturing' methodology where actual arbitrators were asked to make an award in one or more hypothetical disputes. In the Bazerman and Farber study the subjects reviewed twenty-five disputes and made both a conventional and final offer award in each of the disputes. While not without problems (Olson 1988), this design provides some important statistical benefits. Since each arbitrator made a decision under both regimes for a set of *identical* disputes, the analysis could take advantage of both the within and between arbitrator variability in awards across the two forms of arbitration. In the empirical analysis Bazerman and Farber specify to be a function of the squared difference between the final offers because, they argue, arbitrators are likely to pay more attention to the positions of the parties when the offers are close together than when one (or both) side has made an 'extreme' final offer. They find that most of the weight is placed on the facts of the case. For an average case they estimate α to be 0.9.

Bloom is critical of the Farber and Bazerman study because the final offers were constructed to be orthogonal to the observed facts of the case. Since this does not fit reality, when making conventional awards the subjects may have discounted the offers more than would be the case in actual disputes. Bloom conducted a simpler experiment based study where four scenarios were constructed and *different* sets of final offers were constructed within and across the four cases. Arbitrators were then sent one of the four scenarios and asked to make a conventional award in the hypothetical dispute. Bloom obtained results significantly different from the Bazerman and Farber results; he found the offers had a far greater impact on decisions than the facts of the case. While there are several possible explanations for the discrepancies between the two studies (Bloom 1986, Olson 1988) that could be evaluated, this topic has not been pursued.

The policy-capturing methodology is a powerful method for modelling arbitrator decision-making because of the control the researcher has over the information available to the arbitrator. Because the researcher defines the facts included in each scenario, there is no need to be concerned about possible omitted variables that may bias the parameter estimates. On the other hand, the hypothetical disputes cannot replicate the information complexities and pressures an arbitrator faces in an actual dispute. In actual cases the 'facts' may be disputed (e.g. how should comparability be defined and measured) and the arbitrator knows his decision may have an impact on subsequent decisions or the probability of being selected in other disputes.

A recently published study by Olson *et al.* (1992) has investigated this issue using data from a policy-capturing experiment (Dell'Omo 1989) and the field data used in Olson and Jarley (1991). In this study the Wisconsin arbitrators used by Dell'Omo in his policy-capturing experiment were the same individuals that decided the vast majority of disputes involving local school boards and teachers in the state of Wisconsin. By merging these two data sets, we were able to compare how the *same* group of arbitrators made decisions in a sample of 'real' teacher disputes and a sample of hypothetical police wage disputes. When the sample of field cases was confined to disputes involving wages, except for an intercept term, there was no significant difference in the decision model used in the experiment and the decisions in actual cases. This result provides strong, direct evidence of the external validity of policy-capturing experiments where the subjects are practising arbitrators.

Two major studies have investigated arbitrator decision-making using field data. The first study, by Ashenfelter and Bloom, used data from the first three years under the New Jersey interest arbitration statute. This law requires that the parties use final-offer arbitration unless both sides agree to substitute conventional arbitration. While both procedures have been used by the parties, Ashenfelter and Bloom were unable to collect data on the arbitration positions of the parties that decided to use conventional arbitration. This made an evaluation of the relative importance of offers versus facts impossible. They do, however, estimate the fair wage belief function separately for each of the three years. Unfortunately, firm conclusions about the beliefs of arbitrators are difficult to make because their estimates varied dramatically from year to year.

The Olson and Jarley study expands on Ashenfelter and Bloom in two important respects. First, wage comparability was not included in the Ashenfelter and Bloom model of arbitrator fair wage beliefs. Olson and Jarley include and measure wage comparability as the negotiated wage increase received by other teachers in the set of school districts the school competes against in high school sports. These athletic conference groupings are exogenous to the bargaining process and define a set of districts that are approximately the same size and located in the same geographic region of the state. Except for the largest districts in the state, the written awards of numerous arbitrators repeatedly use the athletic conference to define wage comparability (Halm 1985). This variable was found to be the most important determinant of the fair wage beliefs of arbitrators – a result consistent with all of the policy-capturing experiments that have manipulated this variable (Farber and Bazerman 1986, Bloom 1986, Dell'Omo 1989) and also an older institutional literature (Bernstein 1954, Miller 1967).

The second key result reported in Olson and Jarley and elaborated on by Olson (1992) is the complexity of arbitrator decision-making where the package of each party includes more than one issue. The model described by equations (1) and (2) assumes that the only disputed issue is the wage rate or, if there are multiple issues, these issues can all be summarised along a single monetary dimension. While this model is clearly appropriate in the previous policy-capturing experiments because the designs manipulated only wages, in jurisdictions where the final offers may include positions on wages *plus* fringe benefits (e.g. health insurance) and contract language issues (e.g. seniority, grievance procedures, etc.), the single issue model is inappropriate unless arbitrators ignore all of the non-wage issues included in the package.

The importance of this problem is illustrated in Olson and Jarley, where Wisconsin arbitrators must pick either the entire employer or union package of offers and a majority of the wage disputes also included at least one other issue. When the single wage model is estimated using the pooled sample of single issue and multi-issue wage cases, the estimate of arbitrator uncertainty is very inconsistent with other research and the observed difference between the offers of the parties. On the other hand, a very plausible set of estimates are obtained if the single issue model is estimated on the subsample of wage-only disputes. Furthermore, the appropriateness of the single issue model is clearly rejected in multi-issue disputes (Olson 1992). Since arbitration in most jurisdictions is not confined to just wages or even 'economic' issues, future research needs to investigate arbitrator decision-making in more complex, multi-issue disputes.

An issue closely related to the decision process of arbitrators is the selection of an arbitrator by the parties. The selection process is linked to the decision models of arbitrators because the parties undoubtedly make predictions about the decisions of arbitrators when they select from the arbitrator pool. The process used to select an arbitrator is usually spelled out in the state statute that mandates the use of arbitration and in most jurisdictions the neutral state agency responsible for administrating the law supplies the parties with a short list of possible arbitrators. The key published study of this process by Bloom and Cavanagh (1986) uses data from New Jersey, where the list includes seven names and each side vetoes two names and ranks the remaining five names. The most important result from their study is the very high degree of agreement between the parties over who would make the better arbitrator. This is illustrated by the vetoes each side exercised. Of the 225 vetoes cast by both sides, the parties veto the *same* name 49 per cent of the time ($n=110$)!

The procedure used to select an arbitrator in New Jersey provides substantial information about the parties' preferences but the veto/rank procedure used in New Jersey is unusual. Under the more typical procedure the parties receive a list of five names and then alternate striking a name from the list until one name remains. Administrative records from this procedure provide far less information about the preferences of the parties than the information available in New Jersey. Typically the only information available is the identity of the panel and the selected arbitrator. Information is not available on which side struck first from the list or the order in which arbitrators were eliminated. This makes it very difficult to make inferences about the preferences of the parties.

A recently completed but unpublished study (Babcock and Olson 1992) carefully evaluates what can be inferred from the alternate name striking system and then investigates the selection of arbitrators in 272 panels sent to teachers and local school boards in Wisconsin over the period 1977–86. This study confirms Bloom and Cavanagh's major conclusion that the preferences of the parties are positively correlated. A model which assumes that the parties' preferences are perfectly negatively correlated is only able successfully to predict 15 per cent of the decisions while a model assuming perfectly positively correlated preferences predicts 37 per cent of the selections. The finding that the parties' preferences for arbitrators are positively correlated seems inconsistent with a selection procedure that is designed to produce a compromise arbitrator (e.g. the middle arbitrator for each side) when the parties have opposite preferences. This apparent inconsistency is explained by the selection process that determines which individuals are on the panel from which each list is drawn. Most individuals on the panel of a neutral agency are individuals with established arbitration credentials or, in the case of new arbitrators, there is some *prima-facie* evidence establishing their neutrality and qualifications. As a result, each list sent to disputing parties is dominated by 'surviving' arbitrators that have at least occasionally been selected; potential arbitrators always vetoed by one or both parties can never become arbitrators! This suggests the selection procedures are designed to protect the parties from the possibility that a biased individual is put on the panel by the agency and to help ensure the neutrality of existing panels members by providing a mechanism that prevents the appointment of individuals that develop a bias towards one of the parties.

THE IMPACT OF ARBITRATION ON WAGES

One type of research that has investigated the relationship between arbitration and wages has focused on how coverage under a compulsory arbitration law changes wages relative to what would occur under some other dispute resolution procedure. Studies of this type typically assume the difference in wages between parties that use and do not use arbitration is likely to be negligible because negotiated settlements tend to be centred on the fair wage beliefs of arbitrators for reasons discussed by Farber and Katz (1979). As a result, the key comparison in these studies is between negotiations where one party can invoke arbitration and negotiations where compulsory arbitration is unavailable. This research is motivated by two considerations that lead to a prediction that wages may be higher under an arbitration system. First, public-sector unions have been the key sponsors of compulsory arbitration laws and are only likely to endorse arbitration if it has an impact favourable for their members. Second, existing research suggests arbitration has been very successful at preventing public-employee strikes (Ichniowski 1982, Olson 1986). If arbitration awards were consistently smaller than the settlements workers could get by striking illegally, substantial illegal strike activity should occur in jurisdictions with compulsory interest arbitration and less public-sector union support for arbitration. These factors suggest the outcomes under arbitration are more favourable to workers than what is possible without arbitration and a prohibition on strikes.

The data support this conclusion. Using data from US police departments that spans the period 1965 to 1978, Ichniowski, Freeman and Lauer (1989) find the total compensation differential between collective bargaining settlements negotiated under a compulsory arbitration was 4–5 percentage points greater than contracts negotiated under a duty to bargain statute or a statute that permits bargaining. The average differential was about 10 percentage points between contracts settled under a compulsory arbitration law and contracts settled in jurisdictions without any law. Since all jurisdictions in the US prohibit police strikes, these estimates also measure the arbitration versus strike prohibition differential. Using Canadian data Currie and McConnell (1991) also find settlements higher under compulsory arbitration than under a no law regime and a law with the duty to bargain but without arbitration or the right to strike.

Theoretical predictions regarding the difference between wage settlements for parties that use and do not use arbitration were first developed by Farber and Katz (1979). In their model the beliefs of the arbitrator about what is a fair award and the risk aversion of the parties determines the position and size of the contract zone. If the parties are equally risk-averse then the centre of the contract zone is equal to Z in equation (1) and a variety of theoretical models predict that the negotiated settlement is concentrated around Z. Thus, if the costs of arbitration are the same for the two sides, there will be no difference between the average negotiated settlement and the expected fair wage belief of arbitrators. On the other hand, if the parties are risk-averse, negotiated settlements will be biased against the more risk-averse party relative to the expected fair wage belief of arbitrators. Thus, mean differences between negotiated settlements and the fair wage beliefs of arbitrators suggest one side is more risk-averse than the other. In a conventional arbitration system this hypothesis is easily tested by comparing mean negotiated settlements with the mean conventional arbitration award (both conditional on the observable facts). The analysis is slightly more complicated where the parties use final-offer arbitration because the appropriate comparison is between negotiated settlements and the expected fair wage belief of the arbitrator and *not* the final offer chosen by the arbitrator.

Current research I am doing with Babcock and Farber suggests that negotiated settlements do look very similar to the expected outcome from arbitration. In Wisconsin teacher negotiations only about half of the disputes where the parties have agreed to final-offers are ultimately settled by a final-offer decision. In the other half of the disputes the parties reach either a negotiated agreement or agree to a consent award which is a negotiated agreement between the parties that is different from the parties' final offers. These settlements are called consent awards because the parties ask the arbitrator to put the settlement in a written arbitration award. This is done for political reasons because the arbitration award is legally binding on the parties and neither side needs to have the agreement ratified by its constituency. *After* the parties have agreed to final offers the expected arbitration award is simply a weighted average of the two offers where each offer is weighted by the probability that it will be selected. These weights can be estimated from the parties' final offers and estimates of the fair wage beliefs of arbitrators can be made from the cases where a final-offer selection is made (e.g. see equation 1). This information is combined to form an estimate of the expected arbitration outcome. Our preliminary results are consistent with the Farber and Katz prediction and show the negotiated and consent awards are very close to the estimated expected arbitration outcome.

The Farber and Katz model does not identify where the parties get their arbitration expectations. These expectations must be learned by observing the arbitration outcomes in other disputes or through personal experience with the procedure. This learning is important if arbitrator beliefs about what is fair change over time because awards provide important new information about the evolution of arbitrator beliefs. One empirical study that has investigated this issue (Olson and Rau 1992) finds the information gained from a final-offer decision has a significant impact on wage settlements in later bargaining rounds. When a final-offer selection is made by the arbitrator the parties learn if the fair wage belief of the arbitrator falls above (union victory) or below (employer victory) the mean of the parties' final offers. If this selection provides the parties with new information about the beliefs of arbitrators, then negotiated settlements in the next bargaining round should be higher when the union's final offer is chosen than when the employer's offer is selected. Olson and Rau find evidence consistent with this prediction. Negotiated settlements are about 2 percentage points greater when the union's final offer is chosen than when the employer wins. They also find in the round following arbitration the variance in negotiated settlements declines and the structure of negotiated settlements converges to the estimated structure of arbitrator beliefs. These results suggest important learning about the beliefs of arbitrators occurs when the parties receive an award.

FUTURE RESEARCH ISSUES

It is customary to conclude a review paper with a discussion of future research issues and this chapter is no exception. While important progress has been made in our understanding of interest arbitration, many issues remain unresolved. Perhaps the most fundamental issue lies in the answer(s) to the simple question: why do parties use arbitration? This question can (and has been) asked of all dispute settlement procedures that are costly to use, including the reasons for strikes and litigation. In all three cases rational parties with 'complete information' would be better off settling the dispute and splitting the resources that are lost using the costly procedure (e.g. forgone profits and wages, attorney fees and uncertainty costs). Since parties continue to use arbitration (and to strike and litigate), the simple rationale model cannot explain arbitration usage.

One possible explanation for arbitration usage that has not received much attention is the pressure negotiators face from their constituencies. While 'political factors' have been widely discussed as an explanation for arbitration usage, there are several recent pieces of evidence that seem to confirm its potential importance in explaining the use of arbitration. The widespread use of consent awards in Wisconsin teacher negotiations (Babcock and Olson 1992) and New Jersey (Frend 1992) police and firefighter negotiations suggest negotiators frequently try and shift responsibility to the arbitrator for a settlement the negotiators have agreed to. The negotiators do not have to have the award ratified by their constituents and can 'blame' the arbitrator for the settlement by having the arbitrator make an award that reflects the negotiated agreement between the parties. McCall (1990) has developed a formal model that begins to address some of these issues. This possible explanation clearly deserves some careful empirical analysis.

Uncertainty about the fair wage beliefs of the arbitrator has been important in recent arbitration research. Research has not, however, carefully examined how uncertainty changes as the parties progress through the arbitration steps and how this change in uncertainty affects the bargaining behaviour of the parties. For example, the uncertainty the parties face *after* an arbitrator is appointed may change dramatically (in either direction) depending on how different arbitrators vary in their fair wage beliefs. Unlike conventional arbitration, under final-offer arbitration *after* two equally risk averse parties have exchanged final offers, uncertainty about the arbitration outcome no longer depends on the predictability of the arbitrator's beliefs (e.g. the variance of ε). This suggests that an analysis focuses on how changes in uncertainty at different stages of the arbitration process could be useful in understanding the role of uncertainty in explaining the use of arbitration.

Results which show (Olson and Rau 1992) that the parties learn about the beliefs of arbitrators when they receive an award suggest that this learning process may explain why some parties use arbitration. This may be particularly important when new issues in negotiations arise because of a rapidly changing environment. In a rapidly changing environment the parties need to update their arbitration expectations and observing awards is the only way to determine the views of arbitrators in the new environment. Some casual evidence on this point is provided by changes in the issues arbitrated by teachers in Wisconsin beginning in the mid-1980s. During this period health-care costs and the share of future health-care costs that would be assumed by teachers became an important issue in negotiations as employers tried to change the widespread practice of 100 per cent employer payment of health insurance premiums to a system where they paid either a fixed dollar amount or shared the cost of health insurance with employees. These health insurance issues have become the major non-wage issue heard by arbitrators and may reflect the parties' uncertainty over how arbitrators will handle this issue. As arbitrators develop a consensus view on this issue I would expect fewer arbitrations over this issue because the parties will have better defined expectations of the beliefs of arbitrators.

Finally, researchers need to continue to pursue a diverse set of research designs. We have learned a great deal about arbitration using designs that take advantage of the benefits of experimental design. The policy-capturing experiments and the lab bargaining experiments are powerful designs for studying arbitration because of their ability convincingly to rule out alternative explanations. This should continue. On the other hand, some issues will continue to require the collection of field data. Investigating, for example, the impact of political factors on arbitration usage may only be done in a convincing fashion by studying the experiences of the parties. However, this has not been done in the arbitration arena. Researchers should try to convince policy-makers to undertake field experiments that take advantage of some of the benefits of experimental design (e.g. random assignment) but use 'real world' participants as actors. For example, it has been very difficult to evaluate different arbitration schemes using across-state variation in procedures because there are usually many other differences between states that could account for differences in dispute rates or other outcome measures. However, a single experiment conducted *within* a state where half the parties were randomly assigned to negotiate under the threat of final-offer arbitration and half the parties negotiated under conventional arbitration would provide evidence on the different effects of these two procedures more valuable than *any* of the previous research comparing these two regimes.

NOTES

1 See Burton and Thomason (1988) for a review of the data on public-sector unionism and the research on the relationship between bargaining legislation and unionization.
2 A recent summary of state laws can be found in Valletta and Freeman (1988). These tabulations summarise the legal developments through the mid-1980s. There have been only modest changes in public-sector collective bargaining laws since 1984.
3 Valleta and Freeman classify some arbitration laws as discretionary where a neutral state agency must order arbitration before it can be used. These laws are compulsory arbitration laws using the defination of this paper – either labour *or* management may petition the agency for arbitration.
4 See Grodin and Najita (1988) for a review of the state judicial response to arbitration.
5 There simply have not been enough different states with similar laws (and data) to identify both the effect of the arbitration law and state fixed effects.
6 There was also a treatment cell where the parties negotiated under a tri-offer arbitration system used only in Iowa. This is a very unusual design and the results under this procedure are not discussed here.

REFERENCES

Ashenfelter, O. and Bloom, D.E. (1984) 'Models of Arbitrator Behavior' *American Economic Review*, 74: 111–24.
Ashenfelter, O., Currie, J., Farber, H.S and Spiegel, M. (1992) 'An Experimental Comparison of Dispute Rates in Alternative Arbitration Systems', Working Paper No. 237, Industrial Relations Section, Princeton University, forthcoming in *Econometrica*.
Babcock, L.C. (1988) *Negotiation Under the Threat of Final Offer Arbitration: A Theoretical and Empirical Analysis*, unpublished dissertation, Department of Economics, University of Wisconsin.
Babcock, L. and Olson, C.A. (1992a) 'An Analysis of the Causes of Impasse in Labor Disputes', *Industrial Relations*, 31: 348–60.
—— (1992b) 'Do Labor and Management Agree on What Makes A Good Arbitrator', unpublished paper, September.
Bazerman, M.H. and Farber, H.S. (1985) 'Arbitrator Decision Making: When are the Final Offers Important', *Industrial and Labor Relations Review*, 39: 76–89.
Bernstein, I. (1954) *Arbitration of Wages*, Berkeley: University of California Press.
Bloom, D.E. (1986) 'Empirical Models of Arbitrator Behavior Under Conventional Arbitration', *Review of Economics and Statistics*, 68: 578–85.
Bloom, D.E. and Cavanagh, C.L. (1986) 'An Analysis of the Selection of Arbitrators' *American Economic Review*, 76: 408–22.
Breger, M.J. (1991) 'Realizing the Potential of Arbitration in Federal Agency Dispute Resolution,' *Arbitration Journal*, 46: 35–40.

Butler, R.J. and Ehrenberg, R.G. (1981) 'Estimating the Narcotic Effect of Public Sector Impasse Procedures', *Industrial and Labor Relations Review*, 35: 3–20.

Burton, J.F., Jr. and Thomason, T. (1988) 'The Extent of Collective Bargaining in the Public Sector' in B. Aaron, J.M. Najita and J.L. Stern (eds) *Public Sector Bargaining*, 2nd edition, Madison: IRRA.

Crable, S. (1991) 'Employing ADR to Resolve Complex Environmental Disputes' *Arbitration Journal*, 46: 48–58.

Currie, J. (1989) 'Who Uses Interest Arbitration: The Case of British Columbia's Teachers, 1947–1981', *Industrial and Labor Relations Review*, 33: 363–79.

Currie, J. and Farber, H.S. (forthcoming) 'Is Arbitration Addictive: Evidence from the Lab and the Field', Madison: *Proceedings of the 44th Annual Winter Meetings of the IRRA*.

Currie, J. and McConnell, S. (1991) 'Collective Bargaining in the Public Sector: The Effect of Legal Structure on Dispute Costs and Wages', *American Economic Review*, 81: 697–718.

Dell'Omo, G. and Gregg, G. (1989) 'Wage Disputes in Interest Arbitration: Arbitrators Weigh the Criteria,' *The Arbitration Journal*, 44: 4–13.

Domenici, P.V. and Everett Koop, C. (1991) 'Sue the Doctor? There's A Better Way', *New York Times* (6 June).

Farber, H.S. (1980) 'An Analysis of Final Offer Arbitration', *Journal of Conflict Resolution*, 24: 683–705.

—— (1981) 'Splitting-the-Difference in Interest Arbitration', *Industrial and Labor Relations Review*, 35: 70–7.

Farber, H.S. and Bazerman, M.H. (1986) 'The General Basis of Arbitrator Behavior: An Empirical Analysis of Conventional and Final-Offer Arbitration', *Econometrica*, 54: 1503–28.

Farber, H.S. and Katz, H.C. (1979) 'Interest Arbitration, Outcomes and the Incentive to Bargain', *Industrial and Labor Relations Review*, 33: 228–40.

Frend, P.J. (1992) 'Interest Arbitration and Experience Under New Jersey's Arbitration Statute', unpublished undergraduate thesis, Department of Economics, Princeton University.

Grodin, J.R. and Najita, J.M. (1988) 'Judicial Response to Public-Sector Arbitration' in B. Aaron, J.M. Najita and J.L. Stern (eds) *Public Sector Bargaining*, 2nd edition, Madison: IRRA.

Halm, F.P. (1985) 'Athletic Conference: The Question of Comparability', Wisconsin Public Employer Relations Association, March.

Ichniowski, C. (1982) 'Arbitration and Police Bargaining: Prescriptions for the Blue Flu', *Industrial Relations*, 21: 149–66.

Ichniowski, C., Freeman, R.B. and Lauer, H. (1989) 'Collective Bargaining Laws, Threat Effects and the Determination of Police Compensation', *Journal of Labor Economics*, 7: 191–209.

Lester, R.A. (1984) *Labor Arbitration in State and Local Government*, Industrial Relations Section Monograph, Princeton University.

McCall, B.P. (1990) 'Interest Arbitration and The Incentive to Bargain: A Principal–Agent Approach', *Journal of Conflict Resolution*, 34: 151–67.

Meierhoefer, B.S. (1990) *Court Annexed Arbitration in Ten District Courts*, Washington, DC: Federal Judicial Center.

Miller, R.U. (1967) 'Arbitration of New Contract Wage Disputes: Some Recent Trends', *Industrial and Labor Relations Review*, 20: 250–67.

Olson, C.A. (1986) 'Strikes, Strike Penalties and Third Party Procedures in Six States', *Industrial and Labor Relations Review*, 39: 539–51.
—— (1988) 'Dispute Resolution in the Public Sector' in B. Aaron, J.M. Najita and J.L Stern (eds) *Public Sector Bargaining*, 2nd edition, Madison: IRRA.
—— Olson, C.A. (forthcoming) 'Arbitrator Decision-Making in Multi-issue Disputes', *Proceedings of the 44th Annual Meetings of the IRRA*.
Olson, C.A. and Jarley, P. (1991) 'Arbitrator Decisions in Wisconsin Teacher Wage Disputes', *Industrial and Labor Relations Review*, 44: 536–47.
Olson, C.A., Dell'Omo, G. and Jarley, P. (1992) 'A Comparison of Interest Arbitrator Decision-Making in Experimental and Field Settings', *Industrial and Labor Relations Review*, 45: 711–23.
Olson, C.A. and Rau, B. (1992) 'Negotiated Settlements and Learning from the Arbitration Experience', unpublished paper, University of Wisconsin-Madison, July.
Saltzman, G.M. (1986) 'A Progressive Experiment: The Evolution of Wisconsin's Collective Bargaining Legislation for Local Government Employees', *Journal of Collective Negotiations in the Public Sector*, 15: 1–25.
Stern, J.L., Rehmus, C.M.J., Loewenberg, J., Kasper, H. and Dennis, B.D. (1975) *Final-Offer Arbitration*, Lexington, MA: Lexington Books.
Stevens, C. (1966) 'Is Compulsory Arbitration Compatible with Bargaining?', *Industrial Relations*, 5: 38–52.
Tebb, A. (1990) 'California's Workers' Compensation Reform: Encouraging the Administrative Approach', in *John Burton's Workers' Compensation Monitor*, January/February, Fort Washington, PA: LRP Publications: 7–12.
Tevelin, D.I. (1992) 'The Future of Alternative Dispute Resolution', *Forum*, National Institute For Dispute Resolution, Winter: 15–16.
Valletta, R.G. and Freeman, R.B. (1988) 'Appendix B. The NBER Public Sector Collective Bargaining Law Data Set' in R.B. Freeman and C. Ichniowski (eds) *When Public Sector Workers Unionize*, Chicago: University of Chicago Press.

9 Do strikes pay?

David Metcalf, Jonathan Wadsworth and Peter Ingram

> The men who constitute the vast army of trade unionists may not be very clever, or, as a rule, far-seeing, but they are hard-headed practical men, and they have a rough and ready way of calculating the advantages and disadvantages of any step which they are about to take, and of the line of conduct which they pursue with so much vigour and effect. They weigh the pros and cons, and balance the probabilities, more closely than many give them credit for doing, and one at least of their deductions has never really been shaken. They have an impression that strikes, in the long run, pay. If they had not this impression they would not risk defeat, spend their hard earned money on them, and endure that privation and suffering which almost always follow in their train.
>
> (George Howell 1879)

Do strikes pay? This is surely the most absorbing and controversial aspect of strike activity, yet for over a century no one in Great Britain has provided an answer. We have been granted access to a rich data source which permits us to clarify – if not finally answer – our question. Although the issue has surfaced periodically (see, e.g., Knowles 1954, Fisher 1973, Gennard 1982, and Gregory *et al.* 1987) to the best of our knowledge this is the first *comprehensive* attempt to analyse the payoff to strike activity since the angry – but illuminating – debate between George Howell (1879) and Phillip Bevan (1880). That debate was the catalyst for the collection of official strike statistics.

The data are discussed and placed in context in the following section. A subsequent section presents information on pay settlements with and without strikes. In the last section these pay settlements are analysed via regression analysis to get at the payoff to strikes.

THE DATA AND BACKGROUND INFORMATION

Our data come from the Pay Databank collected on a quarterly basis since 1979 by the Confederation of British Industry (CBI). The data are unique. The Databank refers to pay settlements and industrial action at the level of the bargaining group. This chapter is based on information from nearly 9,000 pay settlements negotiated during the 1980s.[1]

Each year information is sought from a sample of manufacturing establishments, structured by the number of employees (in the original sample the establishment was chosen randomly from the 1977 Census of Production). The firm involved is not necessarily a CBI member. Each establishment in the sample is asked to provide information on up to three bargaining groups within the establishment (the two largest manual and largest non-manual bargaining groups).

Industrial action is infrequent in non-union workplaces. Therefore our sample of bargaining groups is deliberately drawn only from those workplaces which had collective bargaining (defined by the CBI as those where trade unions were recognised for determining some element of the pay and conditions of at least some of the workforce). The proportion of such establishments was 72 per cent of the CBI Pay Databank sample in 1979 and 70 per cent in 1986. In manufacturing as a whole Millward and Stevens (1986: table 9.2) report using 1984 WIRS data that 55 per cent of establishments employing manual workers and 26 per cent of those employing non-manuals used collective bargaining to determine their pay.

Attrition and consequent replacement of establishments in the sample, non-response and rationalisation of bargaining groups means that only a minority of bargaining groups appear in the sample for five or more of the ten years covered.

The data refer only to industrial action during the course of annual pay negotiations. Further, information is also collected on the threat of action, whether action was taken and, if so, its form – overtime ban, go-slow, strike or other – and duration.

Various indicators of strike activity in British manufacturing in the 1980s are presented in Table 9.1. Around one wage settlement in forty involved a strike (column 1). This strike incidence was noticeably lower in the second half of the decade than it was in the first half. By contrast, the mean size of bargaining groups going on strike (equivalent to 'workers involved' in the official Department of Employment figures) rose substantially over the decade. The mean size of bargaining groups not going on strike was 343 employees (with a range of 319 to 396). Strike durations show no strong pattern over the period. The mean strike lasts twelve working days. These three items are pulled together in column 5 to calculate how much of the total available labour supply was lost due to strikes: the maximum lost was one day per person in the sample in 1983–4 and 1987–8, and the mean labour supply lost was a little over half a day.

Table 9.1 Strike activity in annual pay negotiations in British manufacturing industry

	Strike incidence (%)	*Mean size of striking bargaining groups*	*Strike duration (days)*		*Days lost from strikes as a % of total labour supply*
			Mean	*Median*	
	1	*2*	*3*	*4*	*5*
1979–80	4.88	236	20.2	10.0	0.33
1980–1	2.65	331	10.8	3.0	0.13
1981–2	2.67	403	10.9	6.5	0.14
1982–3	2.67	905	8.6	5.0	0.25
1983–4	3.89	724	12.6	3.5	0.39
1984–5	1.46	1,046	12.3	4.5	0.22
1985–6	2.77	575	7.3	1.6	0.12
1986–7	1.56	658	6.4	1.5	0.08
1987–8	2.26	1,895	7.8	3.0	0.37
1988–9	0.76	1,466	12.6	10.0	0.16
Average 1979–80 to 1988–9	2.56	698	11.6	4.9	0.24

Source: All data from CBI Pay Databank (see text)

Note: Column 1 is the percentage of bargaining groups experiencing a strike. Column 2 is the mean number of employees in striking bargaining groups. This is equivalent to the 'workers involved' category in the official Department of Employment strike figures. Columns 3 and 4 are the mean and median duration (in days) of each strike. Column 5 is days lost from strikes as a percentage of the available labour supply. The numerator for this calculation is (number of disputes multiplied by columns 2 and 3). The denominator is (total number of employees in the sample multiplied by 250 days).

PAY SETTLEMENTS WITH AND WITHOUT STRIKES

Average pay settlements with and without a strike are set out for each year in Table 9.2 and Figure 9.1. It must be noted that these data are settlements. During the 1980s, Department of Employment information shows that outturns were, each year, approximately two percentage points higher than settlements because of bonuses, overtime and the like. Virtually all settlements last for twelve months.

In seven of the ten years settlements involving a strike were higher than those without a strike. On average, for the decade as a whole, real pay increases where there was a strike were 0.7 per cent a year higher than no strike settlements. The same information is presented visually in Figure 9.1. It will be seen that the distribution of settlements with a strike lies mostly to the right of settlements without a strike.

Table 9.2 Pay settlements with and without strikes

Year	*Mean real pay change (%)*		
	Settlements with a strike 1	*Settlements without a strike* 2	*Difference (1–2)* 3
1979–80	0.22	−2.61	2.83**
1980–1	−4.05	−4.13	0.08
1981–2	−3.79	−3.38	−0.41
1982–3	1.00	1.16	−0.16
1983–4	1.75	0.92	0.83**
1984–5	1.75	0.49	1.26**
1985–6	1.69	1.97	−0.28
1986–7	2.09	1.34	0.75**
1987–8	2.37	1.98	0.39
1988–9	1.30	−0.16	1.46
Average 1979–80 to 1988–9	0.46	−0.21	0.67

Source: CBI Pay Databank (see text)

Note: ** denotes significant at 5% level. If the differences in pay settlements with and without a strike are weighted by strike incidence the average rises a little to 0.76%.

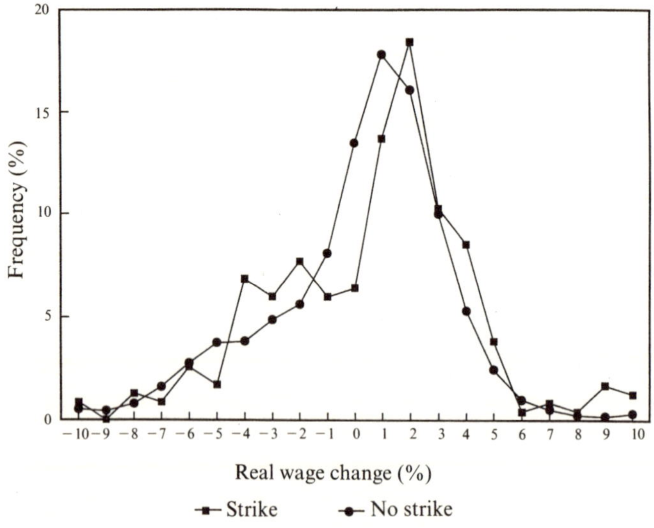

Figure 9.1 Distribution of real wage changes 1979–89

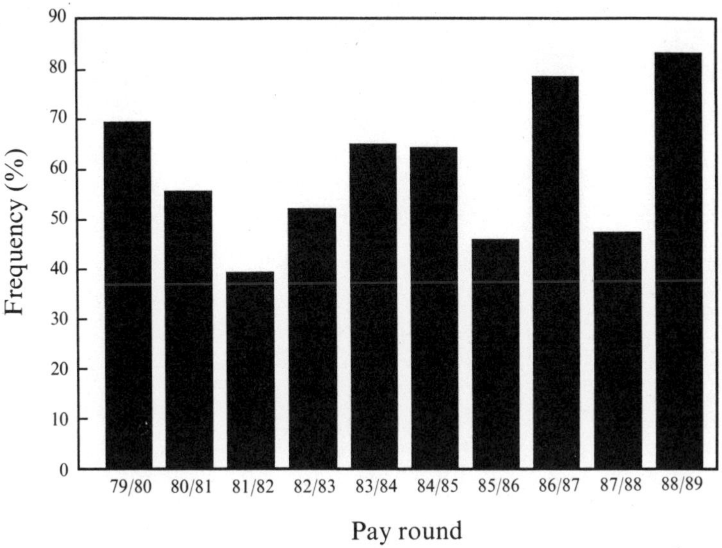

Figure 9.2 Strikes resulting in settlement above mean real wage

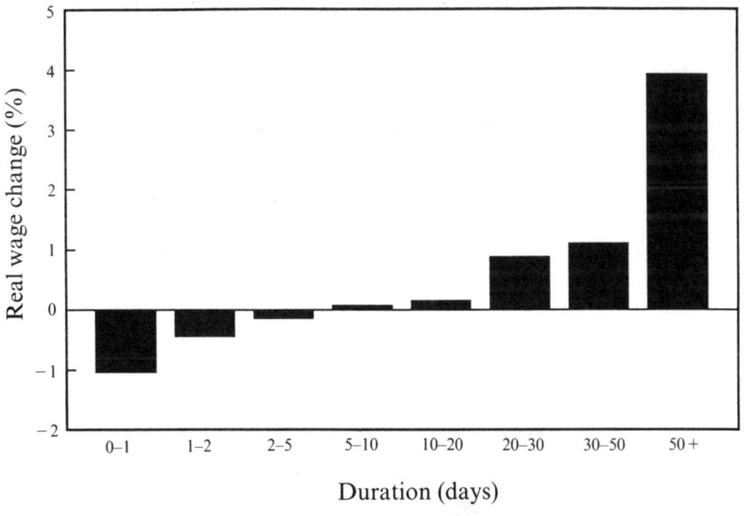

Figure 9.3 Real wage changes and strike duration

Table 9.3 Strike activity and pay outcomes by industry

Industry	*Strike incidence (%)*	*Strike duration (days)*		*Average real wage change (%)*		
		Mean	*Median*	*With strike*	*Without strike*	*Difference*
Food, drink, tobacco	2.46	10.3	3.5	0.32	0.49	−0.17
Coal products, chemicals	1.58	19.2	5.0	0.19	0.61	−0.42
Metal manufacture	1.83	33.8	10.0	3.34	−0.88	4.32**
Mechanical engineering	2.97	11.4	3.5	−0.50	−0.71	0.21
Instrument engineering	3.21	9.4	8.0	1.54	−0.04	1.58
Electrical engineering	4.36	6.9	2.0	−0.76	−0.52	−0.24
Vehicles	4.45	9.6	3.0	0.41	−0.56	0.97
Metal goods n.e.s.	2.65	10.3	5.0	0.30	−0.91	1.21**
Textiles	1.18	9.4	7.7	−2.65	−0.59	−2.06
Leather, clothing	0.56	2.0	2.0	3.60	−0.19	3.79
Bricks, pottery	1.88	11.0	14.0	0.28	−0.41	0.79
Timber, furniture	4.19	3.8	1.0	−1.56	−1.11	−0.45
Paper, printing	1.65	9.9	7.0	0.92	−0.26	1.18
Other manufacturing	2.29	11.5	3.5	1.93	−0.22	2.15**

Source: CBI Pay Databank, 9,117 pay settlements 1979–80 to 1988–9

Note ** denotes significant at 5% level.

The proportion of settlements involving a strike which had above average real wage increases is given in Figure 9.2. It is noticeable (in data not reported) that the average size of bargaining group gaining such above-average increases comprises more employees than striking bargaining groups gaining below average pay rises. However, there is no pattern to the durations. In half the years those achieving above average settlements have longer than average disputes, while in the other half of the sample their strike durations are shorter than average.

Real pay settlements are plotted against strike durations in Figure 9.3. For durations of one hour to ten days (the vast majority of disputes) there is no pattern to pay settlements. However, pay settlements are positively associated with durations beyond twenty days.

Information on the industrial distribution of strike incidence and duration and the associated real pay changes with and without a strike is given in Table 9.3. When strikes take place in metal manufacturing they tend to be relatively long. Further, in that sector real annual settlements involving a strike are some 4.3 per cent higher than those with no strike. This is by far the largest wedge between settlements with and without a strike for any single industry. By contrast, in two of the most strike-prone industries – electrical engineering and timber – settlements involving a strike yield, on average, lower real wage increases than those without a strike.

One important issue concerns the longevity of the gains from striking in any one year. Are such gains quickly eroded or do they last for many years, possibly even increasing because of a credible strike threat? This question is illuminated in Table 9.4. Each entry shows the wage differential the striking group achieved compared with non-strikers. For example, the thirty-six bargaining groups that struck in the 1979–80 pay round got, on average, a 2.71 per cent real wage differential over and above non-strikers. But in the next three years the striking 1979–80 cohort received lower real wage increases than non-strikers. And by the end of the decade the original gain of 2.71 per cent had decayed to 0.18 per cent.

There is no strong pattern. The bargaining groups which struck in 1979–80, 1984–5, 1985–6 and 1987–8 saw their original pay differential from striking eroded over time. By contrast the striking cohorts 1980–1, 1981–2, 1982–3 and 1986–7 built on their pay differential in subsequent years. These results suggest that it is pointless and impossible to predict the duration of the gains (if any) from strike action in any one year.

This information on settlements with and without a strike is useful but does not fully confront the 'do strikes pay?' question. To begin to answer that question we need to know, for a pay settlement involving a strike, what that settlement would have been in the absence of a dispute. It is to this that we now turn.

PAYOFF TO STRIKES

It is necessary to control for factors, other than strikes, which influence real pay settlements. Then we can more nearly get at the net payoff to the strike investment. Such controls are included in the regression analysis of real wage settlements presented in Table 9.5. To be included in this analysis a bargaining group had to be in the sample for at least four

Table 9.4 Real pay differentials achieved by striking groups

		Pay increase: striking groups minus non-striking groups										
		Bargaining round										
Year struck	*Number*	*1979–80*	*1980–1*	*1981–2*	*1982–3*	*1983–4*	*1984–5*	*1985–6*	*1986–7*	*1987–8*	*1988–9*	*Cumulative: strike year plus subsequent years*
1979–80	36	**2.71**	−0.43	−0.45	−0.38	0.00	0.32	−1.14	0.31	−1.00	0.24	0.18
1980–1	27	−1.28	**0.08**	1.36	0.32	−0.05	−0.56	1.33	0.64	−0.53	0.47	3.06
1981–2	22	−2.80	−1.72	**−0.41**	−0.11	0.36	0.93	0.44	0.08	−0.21	−0.26	0.82
1982–3	19	1.53	−0.50	−0.02	**−0.16**	0.24	0.79	−0.19	0.00	0.37	0.67	1.56
1983–4	40	1.57	0.23	0.10	−0.27	**0.82**	0.28	−0.32	0.27	0.79	0.33	2.17
1984–5	14	−2.45	−1.23	−0.82	0.39	1.36	**1.50**	0.19	−0.02	−0.41	0.11	1.37
1985–6	24	−0.12	−1.57	−0.17	−0.90	0.01	0.43	**−0.28**	−0.16	−0.17	−0.57	−1.18
1986–7	14	−1.77	1.04	−2.03	−0.79	−0.60	0.82	1.49	**0.75**	0.76	0.63	2.14
1987–8	19	2.95	−0.77	0.00	0.39	0.98	1.81	0.41	0.78	**0.37**	−0.09	0.28
1988–9	6	–	–	0.58	−0.12	0.71	−1.42	0.12	1.03	0.23	**1.45**	–

Source: CBI Pay Databank, 9,117 pay settlements 1979–80 to 1988–9
Note: Each cell refers to average pay increase achieved by striking group less average pay increased achieved by non-strikers. Thus the diagonal indicates the initial payoff to strike action. Reading across for any given striking cohort, the table notes the annual real pay differentials in settlements prior to the strike, in the year of the strike (the diagonal) and in settlements after the strike year. The number of bargaining groups taking strike action in any given year is indicated but it should be noted that because of sample attrition these groups will not all remain in the sample throughout the ten year period.

Table 9.5 Panel data estimates of real wage changes

Independent variable	*Sample mean*	*OLS equation*	
Constant		0.02	(0.32)
Number of employees times 10,000	394	0.59*	(0.32)
Manual	0.59	0.37**	(0.13)
Non-manual	0.34	0.43**	(0.14)
Number of bargaining groups	2.33	−0.18**	(0.04)
Contract length (months) $t-1$	12.21	0.04	(0.12)
Wage change $t-1$	0.15	0.28**	(0.01)
Strike	0.02	0.30	(0.22)
Unemployment (%)	10.58	0.09**	(0.01)
Industry dummies		65.6**	(15)
R^2		0.163	
Model χ^2		540.3	(8)**
N		3834	

Notes
1 * denotes significant at 10% level.
2 ** denotes significant at 5% level.
3 Standard errors in parentheses corrected for heteroskedasticity. Mean of dependent variable = 0.8%. Excluded category in occupational definition of bargaining group is mixed manual and non-manual group.

continuous years. This permits the use of lags and instrumental variables and comprises a sample size of 3,834.

Real wage increases are (Table 9.5) positively related to the size of the bargaining group, the size of the wage settlement last year and the level of unemployment in the local labour market. Manual and non-manual bargaining groups have larger pay settlements than mixed groups. Pay increases where there are multiple bargaining groups in the workplace are lower than where there is a single bargaining group. There is no association between the duration of the previous contract and the current wage settlement: this is not surprising because almost all contracts run for twelve months. The mean real wage increase in this sample of settlements is 0.8 per cent. The OLS estimate suggests that a strike boosts the real wage settlement by 0.3 per cent.[2]

How long is a strike 'worthwhile'? Our information permits an approximate cost-benefit analysis, from the unions' viewpoint, of strike action. The present value of the post strike wage gains can be compared with the wages lost while the strike is on. This exercise is set out in Table 9.6.

Table 9.6 Present value (£) of wage gains from striking (and maximum length of 'worthwhile' strike)

		Duration of wage gain from striking in years		
		1	*7*	*30*
Discount	2	44	288	997
		(<1)	(5)	(17)
rate	6	42	248	612
		(<1)	(4)	(11)
%	10	40	217	420
		(<1)	(4)	(7)

Notes

1 The regression analysis (Table 9.4) puts the incremental gain in real wages from striking at 0.30 per cent. In April 1991 the average pay of full time workers was £285 per week (DE *Gazette* November 1991: 602). The incremental gain in 1991 from striking was therefore £0.86 per week or £44.50 per year. The present value of £44.50 per year for various durations of benefit and discount rates is presented as the top number in each cell.

2 £285 per week is equivalent to £57 per day. The present value of the wage gains is divided by this figure to calculate the strike duration (in days) such that the wage losses equal the PV of the gains (assuming a five-day work-week when at work).

3 An example: if the gains from striking last seven years and the discount rate is 6 per cent the PV of the gains is £248. The maximum length of strike which would be worthwhile to achieve such a gain is four days.

The present value (PV) of the wage gains associated with strike action depend on (a) how long those gains last and (b) the discount rate. The table uses, for illustrative purposes, gains lasting for one, seven and thirty years. It was shown above that we simply do not know which of these are most nearly correct.

Almost all settlements have a duration of one year so this is a reasonable minimum period. During the 1980s, 2.4 per cent of wage settlements involved strike action. This implies each settlement involves a strike once every forty-two years, on average. This could be the maximum duration of the wage gain from the (previous) strike. However, we know from Ingram, Metcalf and Wadsworth (1991) that a bargaining group which has a strike this year is more likely to experience a strike in subsequent years. Therefore a reasonable ceiling on the maximum duration of wage benefits is thirty years. Seven years is chosen as the intermediate duration of wage gains from strike action because this represents the average remaining duration of jobs currently in progress (Wadsworth 1989). Discount rates of 2 per cent, 6 per cent and 10 per cent are chosen for illustrative purposes.

The regression analysis puts the real wage gain from a strike at 0.3 per cent. This is roughly half the (uncorrected) difference between the mean wage increases from settlements involving strikes compared with those

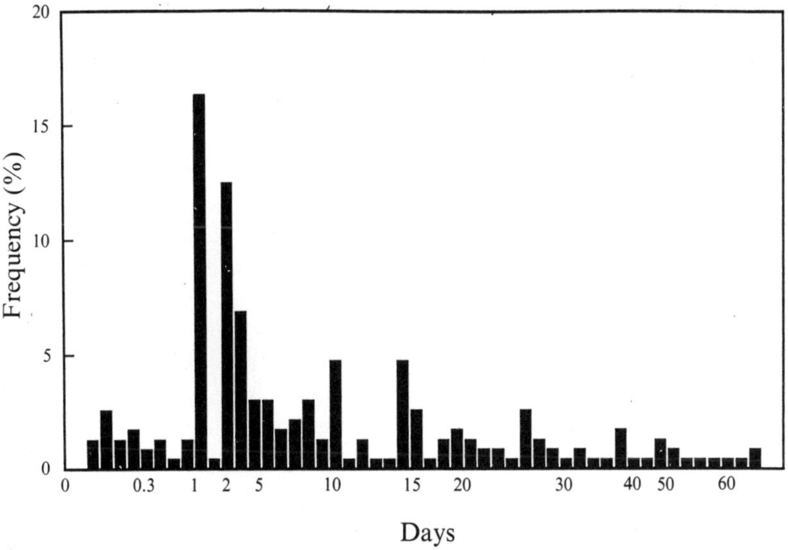

Figure 9.4 Distribution of strike duration: British manufacturing: 1979–89

without strikes (see Table 9.2). The 0.3 per cent figure translates (April 1991) to £44.50 a year. If this payoff to a strike lasted for thirty years and the discount rate was 0.02 the present value of the gross real wage gain from the strike is £997. By contrast if the payoff only lasted one year and the discount rate is 0.10, the present value of the gain is only £40. These present values can be used to calculate how long a strike is a 'worthwhile' investment. Such worthwhile durations are given in brackets under the present value amounts in the table. They are calculated by simply dividing the present value by £57, the average daily amount lost by strike action. On average, if the wage gains from striking last for only one year no strike of over one day is worthwhile. But if the gains last for thirty or more years substantially longer strikes become a worthwhile investment.

The actual distribution of strike durations is given in Figure 9.4. If the wage gain of 0.3 per cent lasts for seven years the maximum 'worthwhile' strike duration is five days (Table 9.6). It can be seen from Figure 9.4 that, on average, 56 per cent of strikes would be a good investment in such circumstances because 56 per cent of strikes in our sample last five days or fewer.

However, the average (mean) strike duration is between eleven and twelve days (see Table 9.1). Such an 'average' strike would, we see from Table 9.6, require the duration of the extra pay settlements to last for thirty years, with a discount rate of 6 per cent or below, for the benefits to at least equal the costs. This hints that the 'average' strike is unlikely to be a good investment.

These calculations are illuminating but merely illustrative. Some caveats must be noted. The payoff to the strike investment could be either greater or smaller than that calculated in Table 9.6. There are at least six reasons why the gain might be understated.

First, the regression results suggest a real wage increase of 0.8 per cent a year without a strike and 1.1 per cent with a strike. The 0.8 per cent figure is the mean of a distribution. Some wage agreements will be settled at the union's demand (with, say, a mean of 1.0 per cent) and some at the employer's offer (with, say, a mean of 0.6 per cent). In this example the gain from the strike is more correctly put at 0.5 per cent (= 1.1 per cent − 0.6 per cent) rather than the 0.3 per cent calculated from the regression.

Second, if relatively few workers go on strike but the gains accrue to all or many employees in the workplace or industry, then Table 9.6 may well be correct for an individual striker but understate the gains to labour in aggregate.

Third, the threat of a strike may ratchet-up pay offers in the 'no strike' group of bargains. This would not be captured by the raw settlement data or the regression. Thus the payoff to the strike weapon would understated.

Fourth, the strike this year might cause future wage settlements to yield a higher increment than the 0.3 per cent assumed in calculating the present value figures in Table 9.6. This might occur because, by striking, the union has issued a credible threat and in future years the firm may settle higher rather than strike.

Fifth, the costs of strike action might be overstated. This would be so if the striker can make good his or her lost pay before or after the strike or if s/he has an alternative source of income during the strike. Strike pay received from the union also offsets lost wages, although this does not come out of thin air, and the striker will normally contribute towards such insurance via union dues.

Finally, the strike may yield some non-wage gains, although the CBI data set is specifically limited to the process of wage determination in the annual pay round.

It is also possible, on the other hand, that the gains from strike action might be overstated. For example, the dispute might have adverse employment consequences in the bargaining group on strike or might have harmful third-party effects such as wage losses caused by lay-offs in other supplier or customer plants.

Further, although our regression controls for lots of influences on pay settlements, it remains possible that bargaining groups which strike have 'stronger' unions, perhaps represented by a pre- or post-entry closed shop or very high density within the bargaining group. It might be union strength, rather than the strike itself, which generates the higher pay settlement.

DATA APPENDIX

The majority of the variables used in Tables 9.1 to 9.6 are taken or calculated from the CBI pay databank. These data are not in the public domain and can only be obtained with permission from the CBI.

The CBI data are designed to provide a continuous picture of the level of wage settlements and related details through time. In any given period the live survey consists of approximately 1,200 establishments in manufacturing. The questionnaire responses are, however, based at the level of the individual settlement group. With an average of 1.7 settlement groups reporting in respect of each establishment, the survey covers around 2,000 groups from which a 60–5 per cent response rate is achieved in any given year. In our sample non-union settlement groups are excluded, comprising around a third of groups each year. Missing information for some groups means that the annual average number of bargaining groups is around 1,000 (see also Note 1). Responses to the survey are obtained in respect of groups of both manual and non-manual weekly paid employees in private manufacturing, where at least one item of the pay and conditions package is modified by determination at company or establishment level. The survey therefore excludes 'national level only' bargainers.

The questionnaire is completed by a member of the management negotiating team who has had direct involvement in the settlement process. In addition to determining the rate of increase in wages as a result of the settlement, the survey asks respondents further questions covering the implementation date and expected duration of the settlement, the level of wage claim and any non-wage dimensions to the settlement. Details are also sought on an extensive list of potential pressures impacting on the wage settlement process including information relating to the use of any industrial action taken in support of the claim. Full details on the composition of the sample are provided by Ingram and Cahill (1989) and Gregory, Lobban and Thomson (1985, 1986).

Definitions of the variables are as follows:

1 Number of Workers in Bargaining Group: defined simply by number of employees.
2 Composition of Bargaining group: manual, non-manual or mixed (default).
3 Action last year: strike, overtime ban, go-slow, none (default) in connection with last year's settlement.
4 Real Wage: annual percentage increase in settlement earnings minus increase in retail price index at date of settlement.

In addition we have supplemented the CBI dataset with information from the following source:

5 Unemployment: monthly unemployment rate disaggregated by ten standard regions. Source: Department of Employment *Gazette*, Table 2.3.

NOTES

1 For complete information on the sample see Ingram and Cahill (1989) and the Data Appendix. The full sample where collective bargaining is used 1979/80–1988/9 contains 9,117 observations (pay settlements). For a full analysis of the structure of bargaining in the original sample (1979) see Gregory, Lobban and Thomson (1986). Subsequent decentralisation of bargaining (to 1986) is reported in Ingram and Cahill (1989). Establishments are excluded from the sample if they abide strictly by the terms of a national (industry-wide) agreement. To be included they have to bargain outside such national agreements or make substantial local modifications to national agreements. It is possible that industrial disputes undertaken in connection with a national agreement to which a bargaining group is a party (i.e. there is some two-tier arrangement), may dominate those attributed to local/plant-level issues. This issue was investigated by cross reference to the associated bargaining pressures cited on the questionnaire. Any national dispute can be identified if, in addition to the dispute, a respondent indicated that a national/district agreement negotiated by an employer organisation to which it is a party, represented an influence on the settlement process. Less than a tenth of all disputes recorded exhibited this combination. It is clear therefore that disputes over national agreements do not dominate strike incidence in this sample. Indeed, even if they did there would not be too much to worry about because the statistical analysis includes time and industry controls.

2 The coefficient on the strike variable in the OLS equation is not quite statistically significant. However, in other equations (not reported here) the data show that settlements with a strike of a day or longer yield significantly higher wage increases than settlements without a strike. These equations are reported in Metcalf, Wadsworth and Ingram (1992). That paper also deals with the following technical issues: the endogeneity of strike action; bargaining group fixed effects such as unobserved union power or human capital in the workforce; and inconsistency caused by the inclusion of the lagged dependent variable in longitudinal estimation.

REFERENCES

Bevan, G.P. (1880) 'The strikes of the past ten years', *Journal of the Royal Statistical Society*, 43, March: 35–64.

Fisher, M.R. (1973) *Measurement of Labour Disputes and their Economic Effects*, Paris: OECD.

Gennard, J. (1982) 'The financial costs and returns of strikes', *British Journal of Industrial Relations*, 20 (2), July: 247–56.

Gregory, M., Lobban, P., and Thomson, A. (1985) 'Wage settlements in manufacturing 1979–84: evidence from the CBI Databank', *British Journal of Industrial Relations*, 23 (3), November: 339–58.

—— (1986) 'Bargaining structure, pay settlements and perceived pressures in manufacturing 1979–84: further analysis from the CBI Databank', *British Journal of Industrial Relations*, 24 (2), July: 215–32.

—— (1987) 'Pay settlements in manufacturing industry 1979–84: a micro-data study of the impact of product and labour market pressures', *Oxford Bulletin of Economics and Statistics*, 49 (1), February: 129–49.

Howell, G. (1879) 'Strikes: their cost and results', *Frasers Magazine*, December: 767–83.

Ingram, P. and Cahill, J. (1989) 'Pay determination in private manufacturing', DE *Gazette*, June: 281–5.

Ingram, P., Metcalf, D. and Wadsworth, J. (1991) 'Strike incidence and duration in British manufacturing industry in the 1980s', Centre for Economic Performance, LSE, Discussion Paper 48, August.

Knowles, K.G.J.C. (1954) *Strikes: a study in industrial conflict*, Oxford: Basil Blackwell.

Metcalf, D., Wadsworth, J. and Ingram, P. (1992) 'Pay settlements, strike incidence and duration', mimeo, Centre for Economic Performance, LSE.

Millward, N. and Stevens, M. (1986) *British Workplace Industrial Relations 1980–84*, DE/ESRC/PSI/ACAS, Aldershot: Gower.

Wadsworth, J. (1989) 'Job tenure and inter-firm mobility in Great Britain', Working Paper No. 1173, Centre for Labour Economics, LSE.

10 The shorter working week in engineering: surrender without sacrifice?

Ray Richardson and Marcus Rubin

In May 1989, after prolonged and complex bargaining at the national level with the Engineering Employers' Federation (EEF), the Confederation of Shipbuilding and Engineering Unions (CSEU) announced a strategy of indefinite strikes at selected factories in an attempt to secure a reduction in the working week in the engineering industry. This strategy was successful, in the sense that a large number of firms subsequently agreed to a shorter working week. It is also true, however, that the great majority of these agreements contained provisions intended to defray some or all of the costs of the reduction in hours. The main aim of our research was to determine the net impact these agreements had on the competitiveness of the firms concerned.

BACKGROUND

The previous reduction in the working week before the CSEU embarked on its campaign in May 1989 had been in 1981. An agreement between the CSEU and the EEF had then been reached only after an overtime ban and a series of national one-day and two-day strikes in 1979. That settlement covered hours and holidays over four years and reduced the standard working week from forty to thirty-nine hours by November 1981. A clause in the agreement committed the parties and their members 'to ensure that productivity is increased so that there are no increases in manufacturing costs as a result of the reduction in working hours'. In its comments on the agreement the EEF stated that management would have two full years to prepare for the reduction in working hours so as to minimise any cost increase and that the cost effects should be negligible in view of the productivity clause. Judging by the EEF's subsequent position, the productivity gains actually achieved were rather less than employers had expected.

The CSEU submitted a further claim for thirty-five hours in 1983, the earliest date allowed under the 1979 agreement. The EEF agreed to consider reducing hours in return for changes to working practices. Accordingly, a joint working party was established, but for some years the only visible progress was an increase in the status of the working party, which became a joint negotiating subcommittee. The unions' representatives on the subcommittee tabled a draft national agreement in June 1986, listing 'possible' concessions, including complete flexibility and an end to demarcation, in return for reduced hours which would only be implemented after local agreement on the concessions.[1] After heated internal union debate, the executive councils of the CSEU unions rejected the position adopted by their representatives. In June 1987 the CSEU Conference was united in insisting on the unified introduction of a 37.5 hour week in two stages in November 1988 and 1989. The EEF was not prepared to offer more than a reduction, subject to local agreement on introducing concessions, in two stages with the 37.5 hour week being achieved by May 1990 after implementation of the concessions. As a result of these differences between the parties the agreement effective from November 1987, which proved to be the last national agreement, contained nothing on hours. In the next year's wage negotiations the CSEU proposed a long-term deal with two one-hour reductions on a self-financing basis. The EEF maintained its position, refusing to accept the thirty-seven-hour week and rejecting any agreement along the lines of 1979, under which member companies had to reduce the working week on a particular date even if the unions had not agreed provisions at company level to offset the costs.

Talks finally broke down in April 1989. The EEF told its members that it refused to continue national bargaining because the CSEU would not accept the 'essential principle' that no company should be obliged to reduce working time without first reaching agreement on offsetting the cost and maintaining output.

In May 1989 the CSEU announced a strategy of indefinite strikes at selected factories. An unusual and imaginative feature of this strategy was that it involved a levy by a union federation of the members of its affiliated unions to finance the payment by the federation of strike benefit. The benefit to be paid by the CSEU was in addition to the usual strike pay of up to £25 a week paid by the unions.

The levy, which was one hour's pay a week, attracted sufficient support for the CSEU to announce in October 1989 that it would pay strikers £125 a week. Later that month strike ballots took place at seven factories belonging to four major companies. In all cases the majority of manual workers voted for strike action. At three factories the manual members of particular unions voted against, and at all seven factories white-collar members who were also balloted voted against, in six cases by very large majorities. The CSEU unions which had delivered majorities for action in the ballots called manual workers out on strike at six factories, three of which belonged to British Aerospace. Non-manual members were also called out in the few cases where the majority of members of a particular union at one of the factories had voted for strike action.

In November 1989, when three factories were already out on strike, an agreement was reached at one of the six, NEI Parsons of Newcastle, immediately before strike action was due to begin there. The agreement provided for an immediate hour's reduction and for the introduction of the thirty-seven-hour week in January 1992. There were extensive cost-offsetting provisions. Similar agreements followed within a few weeks at two of the other five factories.

The three British Aerospace factories experienced strikes of between eighteen and twenty-three weeks. The CSEU reduced the benefit it paid to £60 a week in December 1989 and postponed strike ballots at the next group of eight selected factories until April 1990, when agreements had been reached at the three British Aerospace factories on terms very similar to those of the earlier settlements. Shortly before the ballots the CSEU raised its dispute benefit from £60 to £70 a week. At most of the selected factories there were large majorities for strike action followed by settlements without any industrial action. In addition companies facing no direct strike threat were agreeing to introduce the thirty-seven-hour week. The number of agreements on the shorter working week, generally with extensive cost-offsetting provisions, was far more than the number of strike ballots, which continued throughout 1990.

According to official statistics 662,000 working days were lost in 1989 and 1990 as a result of thirteen strikes over hours of work involving 15,000 engineering workers.[2] Some 611,000 working days were lost through strike action by 9,400 workers at the five factories where strikes had taken place following ballots in October 1989. The vast majority of working days lost were at British Aerospace. The extent of strike action was very much less than in 1979, when official figures suggest that 16 million working days were lost and 1.5 million workers were involved.[3]

In December 1990 the CSEU discontinued the levy, which had been reduced to £1 a week in July. There had been £12 million paid out in dispute benefit and nearly £7 million remained in the fund created from the levy to support strike action where unions could not reach acceptable local agreements on reduced working hours.

The CSEU announced in April 1991 the successful end of 'Stage One of the Thirty-Five-Hour Week Campaign', claiming agreements on a thirty-seven-hour week by early 1992 affecting 1,666 companies or company sites covering 600,000 workers. However, lists of factories supplied by the CSEU in support of its claims about the number of agreements included companies with which CSEU unions negotiated but which were outside the engineering industry.

The EEF reported, also in April 1991, that 595 of its 5,000 members had conceded a shorter working week, not necessarily of thirty-seven hours, for 135,000 manual workers, around 30 per cent of manual workers employed by member firms. Whatever the exact number of engineering factories at which the shorter working week had been agreed, there had clearly been a very significant reduction in standard working hours in the period of 'Stage One' of the CSEU campaign.

INITIAL STEPS

A simple reference case for the analysis of the shorter working week is where standard hours are cut, but actual working hours remain unchanged; the implication is that some hours which were previously paid at the basic rate as part of the standard working week would now normally be treated as overtime hours paid at a premium rate. For example, if the standard working week is reduced from thirty-nine to thirty-seven hours, standard hourly wages are increased by 5.4 per cent (on the assumption that pay for the standard working week remains the same); workers will then be paid for an additional two hours at overtime rates, say at time-and-a-half. The hourly overtime rate will be 158 per cent of the old basic rate (1.5 times the new basic rate, which is 105.1 per cent of the old basic rate). So, in terms of the old basic hourly wage rate, workers are paid for an additional 3.2 hours even though their actual time at work is unchanged. This represents an increase of slightly more than 8 per cent in the wage costs of the workers concerned.

There are many refinements to this simple reference case that may be appropriate. First, there are labour costs other than wage costs. In many cases, as with holiday pay and most pension arrangements, these are directly linked to weekly earnings. Such non-wage labour costs would rise in line with the wage costs. In other cases, there is no link to either the hourly or weekly wage, and there need be no additional effect. The overall effect on labour costs for these workers therefore depends on the mix of wage cost-linked and non-wage cost-linked elements. Secondly, if overtime is worked in the initial situation, the percentage increase in wage costs would be a little smaller, even though the original level of overtime is now also paid at the new higher premium rate.[4] Thirdly, the reduction in hours usually refers to only a proportion of the workforce. Others will be entirely unaffected or not affected as much. Thus, management hours might be unaffected whilst other white-collar workers might anyway be working only 37.5 hours per week, and, under a policy of harmonisation, have their hours reduced by only 0.5 hours. The latter would imply, on the above assumptions, a white-collar wage cost increase of less than 1.5 per cent. Overall, the average increase in total wage costs for the firm would be very sensitive to the mix of employees. Finally, it is common for many workers to be 'carried' or 'hoarded' at some stages of the business cycle. This means that they are then not producing a full standard week's work even if they are being paid for one. In this case it may not matter that they are being paid for thirty-seven rather than thirty-nine hours, because they are not fully productive in either situation and their output may be the same in both. Here, there would be no obvious cost implications of the shorter working week.

There are, therefore, a number of conditions that determine the first-round cost implications of a reduction in the standard working week, even in this simple reference case. In addition, we must consider a whole series of possibilities which might affect output per hour worked.[5] Some of these might be an automatic consequence of a shorter working week; others will require negotiation and specific implementation.

Much of the research on previous shorter working week campaigns, especially that done by economists, has concentrated on their employment consequences. Typically, this research has implicitly assumed that the reductions in hours come as exogenous events, pushed by unions into a situation where firms are in some sense 'stable' and 'efficient'. An example is given in Allen (1980), which, it is important to recognise, takes as its starting point the hypothetical situation of production being initially unchanged by the shorter working week. Logically, this could be the case only with some combination of three responses, namely (a) actual hours not falling as much as the basic working week, (b) additional employment, and (c) higher output per hour of work. Allen makes the seemingly reasonable assumption that the basic weekly wage is not reduced in line with the shorter working week, which implies that the hourly wage goes up, at least as a first-round effect.

These assumptions together imply a rise in unit labour costs unless the whole adjustment comes via an increase in output per hour of work. Any rise in costs threatens profit margins and subsequently puts upward pressure on prices and downward pressure on employment. Allen's basic purpose is to estimate the effect on the level of employment under differing macroeconomic conditions. For our purposes, however, the important point is that he does not estimate the size of the three conditions noted above, but instead *assumes* values for them, based on judgements about previous responses to hours reductions. His discussion here is revealing.

First, he notes that 'actual hours worked in manufacturing (adjusted for cyclical movements in the economy) have tended to fall by between one-half and two-thirds of the reduction in standard hours'.[6] Here, he is referring not to the immediate consequences of specific hours campaigns as such but to steady incremental drift over the years. Second, he notes that 'it is widely believed that as normal hours are reduced there will be an increase in efficiency... because the lost hours are less productive than those that remain and because the remaining hours may now be even more productive . . . under-employment may be reduced and work systems may be beneficially re-organised'. He notes that the 'ability of management to re-organise work systems will be increased if... there is a significant interval between reaching agreement with the unions and the actual implementation of shorter hours', and that 'the incentives to re-organise may be stronger when . . . industry is subject to severe competitive pressures ... Against this, certain radical changes in work practices (e.g. a major extension of shift working) may be difficult to achieve in the face of strong union opposition'.[7]

In deciding how much weight to assign these two arguments he suggests that of the total potential forgone output implied by a cut in the standard working week, 40 per cent will be offset by more overtime working and 30 per cent will be offset by higher output per worker – he describes the second assumption as 'arbitrary'.[8] The initial assumption of unchanged production means that the remaining 30 per cent of potential lost output is recovered by higher employment. But the whole process is seen to generate additional inflation which sets 'forces in motion that wholly, or largely, offset any first round gain in employment'.[9] In conclusion, Allen finds that employment will eventually be reduced below what it would otherwise have been unless the authorities are prepared to tolerate an increase in inflation.[10]

It is not our purpose in this chapter to go into the macroeconomic effects of the shorter working week, important as these are. Rather, we prefer to stay with the micro-consequences. For these, Allen is quite correct to emphasise the possible importance of the relabelling of hours (from standard time to overtime) and the rise in output per worker. A key issue is, how large are these effects likely to be?

White, in a number of publications (e.g. White 1980, 1981 and 1987), has written very perceptively about the complexities involved in judging the consequences of reductions in the working week. Perhaps the core of his analysis is the emphasis he places on the potential for the growth in labour productivity which the shorter working week generates. As he notes after a review of the literature, 'in a variety of countries and time-periods, therefore, reductions in hours have been followed by productivity increases sufficiently large to cancel any effect of employment creation'.[11] White groups the sources of productivity growth in response to the shorter working week into five categories.[12] First, there are physiological and psychological changes that may take place in workers. There is some evidence showing that these physiological effects (which are seen, in a sense, as an automatic consequence of shorter hours and lead to a rise in effort) do *not* disappear once the working week falls below eight hours a day.[13] If true, this could be highly relevant to a fall below thirty-nine hours per week. The psychological effects seem to depend in part on the way the shorter working week is bargained over and introduced. The process seems to have an effect on the outcome.[14]

White's other categories are:

1 a range of steps concerned to enhance the productive utilisation of time,
2 new patterns of working time, such as flexible hours systems,
3 the introduction of new methods of production, changes in organisation and more efficient working practices, and
4 the early introduction of changes in productivity which were already in train.

These all revolve around the content of the agreement that may be negotiated in connection with the shorter working week. It is with these deals that the present enquiry is mainly concerned.

In discussing time utilisation, White makes the important point that much time spent at work is not spent in direct productive activity. He specifies lunch and other refreshment breaks, time allowed at both ends of the day for preparing for work and washing up etc. after work, and time spent waiting for materials etc. He suggests (no source given) that in engineering it is common for between 20 and 40 per cent of time to be spent non-productively in one way or another.[15] This obviously provides a rich area for employers to seek an offset to any adverse cost implications of the shorter working week.

White (1980) reports the results of a survey done on various aspects of the shorter working week in 1979. Only about 10 per cent of his sample of 401 manufacturing firms already had the shorter working week (then defined as less than forty hours). The information he collected was a little rudimentary for some purposes, but one of his conclusions was that recent increases in the size of the workforce or the amount of overtime working had been much more linked to product market demand and specific structural characteristics of the industry than to the fact of the shorter working week. Indeed, *ceteris paribus*, he judged the latter to be unconnected with increases in the workforce or overtime working. The same was true of any tendency towards lower output, to an increase in the use of subcontracted labour and to new capital investments.[16] Instead, in this and the companion study (White 1981), he takes the view that there was an intensive and largely successful search for productivity enhancing devices in the plants where the shorter working week had been introduced. Indeed, he concludes from his case studies that 'there was substantial evidence of offsetting measures and productivity improvements, and also in some cases of wage 'trade-offs'. It is not surprising, therefore, that the case studies gave little indication of increased costs arising from the shorter working time'.[17]

White's work on the 1981 reductions of the working week in the engineering and printing industries produced somewhat different results (White 1982, 1983 and White and Ghobadian 1984). Productivity improvements, although still very significant, appear to have been rather less successful in offsetting increased costs. In engineering, 47 per cent of managers interviewed thought that labour costs had risen as a result of the shorter working week, 48 per cent that they had stayed the same and 5 per cent that they had decreased. The conclusion that a little over one-half of engineering firms suffered no increase in costs is subject to an important qualification. There was no clear link between the productivity improvements achieved in 1982 and the introduction of a shorter working week the previous year. Firms where managers had said in 1981 that they did not intend to make any change to offset the cost of reduced hours or where managers reported in 1982 that they had not made the changes they had intended had larger improvements in productivity than firms where an intention to make changes to offset costs had been carried out. White comments on the difficulty managers may have had in distinguishing productivity improvements linked to shorter hours from those which would have occurred anyway.

Another important point made by White is that industrial capacity in 1981 was not being fully utilised. Labour productivity was at the level of six years earlier. So, there was potential to absorb reduced hours without increased costs. It is not obvious that the same would still be true in 1989–91 after the 'productivity miracle' of the 1980s.

It was our main intention to establish the unit labour cost consequences of the 1989–91 campaign. This is no easy task. First, the process of responding to the campaign was by no means complete. Many firms introduced the shorter working week in three phases over two years. Some of the productivity offsets which had been negotiated were still in the process of being operationally defined and implemented and had almost certainly not had their full eventual effect.[18] Certainly, the complete impact is not yet reflected in official data series. A second problem is that the reduction in hours came at a relatively turbulent time for many companies. Manufacturing industry generally entered an unusually deep recession shortly after the first agreements were signed. The second, and often most complex and important, phases of the process were frequently being negotiated just when product demand conditions were manifestly deteriorating very sharply. The recession limited the scope for some of the possible responses, such as wage offsets and increased overtime working. It is extraordinarily difficult to standardise for this even with a good run of official data. The recession is also likely to have a powerful effect on the negotiations surrounding the implementation of any offsets to the costs of the shorter working week. One response to this is to conclude that nothing of interest can be done until there has been a sufficient passage of time to allow the more durable consequences of the campaign to be revealed. The problem with delay is that as time passes managers will find it increasingly hard to isolate the effects of one of several major changes. White suggested that this might be a problem with interviews a little less than a year after a reduction in hours.

Our view was that an early enquiry had merit. We felt that we might be able to get useful insights from a three-pronged research approach. First, we looked at a number of the collective agreements which had been signed. Secondly, we carried out a small number of factory visits to put some flesh on the bare bones of the agreements. Finally, and using the insights gained from the factory visits, we distributed a questionnaire to give us more extensive coverage. We discuss these three elements in turn.

THE COLLECTIVE AGREEMENTS

The first stage was to examine reports of agreements by Industrial Relations Services and Income Data Services, supplemented where possible by looking at the actual text of the agreements. The same categories which White had used were again in evidence and formed the basis of our analysis. Specifically, we saw:

1 reallocations of time,
2 changes in working practices,
3 certain savings which did not affect hours or working practices, and
4 employer finance.

Time reallocation In many agreements, provision was made for workers to give up 'non-productive' time, e.g. officially recognised breaks which count towards the basic working hours, or agree to the introduction of bell-to-bell working and revised clocking procedures in exchange for the shorter working week. The most common forms in the agreements we looked at were the elimination of one ten-minute break each working day and the abolition of paid washing time.

Time given up in this way can have complex effects. Hours spent at work fall for any given level of output per worker, i.e. measured output per hour spent at work rises. But, as a first approximation, unit labour costs are unaffected, because weekly earnings and actual working time stay the same. As refinements, it is possible that longer periods of continuous working could lead to lower productivity because of fatigue; on the other hand, and particularly where machines are being stopped and started, breaks may reduce output by more than their share of basic hours would suggest. Further, because the reduction in the standard working week normally leads to a rise in the basic wage, (because, as a first approximation, standard weekly earnings are not affected) existing overtime hours would still become more expensive.

Changes in working practices The most common examples in the agreements we monitored were increased flexibility in the nature and place of work and multi-machine operation.

Savings which did not affect hours or working practices The main examples were cashless pay, changes to sick pay schemes and penalties for lateness.

Employer finance Agreements seldom specified that the employer was financing the reduction in working hours, but the nature or absence of offsetting provisions often strongly suggested that the costs of the reduction were being financed by the employer.

Finally, many agreements included a commitment to the very general objective (e.g 'to maintain output' or 'not to increase cost') without any indication of how this was to be achieved.

We classified the eighty-three agreements reported in sufficient detail, somewhat arbitrarily, by their major method of finance as shown in Table 10.1. In ten cases we judged the agreement to have had two major methods of finance.

An examination of some 400 agreements made available at the AEU head office showed that the reported agreements were broadly representative of the larger companies, but that agreements by smaller companies were much less likely to have offsetting provisions.

It was rare for agreements to specify that the employer was meeting the bulk of the costs of the reduction in working hours. In most cases

Table 10.1 Major method of finance in reported agreements

Method	%
Time reallocation	28
Specific change(s) in working practices	41
Employer finance	27
General commitment	17

classification to this category was based on the absence or limited nature of other provisions. A few agreements indicated why the employer was financing the reduction. One referred to 'very significant improvements in flexibility and working practices . . . from committed cooperation of the manufacturing partners. For this reason no additional steps are proposed for funding the reduction'. Another stated that improved working practices had already been bought out. In a third agreement the employer was content with a commitment 'to continue the AEU's current practice of cooperation and assistance'.

We were initially highly sceptical of the agreements whose main method of finance was a general commitment to avoid any increase in costs. They appeared to be exactly the type of agreement which the EEF had refused to accept at a national level. In their publicity material on the dispute the EEF stated: '[P]roductivity deals were not always as effective in practice as they promised on paper. . . . Employers gave but received little in return. . . . We have learned the lesson. . . . Employers are still ready to give. But only in return for specific commitments, not mere statements of good intent.'

FACTORY VISITS

We conducted twelve factory visits, each lasting for up to half a day, and, in the case of the smallest firm, a telephone interview, giving us a total of thirteen cases. In all cases our discussions were confined to managers. Sometimes, we saw a number of managers with different functions and in other cases the factory manager or personnel manager alone. The main purposes of the visits was to go behind the collective agreements, to get the perspectives of management on the process surrounding the shorter working week and to make our subsequent questionnaire a more effective instrument. We did not design the visits to be in any way representative of the engineering industry as a whole. Rather, we wanted to take advantage of any convenient access that was readily given in order to sensitise ourselves both to the complexities of the objective situation and to the subjective viewpoints of management. Perhaps, the best way to report the insights we gained from the visits is to start by summarising the material from six cases, which illustrate the variety of management responses which we found.

Firm 1 One of our companies was a very straightforward example of the shorter working week being fully financed by the employer. This firm had agreed to the whole reduction (from thirty-nine to thirty-seven hours) in one go, and had bargained for nothing in return. We were assured that they had additionally paid something like the going rate in the same negotiation, i.e. that there was no trade-off on wages from the hours concession. The personnel director who had negotiated this deal was no longer with the company, one of several management changes as a result of new ownership following the retirement of its founder. His successor was trying to pick up the pieces but saw little prospect of belatedly capturing some offset; those negotiations were water under the bridge; maybe the recession, which was beginning to bite hard at the time of our visit, would give him an occasion, but he was not optimistic. This was a classical case of profit-margin pressure. The consequences for employment were unclear, particularly in view of a second change in ownership shortly after our visit.

Firm 2 The outcome in a second company was radically different. This company, the UK branch of a US multinational making fairly complex machinery, had what looked to be a sophisticated financial control system. Their approach was to estimate their likely sales over the coming twelve to twenty-four months, gauge the prices they could probably charge for their output, judge what was likely to happen to productivity growth and their non-labour costs and derive how much the company could 'afford' to increase its 'total labour costs'.

In 1990, the year prior to our interview, this procedure had led management to conclude that it could afford an increase of 9.4 per cent to its hourly paid employees. Its practice, we were told, was to tell this to the unions (mostly the AEU but with some GMB representation), give them access to the calculations which underlay it and then invite them to 'review', not to negotiate, the ways in which the increase might be split up. Here, there was a definite trade-off between wage increase and hours reduction. The firm estimated the hours reduction that was then on offer (the first half-hour) to cost 1.4 per cent on the wage bill of the hourly paid workers (the whole two-hour reduction from an initial 38.75 hours was costed at 5.4 per cent of the wage bill). We were told that management was not hostile to the shorter working week as such, it just did not want its introduction to reduce the firm's competitive position from what it would otherwise have been.

The overall 9.4 per cent offer was subject to keen 'review' and resulted in a failure to agree. The unions finally accepted it, and chose a package of 8 per cent on wages plus the equivalent of 1.4 per cent in fewer hours; the manager we interviewed thought that many of the shop-floor workers would have preferred the 9.4 per cent all in cash (we were told that management would have been equally content with an all-cash settlement) but that the shop stewards felt a loyalty to the union and the national campaign and therefore took the hours reduction. The deal was subsequently accepted in a ballot of the workforce by a ratio of 70:30. We were also told that the 9.4 per cent was independent of the hours issue, and that its original size had not been affected by that issue. The management claimed that it had built up the 'credibility' of this procedure and that there had been no budging on the total during a rather difficult 'review process'.

The 1990 negotiations, in fact, produced a two-year deal. The second year had a similar trade-off, with the workforce absorbing 2.1 per cent of their pay increase in the form of a further three-quarters of an hour reduction in the work week. In a subsequent telephone conversation with the same manager we were told that another, qualitatively similar two-year deal was signed in 1992. In this, a further quarter of an hour reduction in the working week was scheduled in each of the two years, with the same terms of trade between hours and pay.

This was the only one of our thirteen cases where management reported that the workers had paid for the whole perceived cost of the hours reduction in the form of lower wage increases. There was no productivity deal specifically tied to these negotiations, so the firm was left with the problem of how to maintain output levels at a time when the standard working week was being reduced. One possibility was increased overtime, but management felt that the determinants of the rate of overtime working were so complex and variable in this firm that they would never be able to identify a shorter working week effect. Historically, the firm had operated on very high levels of overtime, but these, we were told, had been reduced from an average of no less than 36 per cent of the basic working week of manual workers in 1989 to 20 per cent in 1990. The reduction was not due to a fall in the level of production, as the business had been equally successful in both years. Rather, it was made possible by changes in the methods of manufacture, the work becoming more like an assembly line with a 'sequence-build' philosophy. In the context of changes on this scale, management felt that any increase in overtime as a result of the shorter working week would be very hard to detect, even if the level and composition of production themselves were stable, which was by no means likely to be the case.

Firm 3 A third company exemplified the dangers of relying on the single research approach of analysis of collective agreements. This company was a part of a large group that had fairly recently been taken over by an even larger group. It employed more than 650 workers, about half of them manual, in the design and manufacture of engines. The workforce was highly skilled, probably the most skilled in the area. The manual workforce was 100 per cent organised by the AEU. Management judged its relations with the union and the workforce to be generally good.

Hours had been an intense demand during the negotiations at the end of 1989, but management felt that it had resisted successfully. Management's view was that the workers saw the shorter working week as a subtle way of obtaining a pay increase. The negotiations on the shorter working week in this firm were prolonged and said to be unusually difficult. Again, there was a failure to agree and the matter had been referred back for an in-house settlement. In the judgement of our informant, the full-time union officials had given up on hours in this firm. Management was about to indicate that more money would be available if the hours demand was withdrawn when a sister company in the group reached a settlement. In management's words, 'Our ground was taken from us.'

The firm was then instructed by head office to negotiate a working week on terms no less favourable than those of the sister company, that is at no net cost. In effect they had to start their negotiations afresh. One result, we were told, was that the settlement gave a smaller pay increase than it would otherwise have done. The firm's problem was that when they examined the details of the agreement in their sister company, they discovered that the concessions listed there were not applicable in their factory as they reflected already established practice. Yet they were under head office pressure to get a deal that was not worse. The result, we were told, in what seemed a remarkably frank interview, was that the firm's management had to change its tactics: 'Our aim was damage-limitation. We had nothing to claw back.' Effectively they engaged in a charade. As an example, what seemed on paper in the agreement to be a useful concession to management on training, was no such thing because there was nothing in it which the firm could not do already if the issue had been approached correctly. There was possibly some marginal benefit in having a written agreement on this with the union; a few workers might co-operate more because the union had reached agreement. But this was insignificant when compared with the costs of the hours reduction. The agreement contained several provisions based on the sister company's agreement which had absolutely no implications for the factory or the workers employed there.

The one significant concession the management in this firm saw in its negotiations on the reduction in hours was that they secured a wage settlement that was 'perhaps 1 to 2 per cent lower' than it would otherwise have been. This should be compared to the 8 per cent they estimated the hours reduction to cost. That apart, what seemed like a typical example of a detailed and serious list of concessions negotiated by management turned out to be something different. Management's candid view was that 'The written agreement was shop-window-dressing. We did not get anything.'

The experience of firms 2 and 3 underlines the desirability of modifying the usual textbook discussion away from the static focus of wage levels to include the possibility that wage increases are significantly affected by the demand for a shorter working week. When wages are anyway changing by 7–10 per cent a year, this is potentially an important change of focus.

The response in each of these first three firms was not inconsistent with the normal analytical framework used by economists, where firms are assumed to be, in some straightforward sense, in a stable and efficient production equilibrium. Many of our other cases, however, were better analysed in the radically different tradition of the behaviourial theory of the firm.

Firm 4 Our fourth firm was a privately owned company where the chairman had recently retired after many years of running the firm. He was described as a man with the common touch but dictatorial and paternalistic: 'His fingers were on all the pulses'; the company had been 'his train set, as we say . . . .nothing was devolved down through the (management) structure'. This management style was combined with strong convictions on how the factory should be operated. So, there was, for example, no possibility of even discussing the introduction of shift work in place of the firm's traditional reliance on extremely high levels of overtime. There was a general absence of many of the usual elements of management systems and of certain kinds of information, which implied a high degree of management ignorance.

As a consequence of the chairman's retirement, the firm was undergoing a profound management change. The shorter working week issue happened to come along while the revolution from the old regime to the new was about to start. As part of this revolution there was anyway going to be an attempt to introduce a whole series of changes, including changes in working practices. In short the underlying situation was fluid, and was very far from exhibiting the kind of stability and optimality which economists take as their normal starting point.

The firm was also, almost certainly, not on its production frontier. It was probably by no means the worst-off of our firms in this respect, but various long-established practices were deemed by management to be in need of radical change. They were therefore keen to introduce electronic time recording and direct entry of job-booking by workers using computer terminals. This, it was claimed, would enable problem areas to be identified and addressed. It would allow 'wasted time' to be located and subsequently acted upon. Management 'knew' that there was a great deal of lost time, but did not know precisely where. This echoes White's point that much time spent at work is not spent in direct productive activity. He included time spent waiting for materials, but conditions in this firm suggests that there are also many other examples. The firm was basically trying to get information to allow it to make subsequent changes.

The managers also wanted to introduce a shift system, which would substantially spread the very large overheads of the plant and significantly reduce the amount of overtime. Together, this whole package of changes was seen by management as the key to greater plant efficiency.

The managers at this firm, like nearly all the others we spoke to, came to regard a concession on hours as inevitable. None actively welcomed it, though some claimed to see that it fitted well with their long-term goal of harmonisation. But one reaction to its appearance was to secure a deal that would phase the reduction over time. Subsequent difficulties in negotiations resulted in the second two stages being deferred for some months. In the case of this firm, there were to be half-hour reductions in February 1990 and February 1991, and a further one hour in February 1992. The phasing achieved two things. Marginally, it made the present value of the cost increase somewhat less. Much more importantly, it gave managers time to get a range of offsets identified and negotiated. The first phase was accompanied by a statement that the subsequent reductions in hours should not damage the firm's competitive position and that they should be self-financing. This was not an anodyne clause in the agreement. Both sides had entered into a serious agreement and the period between the first and second phases allowed the management the time to do much staff work.

The only immediate offset to the first half-hour reduction in February 1990 had been the introduction of cashless pay. Managers agreed that, although this was a convenience, it had little monetary significance for the firm, and certainly failed to offset the impact of even this instalment of the hours reduction on the firm's costs. But in the intervening period they had developed the package of reforms outlined above and, when we visited them were hard at it in negotiations over its introduction. This, it is important to realise, was all in the context of a firm anyway undergoing profound changes. The shorter working week issue became an occasion for a more considered and more urgent review of a number of practices. In a subsequent letter from the managers of this firm we were told that time and attendance recording for everyone and new shift working arrangements had been secured in the 1991 negotiations, and that the costs of the half-hour reduction in 1991 had been further offset by bell-to-bell working and an agreement to move down the path to multi-skilling. By the end of the 1992 negotiations they were still 'working towards the implementation of computerised job tracking', but had implemented the final one-hour reduction in the working week. The costs of this, we were told, were fully covered by a lower wage offer; the firm settled at a wage increase of only 2.1 per cent increase in the weekly wage plus the reduction of one hour (which was responsible for a further 2.7 per cent increase in hourly earnings). The hour's reduction was brought forward to February, the original date, rather than July as had been agreed the previous year.

Management felt wholly unable to cost the organisational and working practice changes with any precision. Their information systems were simply too primitive. However, they were of the view that they were very likely to pay for the hours reduction by themselves. They made another point. The changes they were seeking would have been introduced anyway, sometime in the future. It might, therefore, seem that all they had secured was a somewhat earlier delivery of something they would have got later. This was *not* the view of these managers. They felt strongly that, had the hours reduction not materialised, they would have had to make some other concession, probably in the form of wages, on the occasion of introducing e.g. direct inputting. If they were right, there was a real case of a wage/hours trade-off, but inter-temporal rather than contemporaneous. This therefore is not simply a case of moving some things planned to come in at some time up the agenda. Rather, it is bringing them forward and paying for them in a different way.

This is perhaps particularly likely when the firm is anyway in a turbulent situation. Our fourth firm was in a very turbulent situation. First, as we have suggested, because the chairman had retired after serving for very many years and management was beginning to consider things that had been permanently off the agenda. Second, because the second stage of the phased agreement was being done at a time when the scale of the recession was beginning to be realised by both management and workers.

This has an implication for the union side. Whether at national or even local level, the unions could not know what they were going to be asked to do in return for shorter hours. The consequences for them of their pressure were therefore unpredictable, even after they had secured agreements on the shorter working week in principle. It seemed to us that the unions in this firm were in a cleft stick; they had got one half-hour for free, had built in the anticipation of another ninety minutes with unspecified strings, and were being disagreeably surprised about the strings. They had a failure to agree on the 1991 negotiations (an unusual event in this firm), and the negotiations were certainly tough, but management felt optimistic both at the time and in retrospect.

In many respects, this firm represented the situation in about half of our case study firms. Most said that they were undergoing more or less profound organisational/work practice changes, and were looking for flexibilities, shift pattern changes, etc. The hours negotiations became the opportunity for filling out their operational agendas to include more of what they could conceive of doing in the future.

Firm 5 This is well illustrated by a fifth company. This company made machinery for the paper industry. It was a major player on the world scale in its area of the market, but was still not very large. On the day of our visit, redundancies were being announced, and the firm would soon be down to employing just over 350 workers, about half of them hourly paid. The proportion of unskilled workers was constantly being reduced.

At the same time as the introduction of the shorter working week the company had been undergoing three major changes: accreditation as a world-class manufacturer (BS 5750), the introduction of Material Resources Planning and total integration within the larger group. Before the claim for reduced hours had been received at the end of 1989, the group had decided to concede a shorter working week, as had an unofficial body composed of personnel managers of EEF firms in the locality. Harmonisation was group policy, but there were no specific plans to introduce it. The feeling was that the reduction would have to be conceded at some time. The firm wanted the reduction to be phased over two years. The agreement provided for half-an-hour immediately, followed by an hour a year later and a final half-hour two years later.

In return for the reduction in hours this firm felt that it had bought a lot of co-operation on new working practices and increased flexibility. As well as securing co-operation on the three organisational changes listed earlier, they had introduced a completely integrated clocking system so that workers clocked on and off all jobs. This was important because there were a whole host of controls which depended on record-keeping by operatives.

The agreement also provided for the extension of three-shift working, which had reduced overtime and lead times, and had finally eliminated crane operators. Workers would henceforth operate the crane when they required it, which could have been done twenty years previously. Other provisions meant that up to ten workers would work on installations on customers' sites around the world and that electricians would receive training in electronics at the EETPU college.

Management claimed that all these changes would have been on the agenda in any event, but would not necessarily have been achieved in the 1990 negotiations, and they would have had to have been paid for in other ways whenever they were introduced. It was hard to specify anything which had been added to the 1990 negotiations because of the hours issue. They already had many of the concessions achieved in other firms. There were no tea-breaks (although workers were able to get refreshments) or washing-up time. They had introduced additional controls on bell-to-bell working, which they already had. The procedures for JIT which had been part of the agreement were being implemented at the time of our visit.

This was an interesting and complex case. Management's view was that 'We bought a lot of cooperation [with the hours]. . . . [We are] satisfied all of these [agreed changes have been] delivered by the unions.' They had made almost no calculations of the effects of the various elements in the package, in part because this was almost never their practice, and in part because the external and internal situations were anyway so volatile as to make such calculations seem beside the point. Management felt that the importance of changes in techniques and organisation 'could not be overstated'. As a result, they said, output per employee would be much higher in the next business upturn. In addition managers told us that the January 1991 wage settlement, at 7.3 per cent, was definitely lower because of the reduction in hours.

Management clearly believed that they had come out of the whole process pretty well, mainly because they had played it long in the negotiations and had combed through all the changes they could possibly add to their agenda. They were not quite ready to agree with the rather provocative question that, in retrospect, they had done so well that they must have pleased at the unions' original initiative on the hours question, but our judgement was that they felt that their competitive position had surely not been harmed by the whole sequence of events.

Firm 6 This aerospace firm was part of a large group. In the past, according to the managers we spoke to, it 'had not been run on business lines. . . . We did not worry too much about the profit side. We were good engineers, good manufacturers. We got to the point where we had to be a business. Otherwise, we would not stand up in the future.' But, there had been major changes over the previous three to four years. A presentation by the managing director to the whole workforce in January 1989 set out the company's views of the future, including a sharp run-down of a number of traditional areas, with significant job implications. Workers, we were told, had their questions answered and had an input into the decision-making process, for example through site meetings. Asking workers for their views on the future involved a real change of management style and, it was said, had had quite an effect on the attitudes of the workforce. In addition, management was seeking to apply concepts such as flexibility, intra-plant mobility and cell working. Shop-floor workers from a pilot project had gone on residential training with supervisors and engineers.

The company was highly unionised with the AEU the predominant union. The site was not perceived by management to have been militant, although there had been disputes in the past. Bargaining was said to be 'relatively responsible'. There had traditionally been considerable trade union control over working. The unions, we were told, would say that this was 'done' or 'not done'. This, we were told, had changed and the shop-floor representatives and the majority of the workers now 'accepted the need for change'. Shop-floor representatives had been to the USA a couple of years previously and had seen that the competition worked differently. Interestingly, the managers we spoke to felt that it had been far more difficult to change management than employee attitudes.

Each year the company thought what it could get back from the annual wage negotiations. Their approach to the thirty-seven-hour week, which with output being maintained through overtime they costed gross at about 8 per cent, had been the same. Their target was to recover this cost.

The agreement consisted of a clear but general enabling agreement plus specific changes in working practices. The latter included increased flexibility and intra-plant mobility. In addition, there were commitments on quality improvement, cellular manufacturing and operator approval of work. Finally, they had secured agreement on a movement towards bell-to-bell working which was expected to yield an average of around fifty more minutes' productive time a week. While these changes had not been costed, managers were confident that they would more than offset the costs of the shorter working week. As one of them said, 'If, through this agreement, we get every member of the group working bell-to-bell and flexible, so that we get away from the situation, which I am afraid we have at the moment, of electricians working overtime in one area while they are sitting twiddling their thumbs in another area, we would more . . . than recoup the two hours we are losing off the working week.' They were also strongly of the view that it would have been very difficult to obtain so many concessions from the union in one agreement without the hours concession. As one of them said, the hours claim eventually led to management getting a 'massive package to allow us to change our business the way we wanted to'. Another said that it 'gave us the opportunity to do it all at once. If we had been dealing purely with wage negotiations, it (the package of concessions) would have been very difficult to achieve.' It was also thought that the enabling agreement opened up possibilities for the future. It would allow management to 'route into things we can achieve over next two years: multi-skilling, sub-contracting, make versus buy analysis.'

Conclusions from the factory visits

These six cases illustrate the variety of reactions to the shorter working week campaign, an event which all saw as an exogenous shock. Few easy generalisations are possible but it is obvious, from what we were told, that the net costs of the experience differed markedly amongst firms, as did the nature of the management response.

Our factory visits supported the possibility suggested by the analysis of the collective agreements that one explanation of the variation in costs and response is the number of workers employed. The smallest of the firms had an agreement which provided that the reduction from thirty-nine to thirty-seven hours would be 'funded by an appropriate increase in productivity', but management was unable to specify any benefit to the company from this. Another of the smaller firms felt that there was nothing they could ask of their workers which they were not already getting. A third small company had secured offsets in three areas. The two most important were a reduction in paid 'non-productive time', which seemed to have been rather more than at the other two smaller factories, and the requirement that a specified level of productivity be achieved before the later stages of the reduction were implemented. The manager we interviewed at this third firm, however, acknowledged that the productivity improvement was no more than would have been expected on the basis of recent performance.

It may be that the management of smaller factories are generally satisfied with their working practices and organisation of production and do not see any major scope for improvement. It is also possible that they have less capacity to look critically at their internal organisation and that they introduce changes with less negotiation.

Apart from factory size, it would be no surprise if the variations in costs and response, were related to the general competence of management, hard though this is to measure. Nor would it be a surprise if they were related to a decline in the degree to which trade unions typically strove to resist changes to working practices or organisation. But, the interviews suggested that they might also depend on the degree of internal and external 'turbulence' of the firm. One hypothesis is that the more the firm's internal working practices and organisational arrangements are anyway under pressure to change, for whatever reason, the more will an external shock like a shorter working week campaign be used as the occasion to secure workforce agreement to the changes. These, in turn, will absorb some, or all, or even more than all of the costs of the shock. Where simultaneously there are external pressures, this process might be even greater. It is to these and related questions that our questionnaire material was directed.

THE QUESTIONNAIRE SURVEY

Our survey was sent out at the end of August 1991 to a random sample of 184 establishments listed by the CSEU as having agreed between November 1989 and March 1991 to a reduction of the working week. After a reminder sent in October, a total of 102 completed questionnaires were returned, a response rate of 55 per cent. Appendix 10.1 shows the answers to the questionnaire in detail.[19]

The main purposes of the questionnaire were to establish the perceived costs of the reduction in hours, including the value of any offsets that had been negotiated, as well as to identify some of the circumstances which were associated with high or low net costs. We also wished to learn something about how managers saw the episode.

Management estimates of the gross costs of the shorter working week

All but thirteen of our respondents claimed to have made an estimate of the effect a full reduction to thirty-seven hours per week would have on the total labour costs of the establishment's hourly paid labour force. This is a surprisingly high number in the light of our interviews, and it is possible that some of our respondents made their first explicit calculations only when they received our questionnaire. Some 56 per cent put the labour cost increase at between 4 and 6 per cent; the simple mean value was 5.1 per cent, whilst the mean value weighted by employment size was 5.6 per cent.[20] For most respondents this estimate probably reflects the very straightforward calculation of (39 − 37)/37 = 5.4 per cent.[21] In practice, as is discussed above in the first main section of this chapter, the true figure could well be greater than this but the extent of the difference depends very much on circumstances.

Management estimates of the cost increase varied amongst firms. There was, for example, an industry effect, with 'other transport equipment' (mostly aerospace and shipbuilding) producing higher average estimates than 'electronic and electrical engineering' (5.8 per cent versus 4.7 per cent). More interesting was the association between the estimated costs and the degree of internal or external stability or turbulence facing the firm (as measured by the six questions in part one of the questionnaire). The general result here was a little unexpected in that greater turbulence was associated with higher perceived costs. This was true for plants where working practices were said to be anyway undergoing change (an average increase of 5.8 per cent in plants with substantial change versus 4.8 per cent in those likely to be unchanged, with the difference being significant at the 2 per cent level), for plants where the organisation of production was anyway undergoing change (5.7 per cent for plants with substantial organisational change versus 4.9 per cent for plants likely to experience no change, with the difference being significant at the 6 per cent level), and for plants where the product range was changing (5.9 per cent for plants with substantial product range change versus 4.9 per cent for those with none, significant at the 5 per cent level). There was a similar connection between the estimate of the increase in costs and the degree to which external competitive pressures were perceived to be increasing (5.5 per cent in plants where competitive pressures were becoming much fiercer versus 4.8 per cent elsewhere, with the difference significant at the 4 per cent level). There was, however, no such pattern by the state of the order book.

Management estimates of concessions secured

The above estimates refer only to gross costs, and make no allowance for the value of any concessions negotiated in response to the shorter working week. All but ten of our respondents said that they had obtained such concessions.

The reduction of working time paid for but not previously worked was the most common concession, followed by direct entry job-booking and electronic time-keeping, and a residual category 'other', which included such things as the introduction of cashless pay, annualised hours schemes, operator inspection, total quality management, the introduction of team working, relocation and specific productivity commitments.

There was a clear link between the perceived difficulty of the hours reduction negotiations and the number of concessions eventually obtained. The nineteen factories whose negotiations were seen to be 'much more difficult' than regular wage negotiations finally obtained an average of 4.2 concessions; this compares with an average of 3.3 for the twenty-seven who reported negotiations a 'little more difficult', 2.6 for the forty-two where they were 'about the same', and 2.0 for the twelve with 'less difficulty'. This, perhaps, implies that managers have been generally successful in securing many of the concessions they were seeking. If managers had not secured concessions in proportion to their ambitions, there would be no reason to expect a link between the difficulty of negotiations and the number of concessions.

Managers who estimated the move to a thirty-seven-hour week to involve rather high gross costs also tended to secure more concessions. The 22 per cent whose estimate was over 6 per cent obtained more than four concessions on average, while the 22 per cent whose cost estimate was no more than 4 per cent averaged fewer than three concessions. Those who thought the hours reduction was more costly also reported that their concessions absorbed a higher percentage of the gross costs.

Managers reported that not all the concessions had been achieved in practice. Only 15 per cent reported that they had yet been achieved in their entirety, although another 70 per cent said they had been largely achieved. Assessing why the agreed concessions had not been fully realised in practice was difficult. Only thirty-three, 42 per cent of those who reported that the concessions had not been entirely achieved, gave a reason. One manager commented that it was a good question! The most common reasons were that there had not yet been sufficient time for full implementation and that concessions were difficult to enforce effectively. There were also some complaints of lack of co-operation from unions or workers, but rather more managers attributed the failure to management deficiencies.

Concessions were connected with phasing-in. Sixty-five per cent of our respondents reported that the hours reduction was spread over more than one year. The two major reasons for this were reported to be, first, to defer the costs somewhat and, secondly, to ensure that the agreed concessions were achieved. Other important reasons were (a) to provide the time to identify and plan promising concessions, and (b) advice from employers' associations or head office to phase the reduction.

Management estimates of the net costs of the shorter working week

There were very substantial variations amongst our respondents in the extent to which the value of the concessions was thought to have offset the gross costs of the shorter working week. On average, and taking no account of the size of the firm, concessions were thought by managers to have offset just over half the gross costs. Taking into account those who reported no concessions, the offsets are seen to have defrayed just under half the gross costs for the sample as a whole. On managers' own judgement, therefore, the shorter working week directly added around 2.5 per cent to the labour costs of their hourly paid labour.

The value of the offsets was related to circumstances. In particular, offsets were said to be greater where some of our measures of turbulence had high values. An analysis of variance showed that reported offsets were high where, quite apart from the shorter working week issue, there were substantial changes planned for working practices (significant at the 1 per cent level) and for the organisation of production (significant at the 2 per cent level). Managers also reported relatively large offsets in plants where union resistance to changes in working practices and organisational arrangements was thought to have generally diminished over recent years (significant at the 1 per cent level). Finally, the value of the offsets increased with plant size (significant at the 5 per cent level).

We sought to investigate the determinants of the offsets in a somewhat more sophisticated fashion through regression analysis. Table 10.2 shows some results. Our dependent variables were 'concessions' (equal to the percentage of the gross costs which managers thought their companies would face after taking account of all the negotiated concessions), 'net cost' (equal to gross costs minus the value of the concessions) and 'final cost' ('net cost' minus the estimated reduction, if any, in the next year's wage settlement). We defined 'concessions' in this way so that negative coefficients on the explanatory variables in all three columns represented a reduction in costs.

In all cases our estimates used interval mid-points and 'reasonable' values for the open-ended categories. We experimented with a variety of measures for the explanatory variables. This, together with the precise definition of the variables in Table 10.2, is discussed in more detail in Appendix 10.2. Our intention here was to investigate the hypotheses suggested by the case study material, in particular, that the value of concessions were positively connected with the degree of turbulence experienced by the firm, and with a general decline in trade union resistance.

Table 10.2 shows support for both these propositions. First, firms with a high value on our combined index of internal and external

Table 10.2 Determinants of the value of concessions, and of net and final costs from the shorter working week

	(i) *Concessions*	*(ii)* *Net costs*	*(iii)* *Final costs*
Index of internal and external turbulence	−0.28***	−1.19**	−1.06**
	(−3.34)	(−2.49)	(−2.09)
Index of lower resistance to change from unions	−0.27***	−1.24***	−1.23**
	(−3.42)	(−2.78)	(−2.62)
Firm size	−0.14*	−0.90**	−0.84*
	(−1.82)	(−2.06)	(−1.83)
Constant	0.73***	3.63***	3.11***
	(10.66)	(9.22)	(7.49)
Adjusted R^2	0.30	0.22	0.18
F statistic	12.20***	8.55***	6.80***

Source: Questionnaire material

Notes
1 Figures in brackets are *t*-statistics:
* significant at 10 per cent level.
** significant at 5 per cent level.
*** significant at 1 per cent level.

turbulence claimed to be getting more substantial concessions from their workforce in return for the reduction in working hours. This in turn was seen to have lowered the net costs of the hours reduction. Second, the value of concessions again tended to be high, and net costs low, where management felt that trade union attitudes to change had generally become less resistant in recent years. Finally, concessions were more valuable, and net costs lower, in larger firms.

What about the size of these effects? The coefficients in the second column of Table 10.2 suggest that for firms which were not especially turbulent, which had not seen their unions becoming less resistant to change and which had fewer than 250 workers, the net costs of the shorter working week averaged 3.6 per cent of the wage bill of hourly paid labour. The corresponding figure for larger firms with significant turbulence and less resistant unions, however, was as little as 0.3 per cent.[22] But, that is not the end of the story.

One of the reported concessions (in eighteen firms) was a trade-off against the wage settlement accompanying the initial shorter working week agreement. In addition, twenty-six of our respondents felt that the reduction in hours caused the wage settlement in the subsequent year's negotiations to be reduced below what it would otherwise have been, confirming a finding from some of our factory visits. There is obviously a highly conjectural element in the responses to this question, but, averaged over the whole sample, the size of the reported wage trade-off in the subsequent settlements amounts to around 0.5 per cent of the costs of hourly paid labour. Taking this influence into account, the coefficients in the third column of Table 10.2 imply that the 'final' costs of the whole shorter working week episode were *negative* for at least one group of our respondents! For the average larger firm experiencing significant turbulence and less resistant unions, our findings suggest that unit labour costs actually fell as a result of the shorter working week negotiations. For all the firms in our sample taken together, the average final cost of the shorter working week was between 1.5 and 2 per cent of the wage bill of hourly paid labour; when the final cost is weighted by employment size, the average falls to under 1 per cent.[23]

These estimates are not strongly at variance with the responses to the qualitative question on competitiveness at the start of part 3 of our questionnaire. Twenty-three per cent of our respondents felt that their firm's competitive position had been either marginally or significantly improved by the whole episode, as opposed to 31 per cent who felt that their competitive position had been worsened. The above conclusions on the wage bill might suggest that more should have perceived a fall in competitiveness, but two additional factors should be stressed. First, the wage bill calculations refer only to the labour costs of the hourly paid. These are often a surprisingly small percentage of total costs. A 2 per cent increase in an item that comprises only 10–15 per cent of total costs might not be very significant to management, especially in a world that is extremely changeable for other reasons. Second, the fact that many firms have negotiated a reduction in hours means that at least some of the domestic competitors of any single firm experienced the same pressures, leaving the competitive position of each much less affected.

Another cross-check on the costs of the shorter working week is given in the answers to our 'hypothetical' question at the end of part 3 of the questionnaire. This suggests that, in a stable business environment, a substantial majority of firms would respond to an hour's reduction by increasing overtime working, and that a significant minority would respond by taking on more workers. Clearly, both actions imply that a reduction in the working week would raise costs and lower competitiveness. In both cases, however, it was suggested that these responses would be used to only a small degree. By far the major response – 80 per cent say they would resort to it 'a lot' – would be an attempt to raise efficiency. This too suggests substantial offsets.

A final issue is whether the concessions obtained would have been introduced anyway, either at the same time or at a later date. Thirteen per cent claimed that the concessions would have been introduced at the same time without the hours issue. Nearly 60 per cent said that the concessions were in their plans anyway but the hours question meant that they had been agreed earlier. On the other hand, more than 60 per cent of our respondents thought that they would have had to raise the wage settlement in order to get these concessions agreed to. So, instead of the concessions causing wages to go up in the future, they seem to have been 'paid for' by a reduction in hours in the present. Averaged over the whole sample, our managers felt that the concessions would have required wage increases of maybe 1–1.5 per cent. If so, this would have been a somewhat cheaper way of paying for the concessions than agreeing to the shorter working week.[24]

CONCLUSIONS

It was not our principal purpose in this project to determine the winners and losers in the shorter working week campaign of 1989–91. As a former chairman of the TUC observed, 'Victories are for boys who play at games',[25] and what constitutes victory or loss in industrial disputes is always exceedingly hard to establish. The popular perception, perhaps, is that the 1989–91 shorter working week campaign was a major success for the engineering unions, at least in 'political' terms. After a number of painful years when trade unions were generally seen to be very much on the defensive, the shorter working week campaign seemed to show that they could still mobilise their members effectively, deploy the strike weapon successfully and secure their stated objective in a large number of firms. The Annual Review Article in the *British Journal of Industrial Relations* referred to 'a quite unexpected degree of union resilience' (Terry 1991). On a more specific point of tactics, selective indefinite strikes, here stimulated by the 1984 legislation, were seen as a very promising trade union weapon, as effective as the limited national strikes in support of reduced hours at the end of the 1970s.

Seen in an 'industrial' or historical context, however, the unions' success is, perhaps, less impressive. First, the employers had already conceded the principle of a thirty-seven and a half hour week by 1987. Eighty per cent of engineering managers interviewed by White in 1982 expected further reductions in the working week within five years. Second, our factory visits and survey strongly suggest that employers substantially achieved their objective on one of the major issues which led to the breakdown of national negotiations, the 'essential principle' that agreement on cost offsets and the maintenance of output should precede any reduction in working time. Finally, as Industrial Relations Services (IRS 1990: 10) commented, 'Some union members may wonder if the hours cuts are worth the greatly increased productivity being contributed by them to their employers'. This is a curious statement, one that could perhaps be made only in the UK, but the proper response to it probably turns on the nature of the concessions made in return for the shorter working week.

The international competitiveness of our engineering industry is too important to be put at risk by the outmoded assumption that collective bargaining is a zero-sum game. In some cases improved productivity may still be achieved by increased effort from workers, but more generally it comes from changes in organisation and working practices such as JIT, TQM and multi-skilling, many of which involve less repetitive work. Unions have a continuing role as partners in change, which now requires a higher level of workforce co-operation to be fully effective. Without agreement, effective change is almost certainly less likely. From our evidence, the shorter working week campaign resulted in more agreement on change. Seventy-eight per cent of our respondents said the campaign had resulted in either earlier change or in changes which would not otherwise have been considered.

It is not clear whether the 1989–91 campaign had quantitatively different effects from earlier episodes. White could find little positive effect on either employment or overtime levels as a result of the 1981 reduction, but believed that he had found a large productivity effect. The negotiating stance of the EEF during the 1980s, perhaps, suggests that he exaggerated the extent of this effect. Certainly, some of the EEF member firms seem to have felt that full productivity offsets had not been realised in 1981 and that, as a consequence, the costs of moving to the thirty-nine hour week had not been zero. Nevertheless, White's findings look broadly correct and it is easier to point to productivity growth than to employment and overtime growth as a result of the 1979–81 campaign.

Would the same be true for 1989–91, particularly in light of the debates on the 'new industrial relations' and the 'productivity miracle' of the 1980s? Qualitatively, we found that it was. Our initial response, bearing in mind the rather grim reputation which UK manufacturing acquired in the 1960s and 1970s for written productivity agreements, was to be highly sceptical of agreements that had very general statements about maintaining competitiveness or containing costs and no indication of how the offsets were to be achieved. But we were wrong. In many cases they were evidently enabling agreements which were subsequently the basis for hard negotiations on productivity. Given the recession, few of those we contacted were thinking in terms of increases in employment or overtime, but most were looking for productivity enhancement. Our own interpretation is that, however new and miraculous the 1980s were, a great deal of organisational slack and inefficiency remained in the UK engineering industry by the end of the decade. The shorter working week campaign was an occasion for a further assault on it.

Our best estimate of the final cost to the engineering industry of the thirty-seven hour week is that it raised the direct labour costs of manual workers by less than 1 per cent. This may be an underestimate, because we are likely to have obtained a lower response to our questionnaire from smaller factories, where costs seem generally to have been higher. Also, factories with stronger unions, the ones targeted by the CSEU, may have had more potential to offset the increased costs than factories which had not agreed a thirty-seven hour week by April 1991. If so, the cost to the whole industry cannot be accurately assessed on the basis of the experience of the factories where hours were reduced early on. Among this latter group, however, there was a significant minority where managers felt that the value of the concessions they secured at least equalled the cost of the reduced working week. For these firms at least surrender to the demands of the CSEU involved no sacrifice of competitiveness.

APPENDIX 10.1 COMPETITIVENESS AND SHORTER WORKING WEEK SURVEY

Part 1

	Per cent (Number)
1 The working practices of hourly paid labour in the establishment were anyway:	
about to undergo substantial change	25
about to undergo minor change	39
likely to remain unchanged	36
	(102)
2 The organisation of production in the establishment (e.g. the introduction of JIT or TQM), as it affected hourly paid labour, was:	
about to undergo substantial change	30
about to undergo minor change	37
likely to remain unchanged	34
	(98)

	Per cent (Number)
3 The establishment's product range was:	
about to undergo substantial change	12
about to undergo minor change	40
likely to remain unchanged	48
	(102)
4 Investments in new technology which were planned for the near future, and which affected hourly paid labour, were:	
substantial	38
fairly minor	44
virtually non-existent	18
	(102)
5 The establishment's order book was:	
much healthier than normal	5
healthier than normal	19
normal	38
weaker than normal	27
much weaker than normal	12
	(101)
6 Competitive pressures from other companies were:	
becoming a lot fiercer	40
becoming a little fiercer	30
normal	27
becoming a little easier	2
becoming much easier	0
	(102)

Part 2

1 What was the standard working week for the majority of your hourly paid employees *before* you signed the agreement?	
more than 39 hours	11
39 hours	75
38.5 hours	1
38 hours	8
37.5 hours	4
37 hours	1
	(101)

		Per cent (Number)
2 Was the reduction in hours spread over more than one year?		
	yes	65
	no	35
		(102)
3 If yes, why did you want to spread the reduction in this way?		(56)
4 How did the negotiations over the shorter working week compare with regular wage negotiations?		
	Much more difficult	19
	A little more difficult	27
	About the same	42
	A little less difficult	7
	A lot less difficult	5
		(100)
5 Did you calculate how much the full reduction to thirty-seven hours would, *in the absence of any offsets you might negotiate,* increase the total labour costs of your establishment's hourly paid labour force?		
	yes	89
	no	11
		(102)
6 If yes, what was the estimated increase in labour costs?		
	4% or less	22
	4.1% to 6%	56
	6.1% to 8%	18
	more than 8%	4
		(91)
7 Did you obtain *any* concessions from your workforce in return for the agreed reduction in hours?		
	yes, in the initial agreement	85
	yes, but subsequent to the initial agreement	3
	no	10
	both in initial agreement and subsequently	2
		(102)

(if no, please go on to part 3; if yes, please go on to the next question)

8 What were these concessions?		
a) reduction of paid time which was not previously worked (e.g. bell-to-bell working, reduction of tea breaks)		78

	Per cent (Number)
b) additional multi-skilling	34
c) manning reductions	13
d) new shift patterns	26
e) additional flexibility in deployment between departments	47
f) direct entry job-booking and electronic time keeping	22
g) generalised commitment to productivity improvements	65
h) a concession on the negotiated increase in pay	18
i) other – please write in	30
	(92)

9 Did you calculate, even roughly, how much these concessions would offset the cost of the reduction in hours?

Yes	89
No	11
	(93)

10 If yes, what percentage of the cost increase did you expect these concessions in total to offset?

less than 25%	25
25 to 49%	12
50 to 74%	22
75 to 99%	23
100% or more	18
	(83)

11 Which of the following best describes how the shorter working week issue affected the time when these concessions were introduced?

a) Not at all; the concessions were already on your agenda and would have been introduced at the same time anyway.	13
b) They were in your future plans but the hours issue meant that you got agreement on them earlier.	57
c) They were not on your agenda but were developed in response to the hours issue.	30
	(91)

12 If the shorter working week had not been an issue, what effect would these concessions have had on the level of the wage settlement?

none at all	38
2% or less	38
2.1% to 4%	14
more than 4%	10
	(90)

	Per cent (Number)

Part 3

1 On balance, how has the reduction in hours, together with any concessions you negotiated, affected your establishment's overall competitive position?

competitive position significantly improved	7
competitive position marginally improved	16
competitive position unchanged	46
competitive position marginally reduced	29
competitive position significantly reduced	2
	(100)

2 In your judgement, has the reduction in hours caused the wage settlement in *this* year's pay negotiations to be lower than it would otherwise have been?

yes	26
no	74
	(99)

3 If yes, by how much was the settlement reduced by this factor?

1.5% or less	38
1.6% to 3%	54
more than 3%	8
	(26)

4 If your agreement contained concessions to help pay the cost of the hours reduction to what extent have the concessions been achieved in practice?

not achieved at all	2
largely not achieved	13
largely achieved	70
entirely achieved	15
	(93)

5 If not entirely achieved, why not? (33)

6 Now, a very important but hypothetical question. Logically, a reduction in the standard working week must by itself lead to a fall in an establishment's output unless more workers are taken on, overtime working increases, or efficiency goes up.

		Per cent (Number)
On the assumption that the market demand for your products was normal, how important would each of the following possible responses to the shorter working week have been? Specifically, how much emphasis would you have placed on:		
i) taking on more workers		
	a lot	7
	a little	27
	none at all	66
		(97)
ii) increasing overtime working		
	a lot	15
	a little	59
	none at all	26
		(101)
iii) raising efficiency		
	a lot	89
	a little	13
	none at all	7
		(102)
iv) allowing output to fall		
	a lot	12
	a little	11
	none at all	76
		(97)

Part 4

1 Is your production *predominantly*:		
	mass production	6
	medium-sized batch production	27
	small-sized batch production	50
	one-off production	17
2 Which of the following industries best describes your establishment's activities?		
	Metal goods not elsewhere specified (hand tools, finished metal goods, etc.)	23
	Mechanical engineering	34

	Per cent (Number)
Office machinery, data processing equipment	0
Electrical and electronic engineering	13
Motor vehicles and parts	11
Other transport equipment (aerospace, ships, etc.)	14
Instrument engineering	1
Other (please specify)	4
	(93)

3 How many hourly paid people work at your establishment?

Fewer than 25	3
Between 25 and 99	31
Between 100 and 249	24
Between 250 and 499	9
Between 500 and 999	9
1,000 or more	9
	(100)

4 Union attitudes to changes in either working practices or the organisation of production differ substantially. Which of the following labels best describes the attitudes to change traditionally shown by the trade unions in your establishment?

highly resistant	11
resistant	22
cautious	41
amenable	20
very amenable	7
	(101)

5 In recent years, have these attitudes to change in your establishment generally become:

much more resistant	1
somewhat more resistant	8
neither more nor less resistant	27
less resistant	41
much less resistant	23
	(102)

APPENDIX 10.2: VARIABLES USED IN THE ANALYSIS OF THE ENGINEERING SURVEY

Dependent variables

Concessions

Question 7 of Part 2, which asked whether concessions had been negotiated, and question 10 of Part 2, which asked what percentage of the cost increase the negotiated concessions were expected to offset, were used to determine CONCESSIONS. The values given are as follows:

Percentage of costs offset	*Value of CONCESSIONS*
No concessions	0
Less than 25 per cent	0.125
25 to 49 per cent	0.375
50 to 74 per cent	0.625
75 to 99 per cent	0.875
100 per cent or more	1.125

Net cost

NET COST was calculated from CONCESSIONS and the answer to question 6 of Part 2, the estimated increase in labour costs of hourly paid workers of a thirty-seven hour week in the absence of any offsets. A numerical value was given to the answers to question 6, as shown below, and this value was multiplied by the difference between one and CONCESSIONS.

Estimated increase	*Numerical value*
4 per cent or less	3 per cent
4.1 to 6 per cent	5 per cent
6.1 to 8 per cent	7 per cent
More than 8 per cent	8.5 per cent

Independent variables

The independent variables used in the analysis were always dummy variables. This was to avoid giving numerical variables to essentially qualitative answers, which would have made interpretation of the results difficult. There would also have been a serious statistical problem of measurement errors in independent variables caused by assigning the same value to all answers in each interval.

Part 1 variables

Preliminary analysis showed that the answers to questions 3 to 5 added very little additional explanatory power to that provided by questions 1, 2 and 6. Factor analysis suggested that there was no strong statistical reason to give the answers different weights.

Four dummy variables were created from answers to questions 1, 2 and 6. Each answer was recoded so that one represented minimum change or least increase in competitive pressure and three the maximum change or greatest increase in competitive pressure. The three categories in question 6, normal, becoming a little easier and becoming much easier (which was an empty cell), were all coded together so that the new variable received the same weight as the answers to questions 1 and 2.

The answers to questions 1 and 2 were added together to give a variable running from 2, least change, to 6. Values of 5 and 6 were classified as significant change. Dummy variables, MUCH FIERCER COMPETITION AND SIGNIFICANT CHANGE and FIERCER COMPETITION AND SIGNIFICANT CHANGE, were created combining significant change with the answers to question 6. Fiercer competition combines two answers to question 6, competitive pressure becoming a little fiercer and becoming a lot fiercer. Much fiercer competition represents just the answer, a lot fiercer. A value of one represents a combination of (much) fiercer competition and significant change and a value of zero the absence of either (much) fiercer competition or significant change or both.

Two more dummy variables were constructed from a composite variable created by the addition of the recoded answers to questions 1, 2 and 6. This composite variable runs from 3 to 9 reflecting the combination of the answers to questions 1, 2 and 6 with equal weights. VERY MUCH COMPETITION AND CHANGE has the value 1 when the composite variable is 8 or 9 and zero otherwise. MUCH COMPETITION AND CHANGE has the value one when the composite variable is 7, 8 or 9.

Part 4 variables

LESS RESISTANT is a dummy variable constructed from the answer to question 5 of Part 4. It takes the value one where union attitudes to change have become much less resistant or less resistant and zero for other answers.

Four size dummy variables were used. SMALL takes the value one for employment below 100; LARGE for employment of 500 or more;

LARGE/MEDIUM for employment of 250 or more; and LARGEST for employment of 1,000 or more.

Indices used in regressions in Table 10.2

The Index of Internal and External Turbulence corresponds to FIERCER COMPETITION AND EXTERNAL TURBULENCE, the Index of Lower Resistance to Change from Unions to LESS RESISTANT and Firm Size to LARGE/MEDIUM. The indices used were selected according to the significance of their coefficients.

Weighting by size

Industry and size were used to estimate the average manual employment of respondents. The three factories in the smallest size group, under 25, were arbitrarily assumed to have 20 manual employees. Average employment for each other size group by industry was calculated from the Summary Report on the Census of Production 1989, PA1002. The calculation assumes that the average manual employment in each size category of manual workers is identical to the average employment of manual and non-manual workers shown in the Report for the corresponding category of manual and non-manual workers.

For plants employing below 500 workers the variation in average employment was very small. In the size category 300 to 499 the average for industries represented among the respondents ranged from 377 to 400. Accordingly, average employment weighted by industrial distribution within the size category was used for each plant employing below 500 manual workers. The size category of 25 to 99 manual workers did not correspond to the Census categories. The Census category of 20 to 49 workers was heavily weighted to plants with less than 25 workers. Accordingly, the size category 50 to 99 was used to estimate employment in respondents with between 25 and 99 manual workers. The Census category 200 to 299 straddled two categories among the respondents. It was assigned to the 100 to 249 category. As a result average employment in this category and in the category 250 to 499 is probably overestimated.

The estimated average figures for employment are:

Under 25		20 (This is an arbitrary figure.)
25 to 99		69
100 to 249		170
250 to 499		385
500 to 999	Metal goods	609
	Mechanical eng.	686
	Office equipment	693
	Other transport	705
	Not specified/other	680
1,000 or more	Mechanical eng.	1,633
	Office equipment	2,318
	Motor vehicles	4,821
	Other transport	4,817

Number of responses used

Responses in which no estimate was made of the increase in labour costs in the absence of any offsets were excluded from the analysis, as were those for which concessions were reported without any estimate of their value.

NOTES

We are grateful for helpful comments from John Kelly, Stephen Wood and participants at CEP Industrial Relations Group and British University Industrial Relations Association Conferences. We should also like to record our appreciation of practical assistance from the AEU, CSEU and EEF. Tony de Launay not only assisted us with access to a number of factories, but was also the discussant when the paper was presented to the Industrial Relations Group Conference.

1 *Financial Times*, 28 June 1986.
2 The number of strikes is rather misleading. Disputes with a common cause are treated as a single strike. Thus, the five initial strikes are counted as one.
3 These figures may be somewhat exaggerated. They suggest that on average the thirteen days of official action were supported by 1,250,000 workers. The EEF put the number of strikers during the final two-day strike at 750,000, while claiming no more than a slow drift back to work (Meredeen 1988).
4 For example, someone who was initially working five hours of overtime and subsequently worked seven would have an increase in weekly earnings of 7.7 per cent; someone who went from no overtime to two hours would have an 8.1 per cent increase in weekly earnings.
5 Unit costs may also depend on the scale of output. So, if output is affected by the shorter week, there may be additional implications.
6 The more detailed analysis by Neale and Wilson (1985), however, suggests that in the long-run actual hours follow standard hours more closely.

7 All the quotations in the paragraph are from Allen (1980: 7).
8 Allen (1980: 15).
9 Allen (1980: 11).
10 For a recent discussion of the employment effects of working time reductions in West Germany in the 1980s see the exchange between Seifert (1991) and Neifer-Dichmann (1991).
11 White (1987: 16).
12 ibid., chapter 3.
13 The evidence is strongest for continuous or highly repetitive tasks such as visual inspection and machine minding (Colquhoun 1978: 684),
14 The importance of the process of negotiation and/or implementation has been noted by a number of authors (for example, Denison 1967: 60). Such process effects seem unlikely to persist in the long-term (Owen 1989: 103–4).
15 White (1987: 50).
16 White (1980: 79–80).
17 White (1981: 76).
18 Our research raises serious doubts about the widespread assumption that the basic weekly wage is not reduced as a consequence of shorter hours. The assumption might be reasonable if weekly wages were static, but wages are generally increased annually. The negotiated wage increase is probably reduced as partial compensation for the reduction in hours. Shorter hours may also lead to wage increases in the future which are lower than they would otherwise have been. The state of the economy may affect how much of the cost of shorter hours is offset in this way. For some evidence on these points see the sections entitled 'Factory visits' and 'The questionnaire survey'.
19 A comparison of the responses with the whole sample gave no sign of response bias in terms of region, employers' association membership, ownership or date of agreement.
20 These calculations require point estimates from grouped responses. For wage increases we used mid-points for the closed intervals, 3 per cent for the lower of the open-ended intervals and 8.5 per cent for the higher. For employment size, see Appendix 10.2.
21 Only seventy-five of our respondents started with a thirty-nine-hour standard working week for the majority of their hourly paid employees. The arithmetic on this point for the other firms would therefore be somewhat different from that in the text.
22 These figures are subject to high standard errors and do not take account of interaction between the independent variables. Some interaction terms were significant, but did not improve the fit of the regression as measured by its R^2. The regression coefficients are not unduly influenced by extreme values. The exclusion of extreme values of 'net cost' from a regression produced very similar coefficients. The average value of 'net cost' for the fifteen firms in the smaller size, the less turbulent and not less resistant categories was 4.1 per cent and for the twelve firms with opposite characteristics 0.1 per cent. So, the regression results do not accentuate the observed differences between the two cells.
23 This is again supported by the observed values, which ranged from -0.2 per cent for the firms of larger size, with turbulence and less resistant unions, to 3.5 per cent for those with the opposite attributes.
24 The impact of this final qualification on the net costs of the shorter working week is quite tricky to calculate. Basically, we should strip out the value of

any concessions that would have been achieved anyway. The net costs could then be calculated from (a) the gross costs, (b) any reduction in present or future wage settlements stemming from the shorter working week, (c) the value of any concessions achieved but which would not have been achieved anyway, and (d) the wage costs that would have been necessary to secure the concessions that would have ben achieved anyway. On the estimates of our managers, this would produce a figure of perhaps 2–2.5 per cent of the wage costs of direct labour for the sample as a whole.

25 TUC, Congress Report, 1969.

REFERENCES

Allen, R. (1980) *The Economic Effects of the Shorter Working Week*, Government Economic Service Working Paper No. 33, Treasury Working Paper No. 14, June.

Colquhoun, P. (1978) 'Working efficiency, personality and body rhythms', *Employment Gazette*, June.

Denison, E. (1967) *Why Growth Rates Differ*, Washington: Brookings Institution.

Industrial Relations Services (1990) *Employment Trends*, 464, (22) May.

Meredeen, S. (1988) *Managing Industrial Conflict*, London: Hutchinson.

Neale, A. and R. Wilson (1985) 'Average weekly hours of work in the United Kingdom 1948–80: a disaggregated analysis', in R. Wilson (ed.) *Hours of Work*, University of Warwick: Institute for Employment Research.

Neifer-Dichmann, E. (1991) 'Working time reductions in the former Federal Republic of Germany: A dead end for employment policy', *International Labour Review*, 130, (4): 511–22.

Owen, J. (1989) *Reduced Working Hours*, Baltimore: Johns Hopkins University Press.

Seifert, H. (1991) 'Employment effects of working time reductions in the former Federal Republic of Germany', *International Labour Review*, 130, (4): 495–510.

Terry, M. (1991) 'Annual Review Article 1990', *British Journal of Industrial Relations*, 29, (1): 97–112.

White, M. (1980) *Shorter Working Time*, London: Policy Studies Institute.

—— (1981) *Case Studies of Shorter Working Time*, London: Policy Studies Institute.

—— (1982) *Shorter Hours through National Industry Agreements*, Research Paper No. 38, Department of Employment.

—— (1983) 'Shorter Hours through National Agreements', *Employment Gazette*, October.

—— (1987) *Working Hours: assessing the potential for reduction*, Geneva: ILO.

White, M. and A. Ghobadian (1984) *Shorter Working Hours in Practice*, London: Policy Studies Institute.

11 Appendix

A century of UK strike activity: an alternative perspective

Simon Milner and David Metcalf

THE DATA

Conventionally the strike activity time series (stoppages, workers involved and days lost) have been reported as a proportion of employees in employment in order to compare the intensity of industrial action over time and among industrial sectors. An alternative, possibly superior, measure of strike activity is presented here. The various series are described 'per union member' to provide a contrast with the 'per employee' basis. We have also calculated the time series for the average stoppage duration, a measure of strike activity which few people have looked at. The data are presented in Tables 11.1 to 11.4 and Figures 11.1 to 11.5.

Although non-union workers may take industrial action occasionally, it is very unlikely that non-union strikes comprise anything like a significant minority of the whole. Knowles (1954) stated that 'it is the organised rather than the unorganised who strike' in his study of stoppages over the period 1911 to 1947, although he did not actually provide data on non-union strikes or strikers. However, statistics were provided in a study of strikes over the period 1966 to 1973, which showed that on average only 3 per cent of stoppages did not involve any trade union members, and only 1.4 per cent of all working days lost resulted from these non-union stoppages (Smith *et al.* 1978: Tables G, H and Q). Further, this study reported that over the decade from 1966, stoppages over union recognition (which might be expected to include both non-unionists and union members) comprised only 1.1 per cent of all stoppages. More recently the Workplace Industrial Relations Surveys reported that in 1980 and 1984, the incidence of strikes in workplaces with no union members was statistically negligible (Daniel and Millward 1983: Table 9.5, Millward and Stevens 1986: Table 10.3). This does not preclude instances of non-union workers striking alongside their unionised colleagues from the same plant, which is less than 100 per cent unionised, but nevertheless suggests that the overwhelming majority of strikers are trade union members. Our primary intention is to report the data, but some notes concerning particularly interesting aspects of the time series seem pertinent.

The dominance of coal

It is worth restating the dominance of coal mining, wholly disproportionate to its employment size, in the industrial action figures. Between 1926, the year of the general strike, and the early 1960s stoppages in coal mining make up on average one half of the total number of stoppages; and coal accounts for 32 per cent of stoppages throughout the complete period 1893–1991 (see Figure 11.1).

In terms of days lost, coal mining also predominates in the peak years from 1893 to 1929 (peak years include 1893, 1911–13, 1919–21 and 1926) and in 1972, 1974 and 1984. The only days lost peak in which coal mining did not play any significant part was 1978–9. Over the past century, strikes in coal mining account for 30 per cent of the total number of days lost.

The contraction of the coal industry in the 1980s, with a loss of 200,000 jobs (70 per cent of the total) since 1979, suggests that the dominance of coal in the industrial action figures is now a thing of the past. Following convention, we adjusted the time series to exclude coal mining and also adjusted the denominators taking out coal mining employment and union membership. Various time series including and excluding coal mining are presented.

Strike activity per union member

Our measure of strike intensity using union membership as the denominator produces some interesting new conclusions concerning the long run trend of industrial action in the UK.

1 *Stoppages* (Figure 11.2) On the per employee basis the late 1960s and early 1970s comprise the all time peak period of activity (with 1969 as the peak year). But on the per union member basis this period looks very similar to the 1910–13 period and substantially lower than the 1890s.
2 *Workers involved* (Figure 11.3) The peak year on both measures is 1979 but the per union member measure provides a alternative picture of other years. On the per employee measure the 1926 peak is half the size of that for 1979, but on the per union member measure it is virtually the same size. Furthermore, the number of workers involved

during the 1911–13 peak now ranks third among the peaks rather than seventh.

3 *Days lost* (Figure 11.4) This time series provides perhaps the most interesting new portrait of strike activity. On the per employee measure, the 1970s (with 1979 as the peak year) appear more strike ridden than any period other than the early 1920s. But per union member, 1979 ranks lower than seven separate years from 1893 to 1926. In terms of the annual average number of days lost per decade, the 1970s average is lower than all decades up to and including the 1920s.

In summary, the per union member strike intensity measure presents a new perspective on the upsurge of industrial action in the 1970s, especially in comparison to the pre-general strike period. The intensity of industrial action during the 1970s went against the post-1926 trend but it never matched, let alone surpassed, the strike activity of the formative years of the trade union movement.

Duration

The duration of stoppages (days lost divided by workers involved) has shown a considerable decline since the late 1920s (Figure 11.5). Note that the data do not include stoppages of less than one day's duration (except where the aggregate number of days lost exceeds 100). Information from the CBI Pay Databank shows that strikes of less than one day comprised about 15 per cent of all strikes over annual pay negotiations in manufacturing industry in the 1980s (Ingram, Metcalf and Wadsworth 1991).

The peculiar 1970s

The 1970s constituted a break in the trend of strike activity from the mid-1920s (Table 11.2). Stoppages per employee were at an all time high this century. Workers involved per union member and per employee were higher than any other decade on record. Days lost were the highest since the 1920s. Memories of the 1970s cloud much of the comment about the decline of industrial action in the 1980s, but the data suggest that it was the 1970s that was the peculiar decade, whereas the 1980s simply saw a return to the underlying trend of strike activity apparent since 1930.

The explanation for the intensity of strike activity in the 1970s probably turns on organisational factors, which impacted on the ability to take industrial action, and on incentives to strike or grievances.

Particular organisational factors include the upsurge in trade union membership and density and the rise of the closed shop, although these might also be seen as another indication of the militancy of the workforce in the decade rather than an explanation of it. Nevertheless, presumably the closed shop and high union density provided organisational factors which assisted industrial action. The legal and economic framework also provided some organisational support for a rise in industrial action, for example by the restoration and extension of immunities for organising industrial action through the Trade Union and Labour Relations Act (TULRA) in 1974 (see Simpson 1986).

Another factor may be the formalisation and decentralisation of collective bargaining in the 1970s following the Donovan Report (1968). Such decentralisation implies more negotiations and therefore more scope for strikes. Further, this process may have created its own grievances as workers and management fought over the formalisation of the frontier of control (Blanchflower and Cubbin 1986).

Various grievances in the 1970s provided an incentive and willingness to strike and presumably also contributed to an explanation of strike intensity. These include: the oil price shock of 1973 which contributed to real wage losses especially when combined with successive incomes policies, and the Industrial Relations Act 1971.

The 1980s

Strike activity was considerably lower in the 1980s than the 1970s but compared to the 1950s and 1960s the decade does not look particularly unusual. In fact on one measure, the annual average of workers involved per employee, the 1980s is second only to the 1970s. Four per cent of employees and 9 per cent of trade union members were involved in industrial action on average each year in the decade, compared to 2.4 per cent and 7.9 per cent respectively, across all previous decades. However, by the end of the decade the number of stoppages (all industry) was the lowest for fifty years.

DATA APPENDIX

Notes and sources

1 Strike activity

Stoppages, workers involved and days lost, UK.

Sources

DEP, *British Labour Statistics Historical Abstract 1886–1968*, London: HMSO 1971, Table 197.
DE, *Gazette*, July 1990, Table 2 p. 337.
DE, *Gazette*, May 1992, Table 2 p. 236.
DE, *Gazette*, various issues 1970–92, strike activity by industry table (for coal mining figures).

Notes

1 See DE *Gazette* July 1991 p. 337, for full definitions. Stoppages involving fewer than 10 workers and those lasting less than one day, are excluded from the statistics except where the aggregate number of working days lost exceeds 100.
2 Stoppages and workers involved from 1893 to 1968 refers to stoppages beginning in year and from 1969 to 1991 to stoppages in progress in year.
3 Days lost refers throughout to stoppages in progress in year.
4 Average duration of each stoppage is days lost divided by workers involved.

2 Employees in employment

UK, June figure, adjusted for seasonal variation.

1893–1950 sources

Feinstein C.H. (1972), *National Income, Expenditure and Output of the United Kingdom 1855–1965*, Cambridge: University Press, Table 57: T125–T127.
Ministry of Labour, *Gazette*, annual issues 1894–1960, for coal mining employment figures.

1950–91 sources

DE, *Gazette*, November 1989, Historical Supplement, Table 1.1: 8.
DE, *Gazette*, June 1992, Historical Supplement, Table 1.1: 4.
DE, *Gazette*, annual issues 1951–92, Table 1.4, Employee in Employment by industry, for coal mining figures.

Notes

1 Note that in the tables and graphs which follow the 1893–1950 figures on 'per employee in employment' are from the adjusted Feinstein series (see Note 2 below) and from 1950–91 they are from the official series.
2 Feinstein's employment figures are for 'total in civil employment' which includes 'employees in employment' and 'employers and self-employed'. No annual breakdown is provided for the two components. However, Feinstein, does provide the employers and self-employed figure for 1931 of 1,996,400. The corresponding total in civil employment was 18,340,000. Therefore employees in employment for 1931 was 89.12 per cent of the total. We adjusted the rest of the time series (multiplying the total in civil employment by 0.8912) to make the time series consistent with the post 1949 series. The figure for 1950 is provided for both the adjusted Feinstein series and the DE series for comparison purposes. Complete information for 1950–9 using the adjusted Feinstein series is available on request.
3 Feinstein's figures for employees in employment before 1920 were adjusted to make them refer to the UK rather than the British Isles (i.e. to exclude the Republic of Ireland). Nineteen twenty adjusted information indicates that 1,134,000 of British Isles employees in employment were in the Republic of Ireland comprising 6.12 per cent of the total. The figures from 1893–1919 were multiplied by 0.94 to make the figures consistent geographically with the rest of the data.

3 Union membership

UK figures, year end.

1893–1950 sources

DEP, *British Labour Statistics Historical Abstract 1886–1968*, HMSO, London, 1971, Table 196.
Arnot R.P. (1949, 1953, 1961), *The Miners*, Vols I, II and III, Unwin, London.

Trades Union Congress, *Annual Report*, 1946–60, Statistical Supplement.

1950–91 sources

Bailey, R. and Kelly, J. (1990), 'An Index Measure of British Trade Union Density', *British Journal of Industrial Relations*, 28, 2, Table 1: 269.

Trades Union Congress, *Annual Report*, 1951–88, Statistical Supplement.

Trades Union Congress, *TUC Bulletin*, July 1989, 1990 and 1991.

Union of Democratic Mineworkers, mimeo, November 1990.

Notes

1 Note that in the tables and graphs the 1950–91 figures on the 'per union member' basis use the Bailey-Kelly figures (updated to 1991) as the denominator because it is more accurate than the official series. Information for 1950 is also presented using the official DE union membership series. Complete information for 1950–9 using the official DE union membership series is available on request.

2 The Bailey-Kelly figures for trade union membership in Great Britain were multiplied by 1.02 to convert them to UK figures, making them consistent geographically with the rest of the data.

3 Figures for membership of the Union of Democratic Mineworkers are from 1986; the union was officially formed on 6 December 1985.

4 Figures on union membership in the coal industry for 1991 were not available so were estimated from the 1990 figures on the basis that union density had remained constant.

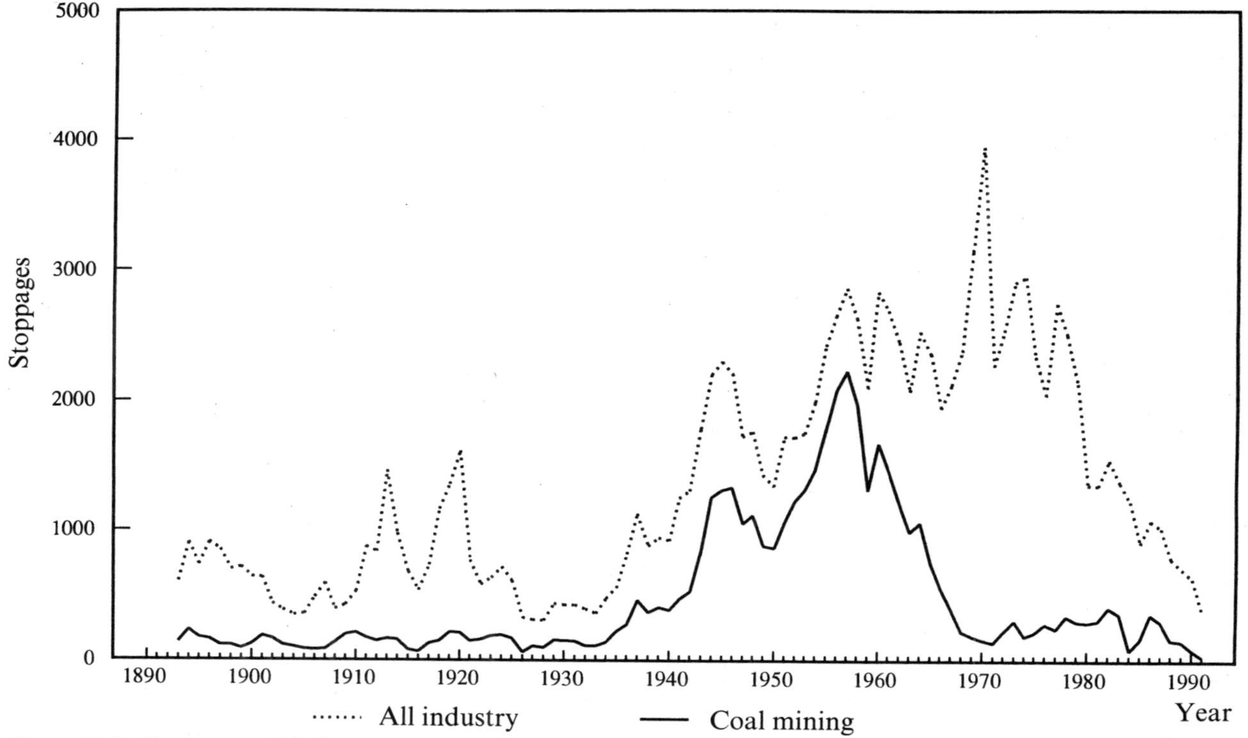

Figure 11.1 Stoppages: all industry and coal mining 1893–1991

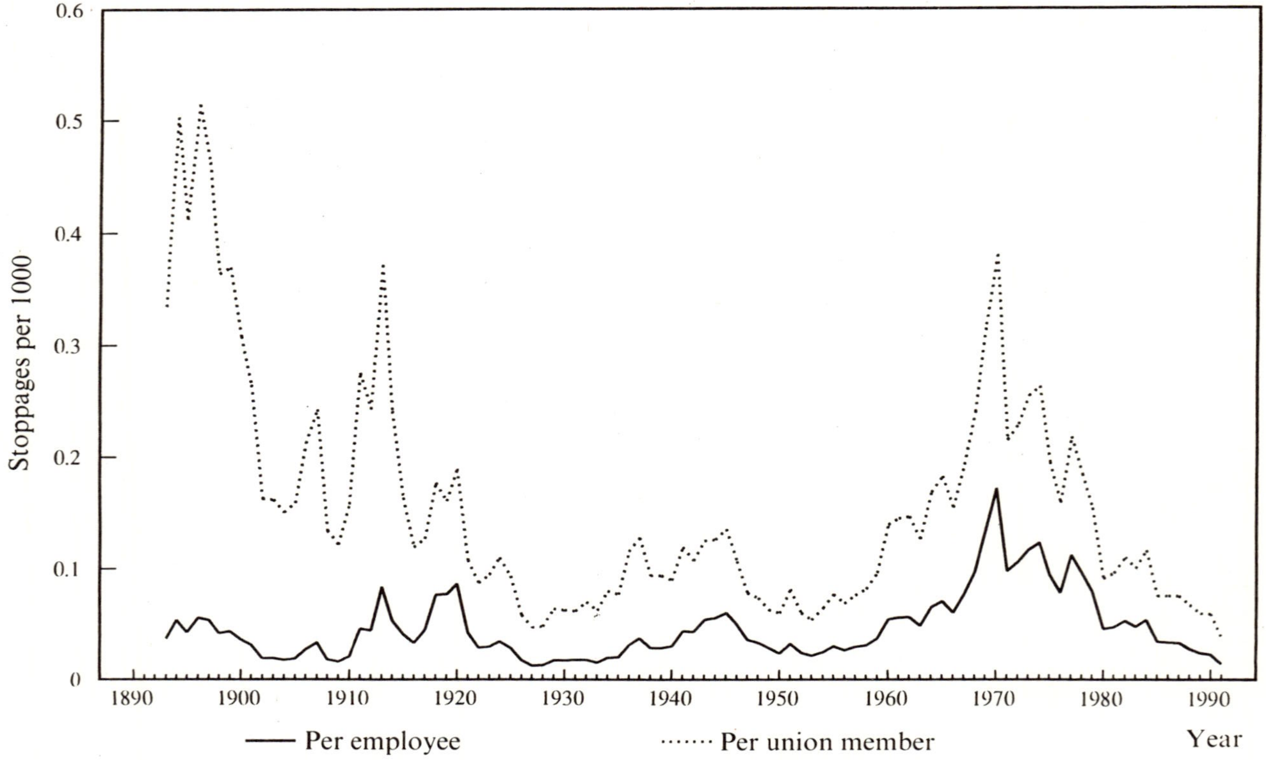

Figure 11.2 Stoppages: per employee and union member excluding coal mining 1893–1991

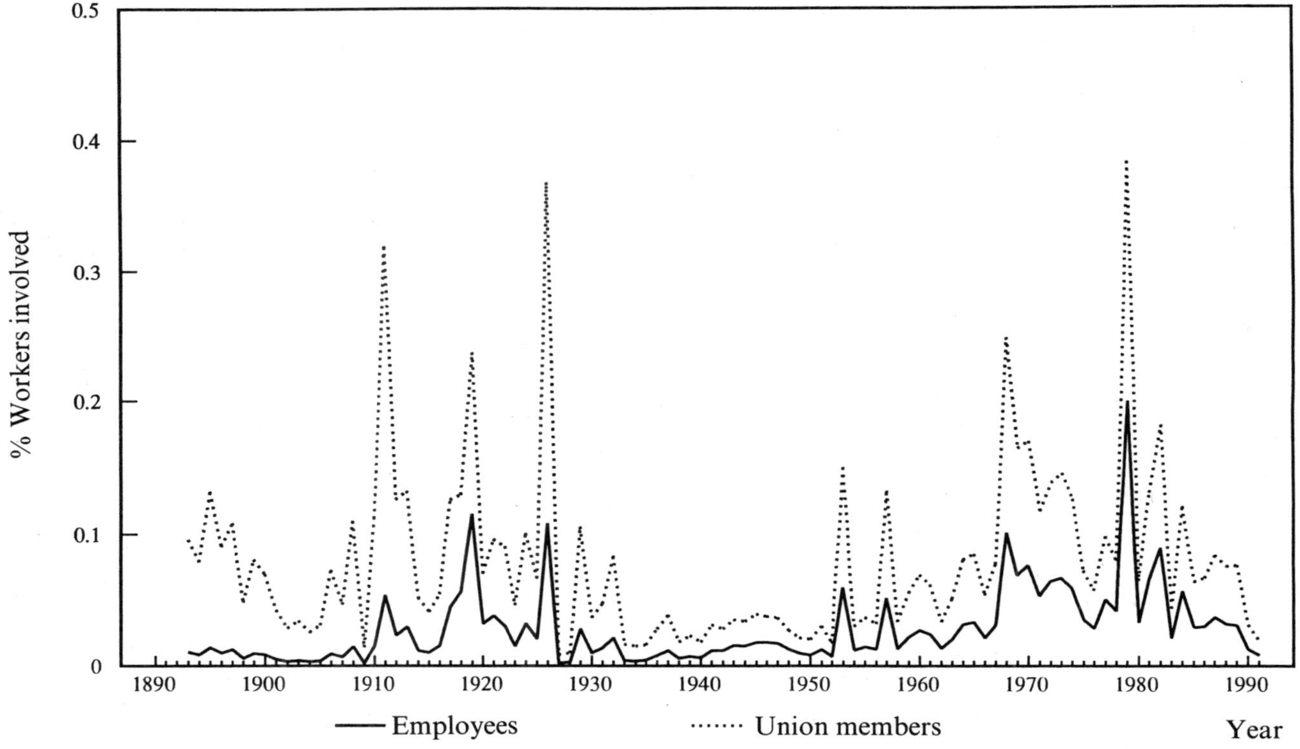

Figure 11.3 Percentage of workers involved excluding coal mining 1893–1991

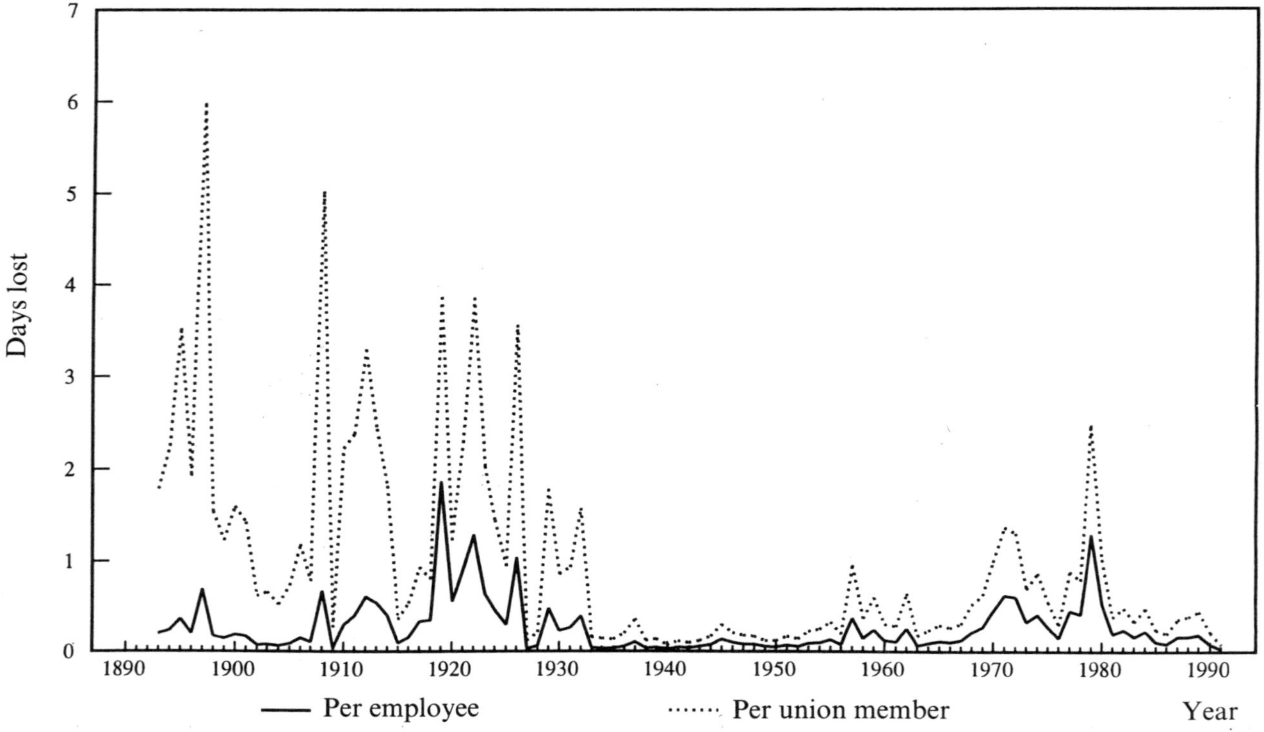

Figure 11.4 Days lost per employee and union member excluding coal mining 1893–1991

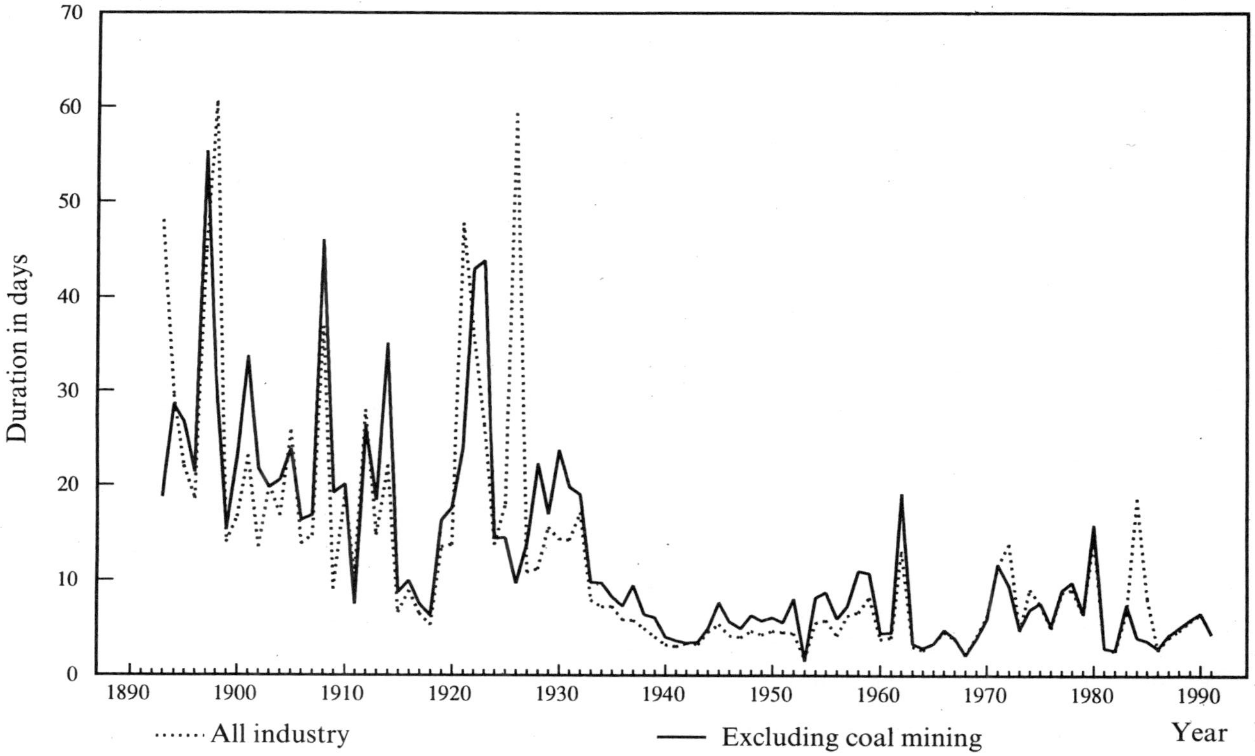

Figure 11.5 Duration of stoppages in days: all industry and excluding coal mining 1893–1991

Table 11.1 UK stoppage activity by decade 1893–1990 *Average annual rates*

Years	*Stoppages per 1,000*		*% of workers involved*			*Days lost*	
	Employees	*Union members*	*Employees*	*Union members*	*Duration in days*	*Per employee*	*Per union member*
A All industries excluding coal mining							
1893–9	0.047	0.423	1.0	9.0	28.3	0.293	2.605
1900–9	0.024	0.191	0.6	4.7	24.1	0.164	1.285
1910–19	0.052	0.203	3.7	13.3	15.6	0.507	1.870
1920–9	0.031	0.090	3.1	9.6	22.0	0.579	1.749
1930–9	0.023	0.085	0.9	3.2	11.9	0.125	0.464
1940–9	0.044	0.102	1.3	3.1	4.9	0.068	0.154
1950–9	0.028	0.072	2.1	5.4	7.3	0.120	0.304
1960–9	0.072	0.181	3.7	9.2	5.2	0.143	0.359
1970–9	0.108	0.225	6.7	13.8	7.7	0.494	1.017
1980–9	0.041	0.087	4.2	9.1	5.4	0.200	0.426
1893–1990	**0.047**	**0.156**	**2.8**	**7.9**	**12.6**	**0.265**	**0.961**
B Coal mining							
1893–9	0.210	0.853	23.6	92.4	29.7	10.444	40.779
1900–9	0.145	0.323	11.5	25.0	13.9	1.404	3.144
1910–19	0.137	0.219	35.9	57.7	12.3	5.297	9.182
1920–9	0.133	0.196	39.8	54.4	28.0	22.001	29.944
1930–9	0.304	0.438	22.5	33.2	5.3	1.199	1.808
1940–9	1.287	1.547	37.3	44.8	2.9	1.155	1.381
1950–9	2.170	2.199	31.6	32.1	2.4	0.744	0.759
1960–9	1.587	1.616	26.1	26.9	2.8	0.802	0.856

1970–9	0.768	0.811	35.0	38.1	7.4	5.656	6.289
1980–9	1.269	1.351	61.4	65.3	12.2	12.522	13.214
1893–1990	**0.817**	**0.955**	**32.3**	**44.9**	**11.0**	**5.878**	**9.620**
C All industries							
1893–9	0.056	0.469	2.0	18.3	34.0	0.762	6.818
1900–9	0.031	0.216	1.1	8.5	19.0	0.211	1.601
1910–19	0.058	0.206	5.3	20.2	13.5	0.741	3.135
1920–9	0.038	0.104	5.0	15.5	25.3	1.839	5.791
1930–9	0.036	0.120	1.6	6.2	8.8	0.155	0.601
1940–9	0.092	0.204	2.4	6.1	9.9	0.099	0.244
1950–9	0.098	0.239	3.1	7.5	5.1	0.151	0.366
1960–9	0.108	0.264	4.2	10.2	4.4	0.157	0.383
1970–9	0.116	0.240	7.1	14.5	8.2	0.569	1.163
1980–9	0.052	0.110	4.8	10.1	7.0	0.332	0.700
1893–1990	**0.068**	**0.206**	**3.9**	**11.3**	**12.1**	**0.526**	**1.897**

Table 11.2 UK strike activity 1893–1991: all industry

Year	Stoppages	Workers involved (000's)	Days lost (000's)	Duration in days	Employees in employment (000's)	Union members (000's)	Stoppages		Workers involved		Days lost	
							Per 1,000 employees	Per 1,000 union members	Per employee	Per union member	Per employee	Per union member
	1	2	3	(3/2)	4	5	(1/4)	(1/5)	(2/4)	(2/5)	(3/4)	(3/5)
1893	599	634	30,439	48.0	12,968	1,559	0.046	0.384	0.049	0.407	2.347	19.525
1894	903	322	9,506	29.5	13,202	1,530	0.068	0.590	0.022	0.210	0.642	6.213
1895	728	259	5,701	22.0	13,512	1,504	0.054	0.484	0.017	0.172	0.376	3.791
1896	906	192	3,565	18.6	14,022	1,608	0.065	0.563	0.012	0.119	0.227	2.217
1897	848	229	10,327	45.1	14,181	1,731	0.060	0.490	0.014	0.132	0.649	5.966
1898	695	252	15,257	60.5	14,416	1,752	0.048	0.397	0.016	0.144	0.943	8.708
1899	710	179	2,503	14.0	14,692	1,911	0.048	0.372	0.011	0.094	0.152	1.310
1900	633	185	3,088	16.7	14,667	2,022	0.043	0.313	0.011	0.091	0.188	1.527
1901	631	179	4,130	23.1	14,683	2,025	0.043	0.312	0.011	0.088	0.251	2.040
1902	432	255	3,438	13.5	14,734	2,013	0.029	0.215	0.015	0.127	0.208	1.708
1903	380	116	2,320	20.0	14,826	1,994	0.026	0.191	0.007	0.058	0.139	1.163
1904	346	87	1,464	16.8	14,759	1,967	0.023	0.176	0.005	0.044	0.088	0.744
1905	349	92	2,368	25.7	15,060	1,997	0.023	0.175	0.005	0.046	0.140	1.186
1906	479	218	3,019	13.8	15,428	2,210	0.031	0.217	0.013	0.099	0.174	1.366
1907	585	146	2,148	14.7	15,562	2,513	0.038	0.233	0.008	0.058	0.123	0.855
1908	389	293	10,785	36.8	15,026	2,485	0.026	0.157	0.017	0.118	0.640	4.340
1909	422	297	2,687	9.0	15,177	2,477	0.028	0.170	0.017	0.120	0.158	1.085
1910	521	514	9,867	19.2	15,804	2,565	0.033	0.203	0.029	0.200	0.556	3.847
1911	872	952	10,155	10.7	16,223	3,139	0.054	0.278	0.052	0.303	0.558	3.235
1912	834	1,462	40,890	28.0	16,306	3,416	0.051	0.244	0.080	0.428	2.235	11.970
1913	1,459	664	9,804	14.8	16,658	4,135	0.088	0.353	0.036	0.161	0.525	2.371
1914	972	447	9,878	22.1	16,265	4,145	0.060	0.234	0.024	0.108	0.541	2.383
1915	672	448	2,953	6.6	15,395	4,359	0.044	0.154	0.026	0.103	0.171	0.677
1916	532	276	2,446	8.9	14,809	4,644	0.036	0.115	0.017	0.059	0.147	0.527
1917	730	872	5,647	6.5	14,307	5,499	0.051	0.133	0.054	0.159	0.352	1.027

1918	1,165	1,116	5,875	5.3	14,273	6,533	0.082	0.178	0.070	0.171	0.367	0.899
1919	1,352	2,591	34,969	13.5	15,922	7,926	0.085	0.171	0.145	0.327	1.957	4.412
1920	1,607	1,932	26,568	13.8	17,411	8,348	0.092	0.193	0.099	0.231	1.360	3.183
1921	763	1,801	85,872	47.7	15,522	6,633	0.049	0.115	0.103	0.272	4.930	12.946
1922	576	552	19,850	36.0	15,581	5,625	0.037	0.102	0.032	0.098	1.135	3.529
1923	628	405	10,672	26.4	15,826	5,429	0.040	0.116	0.023	0.075	0.601	1.966
1924	710	613	8,424	13.7	16,070	5,544	0.044	0.128	0.034	0.111	0.467	1.519
1925	603	441	7,952	18.0	16,254	5,506	0.037	0.110	0.024	0.080	0.436	1.444
1926	323	2,734	162,233	59.3	16,259	5,219	0.020	0.062	0.150	0.524	8.892	31.085
1927	308	108	1,174	10.9	16,745	4,919	0.018	0.063	0.006	0.022	0.062	0.239
1928	302	124	1,388	11.2	16,815	4,806	0.018	0.063	0.007	0.026	0.074	0.289
1929	431	533	8,287	15.5	17,063	4,858	0.025	0.089	0.028	0.110	0.433	1.706
1930	422	307	4,399	14.3	16,744	4,842	0.025	0.087	0.016	0.063	0.234	0.909
1931	420	490	6,983	14.3	16,345	4,924	0.026	0.085	0.027	0.100	0.381	1.418
1932	389	379	6,488	17.1	16,425	4,444	0.024	0.088	0.021	0.085	0.352	1.460
1933	357	136	1,072	7.9	16,766	4,392	0.021	0.081	0.007	0.031	0.057	0.244
1934	471	134	959	7.2	17,254	4,590	0.027	0.103	0.007	0.029	0.050	0.209
1935	553	271	1,955	7.2	17,560	4,867	0.031	0.114	0.014	0.056	0.099	0.402
1936	818	316	1,829	5.8	18,110	5,295	0.045	0.154	0.016	0.060	0.090	0.345
1937	1,129	597	3,413	5.7	18,704	5,842	0.060	0.193	0.028	0.102	0.163	0.584
1938	875	274	1,334	4.9	18,703	6,053	0.047	0.145	0.013	0.045	0.064	0.220
1939	940	337	1,356	4.0	19,428	6,298	0.048	0.149	0.015	0.054	0.062	0.215
1940	922	299	940	3.1	18,537	6,613	0.050	0.139	0.014	0.045	0.045	0.142
1941	1,251	360	1,079	3.0	18,359	7,165	0.068	0.175	0.017	0.050	0.052	0.151
1942	1,303	456	1,527	3.3	18,448	7,867	0.071	0.166	0.022	0.058	0.074	0.194
1943	1,785	557	1,808	3.2	18,002	8,174	0.099	0.218	0.028	0.068	0.090	0.221
1944	2,194	821	3,714	4.5	17,557	8,087	0.125	0.271	0.042	0.102	0.189	0.459
1945	2,293	531	2,835	5.3	17,022	7,875	0.135	0.291	0.028	0.067	0.148	0.360
1946	2,205	526	2,158	4.1	1,8091	8,803	0.122	0.250	0.026	0.060	0.106	0.245
1947	1,721	620	2,433	3.9	1,9250	9,145	0.089	0.188	0.029	0.068	0.133	0.266
1948	1,759	424	1,944	4.6	19,717	9,362	0.089	0.188	0.019	0.045	0.088	0.208

Year	Stoppages 1	Workers involved (000's) 2	Days lost (000's) 3	Duration in days (3/2)	Employees in employment (000's) 4	Union members (000's) 5	Stoppages: Per 1,000 employees (1/4)	Stoppages: Per 1,000 union members (1/5)	Workers involved: Per employee (2/4)	Workers involved: Per union member (2/5)	Days lost: Per employee (3/4)	Days lost: Per union member (3/5)
1949	1,426	433	1,807	4.2	19,874	9,318	0.072	0.153	0.019	0.046	0.081	0.194
1950	1,339	302	1,389	4.6	20,125	9,289	0.067	0.144	0.015	0.033	0.069	0.150
1950	1,339	302	1,389	4.6	20,758	8,527	0.065	0.157	0.015	0.035	0.067	0.163
1951	1,719	379	1,694	4.5	20,970	8,753	0.082	0.196	0.018	0.043	0.081	0.194
1952	1,714	415	1,792	4.3	20,916	8,802	0.082	0.195	0.020	0.047	0.086	0.204
1953	1,746	1,370	2,184	1.6	21,041	8,745	0.083	0.200	0.065	0.157	0.104	0.250
1954	1,989	448	2,457	5.5	21,404	8,781	0.093	0.227	0.021	0.051	0.115	0.280
1955	2,419	659	3,781	5.7	21,702	8,942	0.111	0.271	0.030	0.074	0.174	0.423
1956	2,648	507	2,083	4.1	21,965	8,985	0.121	0.295	0.023	0.056	0.095	0.232
1957	2,859	1,356	8,412	6.2	22,058	9,023	0.130	0.317	0.061	0.150	0.381	0.932
1958	2,629	523	3,462	6.6	21,884	8,849	0.120	0.297	0.024	0.059	0.158	0.391
1959	2,093	645	5,270	8.2	21,421	8,834	0.098	0.237	0.030	0.073	0.246	0.597
1960	2,832	814	3,024	3.7	21,899	9,028	0.129	0.314	0.037	0.090	0.138	0.335
1961	2,686	771	3,046	4.0	22,233	9,085	0.121	0.296	0.035	0.085	0.137	0.335
1962	2,449	442	5,798	13.1	22,452	9,076	0.109	0.270	0.020	0.049	0.258	0.639
1963	2,068	590	1,755	3.0	22,509	9,120	0.092	0.227	0.026	0.065	0.078	0.192
1964	2,524	872	2,277	2.6	22,816	9,252	0.111	0.273	0.038	0.094	0.100	0.246
1965	2,354	868	2,925	3.4	23,085	9,346	0.102	0.252	0.038	0.093	0.127	0.313
1966	1,937	530	2,398	4.5	23,257	9,418	0.083	0.206	0.023	0.056	0.103	0.255
1967	2,116	731	2,787	3.8	22,813	9,352	0.093	0.226	0.032	0.078	0.122	0.298
1968	2,378	2,255	4,690	2.1	22,655	9,355	0.105	0.254	0.100	0.241	0.207	0.501
1969	3,146	1,665	6,846	4.1	22,624	9,611	0.139	0.327	0.074	0.173	0.303	0.712
1970	3,943	1,801	10,980	6.1	22,479	10,261	0.175	0.384	0.080	0.176	0.488	1.070

1971	2,263	1,178	13,551	11.5	22,139	10,213	0.102	0.222	0.053	0.115	0.612	1.327
1972	2,530	1,734	23,909	13.8	22,137	10,420	0.114	0.243	0.078	0.166	1.080	2.294
1973	2,902	1,528	7,197	4.7	22,679	10,508	0.128	0.276	0.067	0.145	0.317	0.685
1974	2,946	1,626	14,750	9.1	22,804	10,791	0.129	0.273	0.071	0.151	0.647	1.367
1975	2,332	809	6,012	7.4	22,723	11,185	0.103	0.208	0.036	0.072	0.265	0.537
1976	2,034	668	3,284	4.9	22,557	11,361	0.090	0.179	0.030	0.059	0.146	0.289
1977	2,737	1,166	10,142	8.7	22,631	11,792	0.121	0.232	0.052	0.099	0.448	0.860
1978	2,498	1,041	9,405	9.0	22,789	12,037	0.110	0.208	0.046	0.086	0.413	0.781
1979	2,125	4,608	29,474	6.4	23,173	12,199	0.092	0.174	0.199	0.378	1.272	2.416
1980	1,348	834	11,964	14.3	22,991	11,885	0.059	0.113	0.036	0.070	0.520	1.007
1981	1,344	1,513	4,266	2.8	21,892	11,113	0.061	0.121	0.069	0.136	0.195	0.384
1982	1,538	2,103	5,313	2.5	21,414	10,643	0.072	0.145	0.098	0.198	0.248	0.499
1983	1,364	574	3,754	6.5	21,067	10,314	0.065	0.132	0.027	0.056	0.178	0.364
1984	1,221	1,464	27,135	18.5	21,238	10,093	0.057	0.121	0.069	0.145	1.278	2.689
1985	903	791	6,402	8.1	21,423	9,934	0.042	0.091	0.037	0.080	0.299	0.644
1986	1,074	720	1,920	2.7	21,387	9,675	0.050	0.111	0.034	0.074	0.090	0.198
1987	1,016	887	3,546	4.0	21,584	9,616	0.047	0.106	0.041	0.092	0.164	0.369
1988	781	790	3,702	4.7	22,226	9,525	0.035	0.083	0.036	0.084	0.167	0.394
1989	701	727	4,128	5.7	22,756	9,325	0.031	0.075	0.032	0.078	0.181	0.443
1990	630	298	1,903	6.4	22,894	9,131	0.028	0.069	0.013	0.033	0.083	0.208
1991	369	176	761	4.3	22,225	8,844	0.016	0.042	0.008	0.020	0.034	0.086

Notes and Sources: See Data Appendix.

Table 11.3 UK strike activity 1893–1991: coal mining

Year	Stoppages	Workers involved (000's)	Days lost (000's)	Duration in days	Employees in employment (000's)	Union members (000's)	Stoppages		Workers involved		Days lost	
							Per 1,000 employees	Per 1,000 union members	Per employee	Per union member	Per employee	Per union member
	1	2	3	(3/2)	4	5	(1/4)	(1/5)	(2/4)	(2/5)	(3/4)	(3/5)
1893	139	503	27,978	55.6	682	185	0.204	0.751	0.738	2.719	41.023	151.232
1894	227	216	6,479	30.0	704	185	0.322	1.227	0.307	1.168	9.203	35.022
1895	174	82	974	11.9	692	162	0.251	1.074	0.118	0.506	1.408	6.012
1896	159	61	765	12.5	692	155	0.230	1.026	0.088	0.394	1.105	4.935
1897	116	58	867	14.9	681	149	0.170	0.779	0.085	0.389	1.273	5.819
1898	116	175	12,806	73.2	693	159	0.167	0.730	0.253	1.101	18.479	80.541
1899	92	45	450	10.0	728	238	0.126	0.387	0.062	0.189	0.618	1.891
1900	122	70	440	6.3	766	363	0.159	0.336	0.091	0.193	0.574	1.212
1901	186	108	1,742	16.1	792	344	0.235	0.541	0.136	0.314	2.199	5.064
1902	161	207	2,395	11.6	824	343	0.195	0.469	0.251	0.603	2.907	6.983
1903	113	60	1,215	20.3	841	340	0.134	0.332	0.071	0.176	1.445	3574
1904	100	45	598	13.3	847	327	0.118	0.306	0.053	0.138	0.706	1.829
1905	83	40	1,129	28.2	858	324	0.097	0.256	0.047	0.123	1.316	3.485
1906	81	82	793	9.7	882	333	0.092	0.243	0.093	0.246	0.899	2.381
1907	87	50	530	10.6	940	458	0.093	0.190	0.053	0.109	0.564	1.157
1908	136	86	1,275	14.8	987	590	0.138	0.231	0.087	0.146	1.292	2.161
1909	195	270	2,169	8.0	1,013	603	0.192	0.323	0.267	0.448	2.141	3.597
1910	211	295	5,476	18.6	1,049	597	0.201	0.353	0.281	0.494	5.220	9.173
1911	170	139	4,065	29.2	1,066	588	0.159	0.289	0.130	0.236	3.813	6.913
1912	147	1,106	31,561	28.5	1,088	587	0.135	0.250	1.017	1.884	29.008	53.767
1913	163	203	1,298	6.4	1,127	646	0.145	0.252	0.180	0.314	1.152	2.009
1914	158	271	3,718	13.7	1,100	761	0.144	0.208	0.246	0.356	3.380	4.886
1915	79	298	1,641	5.5	1,050	721	0.075	0.110	0.284	0.413	1.563	2.276
1916	67	62	311	5.0	1,016	725	0.066	0.092	0.061	0.086	0.306	0.429
1917	128	274	1,171	4.3	1,041	738	0.123	0.173	0.263	0.371	1.125	1.587

1918	147	368	1,165	3.2	1,006	754	0.146	0.195	0.366	0.488	1.158	1.545
1919	212	906	7,441	8.2	1,191	806	0.178	0.263	0.761	1.124	6.248	9.232
1920	210	1,414	17,424	12.3	1,247	945	0.168	0.222	1.134	1.496	13.973	18.438
1921	147	1,251	72,693	58.1	1,132	889	0.130	0.165	1.105	1.407	64.216	81.769
1922	155	118	1,246	10.6	1,148	802	0.135	0.193	0.103	0.147	1.085	1.554
1923	186	188	1,183	6.3	1,203	756	0.155	0.246	0.156	0.249	0.983	1.565
1924	190	137	1,563	11.4	1,214	791	0.157	0.240	0.113	0.173	1.287	1.976
1925	164	130	3,453	26.6	1,084	804	0.151	0.204	0.120	0.162	3.185	4.295
1926	63	1,105	146,434	132.5	1,097	783	0.057	0.080	1.007	1.411	133.486	187.017
1927	110	73	688	9.4	1,005	751	0.109	0.146	0.073	0.097	0.685	0.916
1928	97	82	452	5.5	921	561	0.105	0.173	0.089	0.146	0.491	0.806
1929	153	79	576	7.3	939	521	0.163	0.294	0.084	0.152	0.613	1.106
1930	150	149	663	4.4	891	530	0.168	0.283	0.167	0.281	0.744	1.251
1931	147	281	2,848	10.1	843	527	0.174	0.279	0.333	0.533	3.378	5.404
1932	111	52	287	5.5	785	498	0.141	0.223	0.066	0.104	0.366	0.576
1933	112	72	446	6.2	779	497	0.144	0.225	0.092	0.145	0.573	0.897
1934	143	73	365	5.0	769	499	0.186	0.287	0.095	0.146	0.475	0.731
1935	217	200	1,368	6.8	769	502	0.282	0.432	0.260	0.398	1.779	2.725
1936	270	182	852	4.7	767	531	0.352	0.508	0.237	0.343	1.111	1.605
1937	457	393	1,496	3.8	792	546	0.577	0.837	0.496	0.720	1.889	2.740
1938	363	174	697	4.0	740	587	0.491	0.618	0.235	0.296	0.942	1.187
1939	404	206	565	2.7	765	588	0.528	0.687	0.269	0.350	0.739	0.961
1940	381	190	505	2.7	748	588	0.509	0.648	0.254	0.323	0.675	0.859
1941	470	154	335	2.2	696	581	0.675	0.809	0.221	0.265	0.481	0.577
1942	526	252	840	3.3	709	599	0.742	0.878	0.355	0.421	1.185	1.402
1943	843	294	890	3.0	706	600	1.194	1.405	0.416	0.490	1.261	1.483
1944	1,253	568	2,480	4.4	710	602	1.765	2.081	0.800	0.944	3.493	4.120
1945	1,306	243	641	2.6	696	557	1.876	2.345	0.349	0.436	0.921	1.151
1946	1,329	217	422	1.9	693	554	1.918	2.399	0.313	0.392	0.609	0.762
1947	1,053	308	912	3.0	732	593	1.439	1.776	0.421	0.519	1.246	1.538
1948	1,116	189	464	2.5	725	635	1.539	1.757	0.261	0.298	0.640	0.731

Year	Stoppages	Workers involved (000's)	Days lost (000's)	Duration in days	Employees in employment (000's)	Union members (000's)	Stoppages: Per 1,000 employees	Stoppages: Per 1,000 union members	Workers involved: Per employee	Workers involved: Per union member	Days lost: Per employee	Days lost: Per union member
	1	2	3	*(3/2)*	4	5	*(1/4)*	*(1/5)*	*(2/4)*	*(2/5)*	*(3/4)*	*(3/5)*
1949	874	248	754	3.0	723	635	1.209	1.376	0.343	0.391	1.043	1.187
1950	860	142	431	3.0	699	631	1.230	1.363	0.203	0.225	0.617	0.683
1951	1,058	135	350	2.6	702	644	1.507	1.643	0.192	0.210	0.499	0.543
1952	1,221	274	660	2.4	718	673	1.701	1.814	0.382	0.407	0.919	0.981
1953	1,307	168	393	2.3	720	703	1.815	1.859	0.233	0.239	0.546	0.559
1954	1,464	204	468	2.3	708	708	2.068	2.068	0.288	0.288	0.661	0.661
1955	1,783	354	1,112	3.1	705	709	2.529	2.515	0.502	0.499	1.577	1.568
1956	2,076	241	502	2.1	703	709	2.953	2.928	0.343	0.340	0.714	0.708
1957	2,224	265	514	1.9	711	717	3.128	3.102	0.373	0.370	0.723	0.717
1958	1,963	249	450	1.8	698	711	2.812	2.761	0.357	0.350	0.645	0.633
1959	1,307	191	363	1.9	668	676	1.957	1.933	0.286	0.283	0.543	0.537
1960	1,666	237	494	2.1	606	623	2.749	2.674	0.391	0.380	0.815	0.793
1961	1,458	249	737	3.0	575	581	2.536	2.509	0.433	0.429	1.282	1.269
1962	1,205	154	308	2.0	557	564	2.163	2.137	0.276	0.273	0.553	0.546
1963	987	152	326	2.1	530	535	1.862	1.845	0.287	0.284	0.615	0.609
1964	1,058	172	302	1.8	503	513	2.103	2.062	0.342	0.335	0.600	0.589
1965	740	118	412	3.5	471	478	1.571	1.548	0.251	0.247	0.875	0.862
1966	553	50	118	2.4	513	443	1.078	1.248	0.097	0.113	0.230	0.266
1967	394	41	105	2.6	488	408	0.807	0.966	0.084	0.100	0.215	0.257
1968	221	30	54	1.8	428	371	0.516	0.596	0.070	0.081	0.126	0.146
1969	186	145	1,039	7.2	383	322	0.486	0.578	0.379	0.450	2.713	3.227
1970	157	117	1,090	9.3	360	303	0.436	0.518	0.325	0.386	3.028	3.597
1971	135	23	63	2.7	354	299	0.381	0.452	0.065	0.077	0.178	0.211
1972	218	340	10,797	31.8	330	294	0.661	0.741	1.030	1.156	32.718	36.724
1973	301	47	90	1.9	318	283	0.947	1.064	0.148	0.166	0.283	0.318

1974	183	306	5,625	18.4	302	277	0.606	0.661	1.013	1.105	18.626	20.307
1975	212	28	52	1.9	293	282	0.724	0.752	0.096	0.099	0.177	0.184
1976	276	38	70	1.8	295	296	0.936	0.932	0.129	0.128	0.237	0.236
1977	239	46	76	1.7	297	295	0.805	0.810	0.155	0.156	0.256	0.258
1978	338	104	195	1.9	293	291	1.154	1.162	0.355	0.357	0.666	0.670
1979	295	53	112	2.1	286	289	1.031	1.021	0.185	0.183	0.392	0.388
1980	289	85	151	1.8	285	293	1.014	0.986	0.298	0.290	0.530	0.515
1981	302	98	235	2.4	275	285	1.098	1.060	0.356	0.344	0.855	0.825
1982	403	225	374	1.7	260	280	1.550	1.439	0.865	0.804	1.438	1.336
1983	355	133	484	3.6	254	241	1.398	1.473	0.524	0.552	1.906	2.008
1984	79	281	22,483	80.0	233	231	0.339	0.342	1.206	1.216	96.494	97.329
1985	160	168	4,142	24.7	212	164	0.755	0.976	0.792	1.024	19.538	25.256
1986	351	87	143	1.6	182	157	1.929	2.236	0.478	0.554	0.786	0.911
1987	296	98	217	2.2	150	138	1.973	2.145	0.653	0.710	1.447	1.572
1988	154	92	222	2.4	128	120	1.203	1.283	0.719	0.767	1.734	1.850
1989	146	25	50	20	102	93	1.431	1.570	0.245	0.269	0.490	0.538
1990	87	15	59	3.9	86	78	1.012	1.115	0.174	0.192	0.686	0.756
1991	32	6	29	4.8	82	74	0.390	0.432	0.073	0.081	0.354	0.392

Notes and Sources: See Data Appendix.

Table 11.4 UK strike activity 1893–1991: all industries excluding coal mining

							Stoppages		*Workers involved*		*Days lost*	
Year	*Stoppages* 1	*Workers involved (000's)* 2	*Days lost (000's)* 3	*Duration in days* (3/2)	*Employees in employment (000's)* 4	*Union members (000's)* 5	*Per 1000 employees* (1/4)	*Per 1000 union members* (1/5)	*Per employee* (2/4)	*Per union member* (2/5)	*Per employee* (3/4)	*Per union member* (3/5)
1893	460	131	2,461	18.8	12,286	1,374	0.037	0.335	0.011	0.095	0.200	1.791
1894	676	106	3,027	28.6	12,498	1,345	0.054	0.503	0.008	0.079	0.242	2.251
1895	554	177	4,727	26.7	12,820	1,342	0.043	0.413	0.014	0.132	0.369	3.522
1896	747	131	2,800	21.4	13,330	1,453	0.056	0.514	0.010	0.090	0.210	1.927
1897	732	171	9,460	55.3	13,500	1,582	0.054	0.463	0.013	0.108	0.701	5.980
1898	579	77	2,451	31.8	13,723	1,593	0.042	0.363	0.006	0.048	0.179	1.539
1899	618	134	2,053	15.3	13,964	1,673	0.044	0.369	0.010	0.080	0.147	1.227
1900	511	115	2,648	23.0	13,901	1,659	0.037	0.308	0.008	0.069	0.190	1.596
1901	445	71	2,388	33.6	13,891	1,681	0.032	0.265	0.005	0.042	0.172	1.421
1902	271	48	1,043	21.7	13,910	1,670	0.019	0.162	0.003	0.029	0.075	0.625
1903	267	56	1,105	19.7	13,985	1,654	0.019	0.161	0.004	0.034	0.079	0.668
1904	246	42	866	20.6	13,912	1,640	0.018	0.150	0.003	0.026	0.062	0.528
1905	266	52	1,239	23.8	14,202	1,673	0.019	0.159	0.004	0.031	0.087	0.741
1906	398	136	2,226	16.4	14,546	1,877	0.027	0.212	0.009	0.072	0.153	1.186
1907	498	96	1,618	16.9	14,622	2,055	0.034	0.242	0.007	0.047	0.111	0.787
1908	253	207	9,510	45.9	14,039	1,895	0.018	0.134	0.015	0.109	0.677	5.018
1909	227	27	518	19.2	14,164	1,874	0.016	0.121	0.002	0.014	0.037	0.276
1910	310	219	4,391	20.1	14,755	1,968	0.021	0.158	0.015	0.111	0.298	2.231
1911	702	813	6,090	7.5	15,157	2,551	0.046	0.275	0.054	0.319	0.402	2.387
1912	687	356	9,329	26.2	15,218	2,829	0.045	0.243	0.023	0.126	0.613	3.298
1913	1,296	461	8,506	18.5	15,531	3,489	0.083	0.371	0.030	0.132	0.548	2.438
1914	814	176	6,160	35.0	15,165	3,384	0.054	0.241	0.012	0.052	0.406	1.820
1915	593	150	1,312	8.7	14,345	3,638	0.041	0.163	0.010	0.041	0.091	0.361
1916	465	214	2,135	10.0	13,793	3,919	0.034	0.119	0.016	0.055	0.155	0.545
1917	602	598	4,476	7.5	13,266	4,761	0.045	0.126	0.045	0.126	0.337	0.940

1918	1,018	748	4,710	6.3	13,267	5,779	0.077	0.176	0.056	0.129	0.355	0.815
1919	1,140	1,685	27,528	16.3	14,731	7,120	0.077	0.160	0.114	0.237	1.869	3.866
1920	1,397	518	9,144	17.7	16,164	7,403	0.086	0.189	0.032	0.070	0.566	1.235
1921	616	550	13,179	24.0	14,390	5,744	0.043	0.107	0.038	0.096	0.916	2.294
1922	421	434	18,604	42.9	14,433	4,823	0.029	0.087	0.030	0.090	1.289	3.857
1923	442	217	9,489	43.7	14,623	4,673	0.030	0.095	0.015	0.046	0.649	2.031
1924	520	476	6,861	14.4	14,856	4,753	0.035	0.109	0.032	0.100	0.462	1.444
1925	439	311	4,499	14.5	15,170	4,702	0.029	0.093	0.021	0.066	0.297	0.957
1926	260	1,629	15,799	9.7	15,162	4,436	0.017	0.059	0.107	0.367	1.042	3.562
1927	198	35	486	13.9	15,740	4,168	0.013	0.048	0.002	0.008	0.031	0.117
1928	205	42	936	22.3	15,894	4,245	0.013	0.048	0.003	0.010	0.059	0.220
1929	278	454	7,711	17.0	16,124	4,337	0.017	0.064	0.028	0.105	0.478	1.778
1930	272	158	3,736	23.6	15,853	4,312	0.017	0.063	0.010	0.037	0.236	0.866
1931	273	209	4,135	19.8	15,502	4,397	0.018	0.062	0.013	0.048	0.267	0.940
1932	278	327	6,201	19.0	15,640	3,946	0.018	0.070	0.021	0.083	0.396	1.571
1933	245	64	626	9.8	15,987	3,895	0.015	0.063	0.004	0.016	0.039	0.161
1934	328	61	594	9.7	16,485	4,091	0.020	0.080	0.004	0.015	0.036	0.145
1935	336	71	587	8.3	16,791	4,365	0.020	0.077	0.004	0.016	0.035	0.134
1936	548	134	977	7.3	17,343	4,764	0.032	0.115	0.008	0.028	0.056	0.205
1937	672	204	1,917	9.4	17,912	5,296	0.038	0.127	0.011	0.039	0.107	0.362
1938	512	100	637	6.4	17,963	5,466	0.029	0.094	0.006	0.018	0.035	0.117
1939	536	131	791	6.0	18,663	5,710	0.029	0.094	0.007	0.023	0.042	0.139
1940	541	109	435	4.0	17,789	6,025	0.030	0.090	0.006	0.018	0.024	0.072
1941	781	206	744	3.6	17,663	6,584	0.044	0.119	0.012	0.031	0.042	0.113
1942	777	204	687	3.4	17,739	7,268	0.044	0.107	0.012	0.028	0.039	0.095
1943	942	263	918	3.5	17,296	7,574	0.054	0.124	0.015	0.035	0.053	0.121
1944	941	253	1,234	4.9	16,847	7,485	0.056	0.126	0.015	0.034	0.073	0.165
1945	987	288	2,194	7.6	16,326	7,318	0.060	0.135	0.018	0.039	0.134	0.300
1946	876	309	1,736	5.6	17,398	8,249	0.050	0.106	0.018	0.037	0.100	0.210
1947	668	312	1,521	4.9	18,518	8,552	0.036	0.078	0.017	0.036	0.082	0.178
1948	643	235	1,480	6.3	18,992	8,727	0.034	0.074	0.012	0.027	0.078	0.170

Year	Stoppages	Workers involved (000's)	Days lost (000's)	Duration in days	Employees in employment (000's)	Union members (000's)	Stoppages		Workers involved		Days lost	
							Per 1000 employees	Per 1000 union members	Per employee	Per union member	Per employee	Per union member
	1	2	3	(3/2)	4	5	(1/4)	(1/5)	(2/4)	(2/5)	(3/4)	(3/5)
1949	552	185	1,053	5.7	19,151	8,683	0.029	0.064	0.010	0.021	0.055	0.121
1950	479	160	958	6.0	19,426	8,658	0.025	0.055	0.008	0.018	0.049	0.121
1950	479	160	958	6.0	20,059	7,896	0.024	0.061	0.008	0.020	0.048	0.121
1951	661	244	1,344	5.5	20,268	8,109	0.033	0.082	0.012	0.030	0.066	0.166
1952	493	141	1,132	8.0	20,198	8,129	0.024	0.061	0.007	0.017	0.056	0.139
1953	439	1,202	1,791	1.5	20,321	8,042	0.022	0.055	0.059	0.149	0.088	0.223
1954	525	244	1,989	8.2	20,696	8,073	0.025	0.065	0.012	0.030	0.096	0.246
1955	636	305	2,669	8.8	20,997	8,233	0.030	0.077	0.015	0.037	0.127	0.324
1956	572	266	1,581	5.9	21,262	8,276	0.027	0.069	0.013	0.032	0.074	0.191
1957	635	1,091	7,898	7.2	21,347	8,306	0.030	0.076	0.051	0.131	0.370	0.951
1958	666	274	3,012	11.0	21,186	8,138	0.031	0.082	0.013	0.034	0.142	0.370
1959	786	454	4,907	10.8	20,753	8,158	0.038	0.096	0.022	0.056	0.236	0.601
1960	1,166	577	2,530	4.4	21,293	8,405	0.055	0.139	0.027	0.069	0.119	0.301
1961	1,228	522	2,309	4.4	21,658	8,504	0.057	0.144	0.024	0.061	0.107	0.272
1962	1,244	288	5,490	19.1	21,895	8,512	0.057	0.146	0.013	0.034	0.251	0.645
1963	1,081	438	1,429	3.3	21,979	8,585	0.049	0.126	0.020	0.051	0.065	0.166
1964	1,466	700	1,975	2.8	22,313	8,739	0.066	0.168	0.031	0.080	0.089	0.226
1965	1,614	750	2,513	3.4	22,614	8,868	0.071	0.182	0.033	0.085	0.111	0.283
1966	1,384	480	2,280	4.8	22,744	8,975	0.061	0.154	0.021	0.053	0.100	0.254
1967	1,722	690	2,682	3.9	22,325	8,944	0.077	0.193	0.031	0.077	0.120	0.300
1968	2,157	2,225	4,636	2.1	22,227	8,984	0.097	0.240	0.100	0.248	0.209	0.516
1969	2,960	1,520	5,807	3.8	22,241	9,289	0.133	0.319	0.068	0.164	0.261	0.625
1970	3,786	1,684	9,890	5.9	22,119	9,958	0.171	0.380	0.076	0.169	0.447	0.993
1971	2,128	1,155	13,488	11.7	21,785	9,914	0.098	0.215	0.053	0.116	0.619	1.360

1972	2,312	1,394	13,112	9.4	21,807	10,126	0.106	0.228	0.064	0.138	0.601	1.295
1973	2,601	1,481	7,107	4.8	22,361	10,225	0.116	0.254	0.066	0.145	0.318	0.695
1974	2,763	1,320	9,125	6.9	22,502	10,514	0.123	0.263	0.059	0.126	0.406	0.868
1975	2,120	781	5,960	7.6	22,430	10,903	0.095	0.194	0.035	0.072	0.266	0.547
1976	1,758	630	3,214	5.1	22,262	11,065	0.079	0.159	0.028	0.057	0.144	0.290
1977	2,498	1,120	10,066	9.0	22,334	11,497	0.112	0.217	0.050	0.097	0.451	0.876
1978	2,160	937	9,210	9.8	22,496	11,746	0.096	0.184	0.042	0.080	0.409	0.784
1979	1,830	4,555	29,362	6.4	22,887	11,910	0.080	0.154	0.199	0.382	1.283	2.465
1980	1,059	749	11,813	15.8	22,706	11,592	0.047	0.091	0.033	0.065	0.520	1.019
1981	1,042	1,415	4,031	2.8	21,617	10,828	0.048	0.096	0.065	0.131	0.186	0.372
1982	1,135	1,878	4,939	2.6	21,154	10,363	0.054	0.110	0.089	0.181	0.233	0.477
1983	1,009	441	3,270	7.4	20,813	10,073	0.048	0.100	0.021	0.044	0.157	0.325
1984	1,142	1,183	4,652	3.9	21,005	9,862	0.054	0.116	0.056	0.120	0.221	0.472
1985	743	623	2,260	3.6	21,211	9,770	0.035	0.076	0.029	0.064	0.107	0.231
1986	723	633	1,777	2.8	21,205	9,518	0.034	0.076	0.030	0.067	0.084	0.187
1987	720	789	3,329	4.2	21,434	9,478	0.034	0.076	0.037	0.083	0.155	0.351
1988	627	698	3,480	5.0	22,098	9,278	0.028	0.068	0.032	0.075	0.157	0.375
1989	555	702	4,078	5.8	22,654	9,232	0.024	0.060	0.031	0.076	0.180	0.442
1990	543	283	1,844	6.5	22,808	9,053	0.024	0.060	0.012	0.031	0.081	0.204
1991	337	170	732	4.3	22,143	8,770	0.015	0.038	0.008	0.019	0.033	0.083

Notes and Sources: See Data Appendix.

REFERENCES

Blanchflower, D. and Cubbin, J. (1986) 'Strike propensities at the British workplace', *Oxford Bulletin of Economics and Statistics* 48, (1): 19–40.

Daniel, W.W. and Millward, N. (1983) *Workplace Industrial Relations in Britain*, DE/PSI/ESRC, London: Heinemann.

Donovan (1968), Royal Commission on Trade Unions and Employers' Associations, *Report*, Cmnd 3623, London: HMSO.

Ingram, P., Metcalf, D. and Wadsworth, J. (1991) 'Strike incidence and duration in British manufacturing industry in the 1980s', Centre for Economic Performance, LSE, Discussion Paper No. 48.

Knowles, K.G.J.C. (1954) *Strikes – a study in industrial conflict*, Oxford: Blackwell.

Millward, N. and Stevens, M. (1986) *British Workplace Industrial Relations 1980–84, DE/ESRC/PSI/ACAS Surveys*, Aldershot: Gower.

Simpson, R. (1986) 'Trade union immunities', in R. Lewis (ed.) *Labour Law in Britain*, Oxford: Blackwell.

Smith, C.T.B., Clifton, R., Makeham, P., Creigh, S.W. and Burn, R.V. (1978) *Strikes in Britain*, Department of Employment, Manpower Paper No. 15.

Index